THE MEASURE OF DEMOCRACY: POLLING, MARKET RESEARCH, AND PUBLIC LIFE, 1930–1945

Politicians, government officials, and public relations officers lean heavily on polling when fashioning public policy. Proponents say this is for the best, arguing that surveys bring the views of citizens closer to civic officials. Critics decry polling's promotion of sycophantic politicians who pander to the whims of public sentiment, or, conversely, the use of surveys by special interest groups to thwart the majority will.

Similar claims and criticisms were made during the early days of polling. When George Gallup began polling Americans in 1935, he heralded it as a bold step in popular democracy. The views of ordinary citizens could now be heard alongside those of organized interest groups. When brought to Canada in 1941, the Gallup Poll promised similar democratic rejuvenation. In actual practice, traditionally disadvantaged constituencies such as women, the poor, French Canadians, and African Americans were often heavily under-represented in Gallup surveys. Preoccupied with election forecasting, Gallup pollsters undercounted social groups thought less likely or unable to vote, leading to a considerable gap between poll results and the opinions of the general public.

Examining the origins and early years of public opinion polling in Canada, Robinson situates polling within the larger context of its forerunners – market research surveys and American opinion polling – and charts its growth until its first uses by political parties.

DANIEL J. ROBINSON is a SSHRC Postdoctoral Fellow in the Department of History, University of Toronto.

DANIEL J. ROBINSON

The Measure of Democracy: Polling, Market Research, and Public Life, 1930–1945

UNIVERITY OF TORONTO PRESS
Toronto Buffalo London

ISBN 0-8020-4274-0 (cloth)
ISBN 0-8020-8109-6 (paper)

Printed on acid-free paper

Canadian Cataloguing in Publication Data

Robinson, Daniel J.
    The measure of democracy : polling, market research, and
    public life, 1930–1945

    Includes bibliographical references and index.
    ISBN 0-8020-4274-0 (bound)   ISBN 0-8020-8109-6 (pbk.)

    1. Public opinion polls – Canada – History.   2. Public
    opinion polls – United States – History.   3. Marketing
    research – Canada – History.   4. Canada – Politics and
    government – 20th century.   I. Title.

    HM261.R62 1999   303.3'8'097109041   C98-932368-4

A condensed version of chapter 1 appeared in the *Journal of the Canadian Historical Association* 8 (1997).

This book has been published with the help of a grant from the Humanities and Social Sciences Federation of Canada, using funds provided by the Social Sciences and Humanities Research Council of Canada.

University of Toronto Press acknowledges the financial assistance to its publishing program of the Canada Council for the Arts and the Ontario Arts Council.

Contents

Acknowledgments

Pollsters rely on the kindness of strangers – respondents – to ply their trade, yet in writing about polling I have depended on many people who, happily, can be acknowledged. An immeasurable debt of gratitude is owed Jack Granatstein, who supervised this project while it was a doctoral dissertation at York University and who has since been a much-appreciated source of scholarly advice and good-humoured encouragement. I was fortunate to have as dissertation committee members Robert Cuff, Marlene Shore, and Reginald Whitaker, whose suggestions and criticisms greatly improved this study. Duncan McDowall of Carleton University, in his capacity as external examiner, provided a rigorous and thoughtful assessment of the dissertation. Christopher Armstrong and John T. Saywell were instrumental in advancing my progress in graduate school, as was Norman Hillmer during my undergraduate years.

I am very grateful to the many people who read parts or all of this manuscript and offered commentary: Brian Adkins, W.J.C. Cherwinski, Sally Clarke, Ken Cmiel, Molly Ladd-Taylor, the late Roland Marchand, Peter Neary, Daniel T. Rodgers, Michael Schudson, Harwell Wells – who helped coin the title – and Robert Young. David Northrup at York's Institute for Social Research helped me unravel the intricacies of survey research, as did Scott Bilder at Rutgers University. The Honourable Bob Rae graciously accommodated my interview requests concerning the polling exploits of his father, Saul Forbes Rae. Irving Crespi, Clara Hatton, John Maloney, and Paul Perry provided compelling interview accounts of their own polling careers. Michael Adams of Environics Research took time to enlighten me about the contemporary polling scene. Joyce Holden at the Canadian Daily Newspapers Association and

Betty Bennett at Canadian Facts were instrumental in facilitating my research. The private records of Byrne Hope Sanders and Wilfrid Sanders were kindly made available to me by Dodie Finlayson, Shannon Sperry, and Cassandra Sanders. Sarah Van Allen and George Gallup Jr at the Gallup Organization in Princeton provided photographs and background material on George Gallup. The staff at the Archives of Ontario and the National Archives of Canada were their usual informative and helpful selves. Harold Averill at the University of Toronto Archives worked diligently to track down materials and photographs. Above all, I wish to thank Jon Hughes, formerly at Gallup Canada, for his help in securing access to early Gallup Poll reports.

Research on American polling was made possible by a Canada-U.S. Fulbright fellowship and by the support of members of the scholarly community at Rutgers University. My sincere thanks to John Whiteclay Chambers, Rudolph Bell, and Lynn Shanko for facilitating my enjoyable stay as a fellow in the Rutgers Center for Historical Analysis in spring 1994. I'm indebted to Karen Balcom and Andrew Bendall, who, though uprooted from Canada and Australia respectively, proved resourceful guides to the attractions of central New Jersey, not the least of which was Friday night bowling. At Duke University, where I benefited from a travel grant from the John W. Hartman Center for Sales, Advertising and Marketing History, I wish to thank Ellen Gartrell, Claire Locke, and John Herd Thompson.

Additional funding for this research was provided by an Ontario Graduate Scholarship and from the Social Sciences and Humanities Research Council of Canada. I would also like to thank the staff at Robarts Library, University of Toronto, where most of the secondary research was done and where, courtesy of a closed carrel, much of the writing took place.

Also at the University of Toronto, I wish to convey my sincere appreciation to Paul Rutherford for his ongoing interest in my work. At the University of Toronto Press, I thank Robert Ferguson, Emily Andrew, and Gerry Hallowell. Judy Williams did an exemplary job of copy editing which saved me from many slip-ups. Of course, as is customary, any remaining errors are mine and mine alone.

Finally, I'd like to acknowledge some friends and family members. My parents, Patricia Robinson and Carman Robinson, have been longstanding sources of encouragement and understanding. So too have friends Jordan Berger, Katia Gianneschi, David Himel, and Lucy Luccisano. Most of all, I thank Paula Maurutto for her love, companionship, and insistence that much else mattered besides this book. For these things and much more, this book is for her.

Daniel Robinson
Fall 1998

Abbreviations

ACA	Association of Canadian Advertisers
AIPO	American Institute of Public Opinion
ANPA	American Newspaper Publishers Association
AO	Archives of Ontario
BIPO	British Institute of Public Opinion
BPI	Bureau of Public Information
CIPO	Canadian Institute of Public Opinion
CDNA	Canadian Daily Newspapers Association
COC	Canadian Opinion Company
CPA	Canadian Psychological Association
GC	Gallup Canada
IFOP	Institut Français d'Opinion Publique
ISR	Institute for Social Research, York University
JWT	J. Walter Thompson
NAC	National Archives of Canada
NLF	National Liberal Federation
NORC	National Opinion Research Center
NSS	National Selective Service
OPOR	Office of Public Opinion Research
PCO	Privy Council Office
PUA	Princeton University Archives
QRC	*Quarterly Review of Commerce*
RCPOR	Roper Center for Public Opinion Research
UTA	University of Toronto Archives
WIB	Wartime Information Board
WPTB	Wartime Prices and Trade Board
WRAC	Women's Regional Advisory Committees
WWSPIA	Woodrow Wilson School of Public and International Affairs

Senior officials of Canada's first opinion polling organization, the
Canadian Institute of Public Opinion, established in 1941 by George
Gallup. From left, Arthur Porter, Gallup, and John Tibbey. (*Canadian
Business*, Dec. 1941; Robarts Library, University of Toronto)

George Gallup, world-renowned pollster and consumer market researcher, who argued that polling strengthened democracy by giving ordinary citizens a greater say in public decision making. (Gallup Organization, Princeton, NJ)

Gallup field worker interviewing a blue-collar worker. Early Gallup surveys were conducted in such locations as street corners, parks, doorsteps, and outside factory gates. (*Maclean's*, 1 Jan. 1943; Robarts Library, University of Toronto)

Gallup interview of householder. Women, while the overwhelming majority of respondents in consumer surveys, were heavily under-sampled in public opinion polls during the 1940s. (*Saturday Night*, 12 April 1952; Toronto Reference Library)

Maclean Publishing senior officials in 1937. From left, Horace T.
Hunter, Col. J.B. Maclean, and Victor Tyrrell. During the 1940s, the
company commissioned readership surveys for *Maclean's* and
Chatelaine magazines. (Archives of Ontario, Maclean-Hunter Collection,
F-138-1-1-22)

Business journalist Wilfrid Sanders joined the Canadian Gallup Poll in 1942, later becoming its first Canadian director. (Cassandra Sanders private collection)

University of Toronto psychologist J.D. Ketchum was one of the first academics in Canada to experiment with sample survey techniques. From 1942 to 1945, he coordinated the Wartime Information Board's use of polling to mobilize public support for the war effort. (University of Toronto Archives, J.D. Ketchum Papers, 98-18#1/B74-0072/003P/01)

THE MEASURE OF DEMOCRACY:
POLLING, MARKET RESEARCH, AND
PUBLIC LIFE, 1930–1945

Introduction

The 1940 release of the polling classic *The Pulse of Democracy* was a milestone for both its authors. For Saul Rae, the twenty-six-year-old Canadian who two years earlier had completed a London School of Economics PhD thesis on public opinion, it was an opportunity to convey polling-related ideas to a wide audience, not just the members of a dissertation committee. Recruited by George Gallup in early 1939 while still in Britain, Rae had spent the past year as a visiting fellow at Princeton University, assisting with Gallup's polling firm, the American Institute of Public Opinion (AIPO), and co-writing the monograph.[1] The book, however, would prove an early capstone to his career as a pollster; soon after its publication, his sense of wartime service activated, Rae left Princeton to join the Department of External Affairs, where he would subsequently hold a number of diplomatic postings throughout his career. For Gallup, who since founding the AIPO in 1935 had written many articles promoting the merits of the representative sample survey, *The Pulse* consolidated his position as the dean of American polling, indeed of polling the world over. More significantly, the book advanced the democratic rationale for polling which during the next half-century, according to one survey researcher, would form the 'philosophical bedrock justifying the dogged efforts of pollsters to measure public sentiment.'[2]

Throughout history, Gallup and Rae posited, the 'central problem' of political governance concerned whether 'the common people' should be 'free to express their basic needs and purposes,' or whether they would 'be dominated by a small ruling clique.' The rise of dictator rule in Europe coupled with the upswing in pressure-group lobbying in the remaining democracies had eroded the political clout and civic involvement of ordinary citizens. Democracy was in crisis, in dire need of 'new techniques' to compete with the wartime 'efficiency' of totalitarian societies, and, in the democracies themselves, fast and accurate measures to 'bridge the gap between the people' and government officials. The representative sample survey, touted repeatedly as a 'scientific' and 'objective' instrument, would tabulate and project the views of average men and women into the chambers of decision makers, thus serving to reanimate public life. While, for many, urbanization and bureaucratization had displaced the immediacy and vitality of political affairs, opinion polling promised a measure of civic renewal, a technocratic revival of grassroots expression suitable to the modern mass society. Not only would civil society benefit from widened democratic expression, but so too would 'experts' and policy makers, for surveys repeatedly showed that ordinary citizens possessed a strong measure of common sense and collective wisdom. This democratizing project was all the more achievable because a related form of polling had for some two decades been part of the American commercial landscape. The rise of market research surveys, and their bearing on opinion polling, is succinctly summarized by Gallup and Rae:

The expansion of American industry had led to specialization. This specialization resulted in the emergence of a group of capable market-research analysts who had been applying statistical methods and techniques to the study of consumers' choices and the needs of the national market. Industry needed to know people's opinions about the goods and commodities which they bought or refused to buy. Advertisers wanted to learn about brand preferences, sizes, amounts, buying habits, consumers' interests. To answer these questions, statisticians were called in to develop sampling methods in order to deal with the attitudes of large populations. The research methods which this market analysis had built up furnished yardsticks by which surveys of public opinion could be checked.[3]

Populist democracy, scientific authority, and marketing know-how coalesced to form an ideological defence of polling equating it with the public good.

This 1940 apologia for polling has transcended time and place. In Canada, Keith Davey, a key Liberal strategist and polling adherent since the 1960s, commented in 1969 that 'any scientific measurement of public attitudes surely points the way to democracy.' As modern society became more complex, polling provided 'an increasingly significant way of determining individual social and economic needs,' and accordingly it was a 'useful tool in the hands of those who seek to understand the nation and improve our government.'[4] Michael Adams, the president of Environics Research Group, a leading Canadian market research firm, argued in 1987 that opinion surveys helped lessen the influence of lobbyists and advocacy groups. Polling, 'like universal suffrage before it,' functioned as 'the natural extension of democratic principles made possible by the combination of advanced technology and an informed citizenry.' More recently, Adams again lauded the sample survey for advancing 'the cause of democratic civilization.'[5] Similarly, fellow pollster Martin Goldfarb wrote that opinion polling belonged 'to the world of universal democracy,' serving to 'create an involved citizenry.' His many years of survey experience had convinced him that 'the source of wisdom rests always with the consumer and the voter. The consumer and the voter react from a fundamental and deeply rooted base of common sense.'[6]

Goldfarb also strikes a resonant chord when noting that 'rarely do people reflect deeply about what pollsters do; what roles they play in the evolution of our society.'[7] This is especially true for historical inquiry. For all its modern-day pervasiveness, opinion polling has received only sporadic treatment by historians, who typically turn to past polls to cull opinion figures on topics of inquiry. Similarly, survey researchers when analysing prior polling generally do so to acquire longitudinal opinion data on contemporary issues – for example, capital punishment. One exception is Jean Converse's 1987 pioneering history of American survey research. Drawing on a broad array of primary sources, Converse, herself a survey researcher, chronicles the development of polling from the social surveys of the 1890s to the academic institutionalization of public opinion research in the 1960s. While Converse occasionally explores the intersection between polling and the broader social and political context, her work is largely an internalist history of American survey research, highlighting such subjects as methodological advances and institutional formation. More recently, Susan Herbst, a mass communications scholar, has probed past American polling to assess how this highly quantitative practice, begun in the 1930s, ultimately became the most authoritative means of assessing public opinion. Drawing on the theories of Max Weber and Michel Foucault, Herbst explores the social and political implications of polling's heightened rationalization of the public sphere. She also discusses how the polls affected the surveillance possibilities and knowledge/power capacities of public and private institutions. A provocative and insightful study, Herbst's work, however, all but ignores opinion polling's most important technological and conceptual progenitor, market research surveys.[8]

There are no historical works on Canadian opinion polling, and studies on contemporary polling contain little in the way of sustained historical analysis. Journalist Claire Hoy's exposé on Canadian polling briefly touches on the Canadian government's wartime use of surveys in the early 1940s, but his account lacks documentation.[9] Guy Lachapelle's volume on polling for the Royal Commission on Electoral Reform and Party Financing is similarly short on historical content, and what is provided is long on factual errors.[10] In 1985, three marketing professors published a history of Canadian market research to commemorate the twenty-fifth anniversary of the Professional Marketing Research Society. A commendable compilation of primary source material and first-hand accounts of early market researchers, the monograph, however, is weakest on the pre-1945 period and generally falls short of situating market research within a broader commercial, social, and political context.[11]

This book was originally conceived as a study of opinion polling's impact on Canadian politics and government from the early 1940s to the mid-1960s. After preliminary research, however, it became apparent that a thorough understanding of opinion polling's origins, operations, and political and social functions was not possible without elucidating two other important, though little-known, historical phenomena: George Gallup's American polling operations, and market research surveys in Canada. The Canadian Institute of Public Opinion (CIPO), Canada's first opinion polling organization, began in 1941 as a Gallup import. Many of Canada's early pollsters were Americans or Canadians trained in the United States. Ideas concerning the social and political applications of polling generally originated in the United States, as did the actual techniques of sample surveying. As the Gallup–Rae collaboration suggests symbolically, the rise of Canadian polling was very much conditioned by its North American context. Similarly, an analysis of market research surveys, which preceded opinion polling in Canada by more than a decade, is a *sine qua non* for understanding the latter's roots and emergence. Indeed, as I argue below, opinion polling developed conceptually and methodologically largely as an adjunct of consumer surveying itself. Accordingly, this study encompasses an earlier time period than originally envisioned – from the late 1920s until 1945. As well, sizeable sections are devoted to American polling, chiefly the activities of Gallup's AIPO. While survey methods are at times discussed, the primary focus is on the use of opinion polls by politicians, government officials, and business executives, and the effect of these fledgling surveys on democratic expression.

This study comprises five chapters. The first describes the origins and emergence of market research surveys in Canada, from the late 1920s until the arrival of Gallup polling in Canada in 1941. Consumer surveys arose as a response to the business 'problem' of marketing in the interwar period. Market research surveys were seen as an efficient means of assessing and anticipating consumer demand, thus enabling enhanced production planning. More important, they were a singular technique for advertisers to probe consumer wants and actions, securing valuable information to augment the effectiveness and 'scientific' basis of advertising itself. Chapter 2 discusses George Gallup's consumer surveying and opinion polling in the United States from 1935 until 1945. Gallup championed opinion polling as a democratic leveller of political power. His polls' sampling design, however, significantly underrepresented women, African Americans, and low socio-economic groups, mainly because these constituencies were seen as unlikely voters. Since the scientific authority and commercial viability of opinion polls (and market research surveys) hinged on their ability to forecast election results, Gallup's sampling framework targeted probable voters and conflated them with the 'general public.' Similarly, when brought to Canada in 1941, as analysed in chapter 3, Gallup polling constructed a sampled portrait of 'voting' Canadians which differed from the adult population. Women and the poor were again underpolled, as were francophones, owing to French-language interviewing problems. Chapter 4 examines the Canadian government's systematic and secretive use of Gallup polling to assess public opinion during the war, roughly 1942 to 1945. By war's end, the CIPO had become an integral feature in the planning and dissemination of wartime information or, less euphemistically, state propaganda. The final chapter probes the use of polling by political parties until the 1945 federal election. The Liberal party was the principal player in this regard: its activities constituted the Canadian genesis of 'political marketing,' the application of market research concepts and methods to party policy formation and electoral politics.

Opinion polling was heralded as a democratizing agent, a tool for social change that would restore a much-needed semblance of power to the politically inarticulate. But this egalitarian ideal was constructed on a commercial foundation that was purposely inegalitarian. Market research surveys were not designed to incorporate a cross-section of the adult population; rather, they targeted specific segments of the 'buying public,' which in many cases meant urban and middle- to upper-class homemakers. Certain consumers were deemed (quite rightly) more equal than others. When viewed in this context, it is understandable, if undesirable, that the market researchers who became opinion pollsters would construct skewed samples of the 'general public.' The perceived 'market' of voting citizens did not conform to the adult population. As well, it proved ironic, if not tragic, that many of the early sponsors and beneficiaries of opinion polling were in fact the very 'Interests' – pols, state propagandists, PR men, advertisers – whose power, according to Gallup and CIPO officials, was meant to be tempered by the sample survey. The polling-generated 'People,' itself a distorted facsimile of the citizenry, constituted more a malleable entity to be acted on or manipulated by others than a virtuous source of democratic authority. By 1945, the Canadian foundations of a polling-inspired marketing polity were in place, which contrasted sharply with the CIPO's populist proclamations.

Finally, a few words on past democracy and present-day polling. Historical inquiry embodies an indispensable paradox. Its empirical approach presupposes a firm grounding in past temporal and spatial context. Explanation, etiology, and historical circumstance are inextricably linked. Universalist assumptions and interpretations are broached warily, if at all. But conjoined with this empirical project is the subjective act of judgment or critique, whose moral and epistemological parameters are defined within the historian's own social and professional milieu. The goal, however elusive, is a form of authorial criticism that is broadened and sharpened by modern knowledge yet devoid of presentist conceit, one which is sensitive to the conditions of and possibilities for social change in a particular place at a particular time. This account of opinion polling's emergence attempts such an accommodation of historical empathy and purposive critique. Wherever possible, I have framed my line of criticism against the pollsters' *own* claims for polling and popular empowerment, while trying not to lose sight of the historical possibilities for democratic advancement in mid-twentieth-century Canada and America. It follows too that insights and conclusions drawn from a pre-1945 analysis of polling do not apply *ipso facto* to modern-day survey research. Such a 'myth of origins,' in which practices and meanings formed during a phenomenon's inception prefigure forever after its development and social purpose, is ahistorical and a pedagogical nonstarter.[12] There are today polling organizations, both non-profit and commercial, whose innovative and reliable surveys produce useful knowledge that serves the public interest. Nor would I want this study to be read as giving *carte blanche* for an attack on the basic idea of polling, past or present. Unlike some critics, I believe there is nothing *intrinsically* wrong with or socially harmful about the use of sample surveys to solicit and measure the opinions, attitudes, or behavioural traits of citizens or consumers.[13] The concern arises, rather, when assessing how survey practices and the subsequent use of polls measure up against polling's purported democratizing mission. In the case of Gallup surveys prior to 1945, the performance belied the promise. This does not preclude outright the prospect, both present and future, of polling-conferred democratic renewal;[14] only that such advocates are unlikely to draw inspiration from polling's formative era.

1

Polling Consumers: The Rise of Market Research Surveys

One of the thoughts uppermost in the minds of all advertising people is research. The past five years have taught us that we cannot afford to spend money blindly. We must know what our advertising dollar is going to bring in and must eliminate much of the waste so prevalent in the past.

Stuart Peabody, 1935

It is now possible to tap the consumer mind with little expense.

Walter A. Thompson, 1936[1]

Consumer surveys, the progenitor of public opinion polling, appeared in the late 1920s as a response to the perceived business 'problem' of marketing. Production methods, assisted by business statistics and scientific techniques, were significantly more rationalized and efficient by the 1920s than previously, especially among large manufacturers. But there were few comparable improvements in the marketing of goods. Consumer sample surveys offered a means of gauging and anticipating consumer wants, thus enabling better production planning. More important, they were a powerful tool for advertisers to penetrate the desires and behaviour of Canada's 'buying publics,' securing data to improve the effectiveness and reliability of advertising itself. Three main groups spearheaded the development of this commercial technique: business school academics, mainly from the University of Western Ontario; advertising agencies and market research firms; and magazine and newspaper owners seeking demographic profiles of readers to showcase their publications' advertising potential.

By the late 1930s, market researchers had acquired the capacity to conduct national representative sample surveys, but rarely did such polls mirror the composition of the general population. Conceiving and conducting their undertaking as neither democratic nor egalitarian, consumer surveyors targeted specific socio-economic groups thought most likely to purchase the product in question. Accordingly, most, though not all, samples overrepresented middle- and upper-income earners, city dwellers, and married women. Such surveys, indicative as they were of advertisers' and manufacturers' depictions of preferred or 'typical' consumers, call into question historical accounts of mass marketing emphasizing broad-based participation. Daniel Boorstin, for example, argues that a salutary feature of American consumerism was the effort by manufacturers and advertisers to 'democratiz[e] the market by inventing ways for the consumer to vote his preferences,' which initiated a 'new science for sampling the suffrage of consumers.'[2] More recently, Richard Tedlow extols the emergence of American mass marketing for 'making products available to the masses all over the nation,' in essence 'democratizing consumption.'[3] From the standpoint of interwar Canadian marketers, however, 'mass' consumption constituted less a universal phenomenon than a variable and stratified one.

Canada's economy experienced massive quantitative and qualitative changes in the two decades preceding the Great War. The GNP grew 112 per cent from 1900 to 1910, from $1.06 billion to $2.24 billion, making the early years of 'Canada's century,' on an aggregate level, decidedly prosperous ones.[4] Staple products – wheat, wood, minerals, and other natural resources – fuelled much of this economic 'Great Boom,' but there were also important structural changes in manufacturing, the result of concomitant industrial and managerial innovations beginning in the 1890s. In some industrial sectors, the drive to lower costs through longer, more efficient production runs gave rise to large, multi-unit enterprises, many horizontally or vertically integrated, and where hierarchies of salaried managers over time supplanted individual entrepreneurs in the office and on the shop floor. Operations were centralized, manufacturing methods standardized, and national and international markets replaced local ones. Such Canadian and foreign-owned companies as Algoma Steel, Canadian General Electric, Canadian Westinghouse, Ford of Canada, and Canada Foundries typified this 'Second Industrial Revolution.'[5]

One consequence of the drive to rationalize production was corporate consolidation; between 1909 and 1913, some 220 firms with assets exceeding $200 million merged, and total capitalization of Dominion chartered corporations rose from $12.9 million in 1900 to $490 million in 1911. Small and medium-sized businesses were by no means eradicated; nearly 70 per cent of manufacturing in 1911 remained in the hands of firms with annual sales under $1 million, and most of these remained untouched by scientific management practices. But in large-scale enterprises there was a significant increase of administrative personnel, prompting Paul Craven to conclude that while the '*fact* of scientific management and "efficiency" penetrated to only a small, if very important, group of industries' from 1901 to 1911, the '*ideology* of those movements was far more widely diffused.'[6]

An emergent feature of the ideology and operation of economies-of-scale manufacturing was the use of business statistics, most of which were supplied by Ottawa. The 1901 census of manufacturers was 'improved immeasurably' from earlier versions, containing broader classifications of industries and inaugural and comprehensive figures on material costs, wages, and miscellaneous expenses. In 1905 the Census and Statistics Office was established, the first semi-permanent federal statistics agency.[7] Reflecting the growing importance of commercial statistics, the office was transferred from the Ministry of Agriculture to Trade and Commerce in 1912. Most significantly, the first annual census of production was conducted in the midst of the Great War in 1917, and provided detailed data on a wide range of economic activity in the manufacturing, construction, fisheries, forestry, and mining sectors. When the Dominion Bureau of Statistics (DBS) was established in 1918, its mandate underscored the growing interconnection of state-sponsored statistics and the marketplace, seen as especially crucial for wartime industrial mobilization. The bureau's purpose was to 'collect, abstract, compile and publish statistical information relative to the commercial, industrial, social, economic, and general activities and condition of the people.'[8] Indeed, dominion statistician R.H. Coats, while discussing the DBS publication *Monthly Review of Business Statistics*, launched in 1926, championed such sources as 'barometric statistics,' enabling a 'scientific gauging' of business conditions and production techniques. To neglect these statistical indices risked incurring the fate of the 'ship that drifts away from the main battle fleet – he is apt to get pounced on.'[9] Similarly, Graham Lowe, in his study of early twentieth-century corporate administrative growth in Canada, describes how managerial and production statistics became a 'highly valued resource for the professional managers who took the reins of corporate capitalism.' In this schema, head offices served as 'organizational nerve centres' that 'collected, processed, stored and communicated mountains of facts and figures indispensable for managerial decision-making.'[10]

While by the 1920s statistical knowledge of production processes was well advanced, far less was known about the product's passage from factory gate to purchasing consumer. As one advertiser underlined in 1928, 'distribution is the most important problem of modern business.'[11] General content with efficient, scientifically engineered production systems was tempered by the perceived haphazard and costly methods besetting marketing. The problem was accentuated by Canada's geographic expanse and small population. In 1924 the DBS sought to ameliorate the situation by conducting a small-scale census of distribution. But the project proved unsuccessful; too many wholesalers and retailers were missed and those who were covered furnished incomplete information.[12] There was scant or non-existent statistical data in most marketing fields, including wholesale and retail practices, product packaging, sales methods, advertising, and consumer behaviour. As a Royal Bank of Canada circular put it in 1930: 'The last half century has witnessed the growth of large scale production and remarkable improvements in productive efficiency, but relatively speaking, distribution has escaped attention.' Furthermore, there were 'no comprehensive statistics' in the marketing field, a problem judged 'most acute.'[13] When American officials moved to combine a census of distribution with the 1930 decennial census, Canadian businessmen – including manufacturers, advertisers, board of trade members, and bankers – seized on this precedent and lobbied for a similar Canadian venture to be part of the 1931 census. Ottawa consented, and a census of wholesaling and retailing, according to one DBS official, was launched 'with the blessings of representative bodies in the business world.'[14]

A watershed in Canadian marketing, the Census of Merchandising and Service Establishments represented the first extensive and systematic overview of wholesale and retail operations in Canada and was a vital source of market research information from the early 1930s on. Lists of wholesale, retail, and service establishments were compiled by population enumerators and from other sources. These businesses were then mailed questionnaires soliciting such information as the commodities they handled, sales totals, employee wages, and supply channels. In total, 125,003 retailers, 13,140 wholesalers, and 42,223 service and amusement establishments were enumerated, along with 4,958 hotel operations; only 5 per cent of eligible businesses were missed, the DBS estimated. In 1933, the bureau began an annual survey of wholesale and retail operations, employing a sampling method that used the 1931 decennial census figures as a benchmark. As well, using smaller samples, monthly surveys of department stores, chain stores, and some independent retailers were initiated.[15]

Flowing from these investigations were numerous studies illuminating merchandising practices. Among monthly DBS publications launched were *Wholesale Trade* (1935–), *Price Movements* (1935–), *Monthly Indexes of Country General Store Sales* (1936–), and *Department Store Sales and Stocks* (1938–). Annual publications included *Price Movements* (1931–), *Retail Trade* (1933–), *New Motor Vehicle Sales and Motor Vehicle Financing* (1935–), and *Advertising Agencies* (1941–).[16] The cumulative result by the late 1930s was a radically improved statistical basis of marketing activities, one that enabled manufacturers to track the movement of goods through distribution channels and pinpoint those areas and retailers where their products sold best. Retailing trends could be monitored, sales quotas recast, transportation systems rationalized. In the Depression-ravaged economy, the promise of tighter control and enhanced efficiency of distribution activities resounded loudly, and DBS merchandising data were consumed eagerly by manufacturers and advertisers.[17] As one commentator underscored in 1935 with respect to marketing in a flaccid economy, advertisers could no longer afford 'to spend money blindly' and needed above all to 'eliminate much of the waste so prevalent in the past.'[18]

Government marketing statistics were a powerful and, for many, indispensable tool for navigating the vast and unpredictable empire of merchandising. But for marketers seeking greater control and profitability of product distribution and sales, DBS figures were only a partial solution, for they revealed little about the consumer purchasing process. Questions that had long preoccupied managers and entrepreneurs lacked definitive answers: Who exactly bought the product – young or old, male or female, rich or poor? Why did they buy it, and from where did they get the idea? Were they likely to keep on buying it? What kinds of appeals could get them to buy more of it? In providing answers, sales figures and price trend data were of limited use; rather, one had to ask consumers directly. And commencing in earnest in the late 1920s, a variety of interests began doing just that: conducting interviews of consumers, usually employing a sampling method, that probed the meanings and associated behaviour of mass consumption. Three groups were closely associated with this project to harness consumer opinions for commercial ends: business school academics, mostly out of the University of Western Ontario; advertising agencies and market research firms, the former hoping to enhance the effectiveness and 'scientific' authority of advertising; and magazine and newspaper owners wanting socio-economic profiles of reader audiences to furnish advertisers in their publications. By the early 1940s, this branch of market research – interview-based consumer research – was well developed, both methodologically and conceptually, evolving into a 'mass feedback technology'[19] that functioned to anticipate, rationalize, and ultimately increase consumer purchasing. It was, in part, the demand-side corollary of mass production techniques long underway. As with the second industrial revolution, the origins of consumer survey research were also American.

Credited as Canada's first full-time market researcher when hired in 1929 by the advertising firm, Cockfield, Brown and Company, Henry King attributed his appointment to vice-president Warren Brown's interest in American market research, which he viewed as 'the coming thing' in Canada.[20] And indeed Americans were well advanced in consumer research by the late 1920s. The first systematic market research operation was started by Charles Coolidge Parlin in 1911 when he took charge of the newly formed research department at the Curtis Publishing Company, publisher of the *Saturday Evening Post* and *Ladies' Home Journal*. His 1912 four-volume study, *Department Store Lines*, was a seminal work in the new marketing 'science.' Parlin conducted 1,121 interviews and logged thirty-seven thousand miles visiting America's largest one hundred cities to compile a detailed report of merchandising in department, dry goods, and men's ready-to-wear stores. The study, coupled with another three years later which in part analysed consumer attitudes towards automobiles, was an early example of consumer feedback techniques: information gleaned from consumer surveys was fed back to producers and designers planning future products and simultaneously fed forward to copywriters devising ads for current goods.[21] By 1916 the *Chicago Tribune* was conducting house-to-house interviewing to determine the socio-economic composition, buying habits, and newspaper-reading traits of Chicago consumers, and in 1922 the *Milwaukee Journal* undertook a similar survey, repeated annually, for the Milwaukee area. Such studies were used to convince consumer goods manufacturers of newspaper advertising's efficiency – it could target specific reading 'publics' or consumer markets – and effectiveness: it could employ the most persuasive selling techniques. Total advertising volume in the United States increased dramatically in the early twentieth century, rising from $256 million in 1900 to $2,987 million in 1929.[22] To ensure that these advertising dollars targeted likely buyers and that ads used the most compelling sales appeals, questionnaire surveys on consumer preference and the purchasing decision-making process took on increased importance.

In light of advertising's close links to market research, it is not surprising that advertising agencies developed extensive expertise in this emerging field. The most notable example was the advertising colossus J. Walter Thompson (JWT), particularly after 1916 when Stanley Resor became president. Resor – a disciple of nineteenth-century positivist philosopher Thomas Buckle, who proclaimed that aggregate human behaviour was observable and predictable only by statistical laws – insisted that advertising be empirically grounded. Soon after assuming office, he created a market research department, and in 1920 added the renowned behavioural psychologist John B. Watson to the company payroll. By the early 1920s, Resor had recast JWT into a 'university of advertising,' owing to its intensive consumer research and employee training programs based on social scientific methods. The company also produced the most exhaustive publication on consumer spending. First appearing in 1912, *Population and Its Distribution* reformulated census data to compile more detailed demographic breakdowns of mostly urban consumer markets. Subsequent editions in 1918, 1921, and 1926 offered additional information on consumer goods retailers and corresponding distribution channels.[23] Another prominent advertiser, Young and Rubicam, conducted regular consumer research under the direction, after 1932, of George Gallup, a recent psychology PhD and leading authority on the testing of advertising copy (see chapter 2).

Two other market researchers are noteworthy, since they, like Gallup, later became public opinion pollsters. A jewellery wholesaler during the 1920s and early 1930s, Elmo Roper had travelled the country extensively, conducting informal market research among dealers and customers. In 1934, he teamed up with Richardson Wood of JWT and Harvard Business School marketing professor Paul Cherington to form the market research firm Cherington, Roper, and Wood. Roper made use of his far-ranging contacts to assemble a nation-wide contingent of survey interviewers who were used for consumer and, after 1935, public opinion surveys.[24]

Archibald Crossley started market research work for an advertising firm in 1918; by 1926 he had set up his own market research firm, Cross-ley, Inc., which maintained a country-wide network of personal inter-viewers. Four years later he organized the Cooperative Analysis of Broadcasting, using telephone interviewing to determine radio audience size and composition by income, sex, and age.[25] During the 1936 elec-tion, Crossley, along with Roper and Gallup, employed survey inter-viewing to gauge voter preferences, successfully forecasting the presidential result. In 1936, *Business Week* estimated annual revenues for the market research business at $4 million. While market research was not entirely based on consumer survey interviews, by the 1930s, accord-ing to Jean Converse, it 'relied on them substantially.'[26]

Market research also made marked inroads in American universities. The country's first university marketing course was taught by Harvard's Paul Cherington in 1908, and three years later Harvard's Graduate School of Business opened a Bureau of Business Research which became a national leader in commercial research. Another Harvard Business School professor in the 1930s, Theodore H. Brown, developed the math-ematical formula governing the relationship between sample size and standard error, which was soon adopted by market researchers design-ing sample surveys.[27] The consumer survey method generally used, both in the United States and Canada, was quota sampling. Interviewers selected predetermined 'quotas' of individuals from control variables like age, sex, class, geography, and telephone ownership, which when tallied together would in theory form a microcosm of the desired con-sumer 'universe.' In most cases, this involved middle- and upper-class urban housewives. Sample sizes could range from a few dozen in one centre to a national survey of five thousand or more. During the 1920s and 1930s, sixteen academic monographs and countless scholarly arti-cles on market research appeared.[28] An analysis of 676 market research projects between 1935 and 1940 revealed that 62 per cent were done by professors or university bureaus of research, 30 per cent were govern-ment sponsored, and only 11 per cent came from business.[29]

The most striking American example of academic-business collabora-tion was the Psychological Corporation, founded in 1921 by James McKeen Cattell as a clearing-house for psychologists conducting research for business and government. By 1923 almost half of all Ameri-can Psychological Association members were shareholders. While its early operations consisted mainly of psychological testing and indus-trial counselling, with the creation of a Market Surveys division in 1930 it entered the field of consumer research, employing undergraduate and graduate students as interviewers. Under the behavioural tutelage of its first director, Henry C. Link, the division established its 'Psychological Brand Barometer,' which tracked consumers' preferences for brand-name goods and their awareness of advertising slogans.[30] By the late 1930s, psychologists were well positioned to profit personally and professionally from market research and advertising's ascendency; they had established scientific authority as experts in human behaviour and mental processes, laying claim to specialized knowledge believed crucial by many on Madison Avenue to identifying consumers' desires and formulating persuasive ad copy.[31]

Against this fertile and diverse backdrop of American market research activity, Canadian researchers worked, often drawing directly on American practices, to develop a similar statistical grasp of consumer thought and behaviour. As mentioned earlier, three distinct groups in Canada – business academics, advertising and market research firms, and magazine and newspaper publishers – were the principal practitioners or sponsors of the fledgling marketing science of consumer surveying. They, as their counterparts in large-scale manufacturing had done before them, worked to regulate and rationalize an important phase of the production-distribution cycle. Consumer surveys would help forecast buyer demand, thus enabling better production planning, and hone techniques, principally advertising, to reinforce and amplify consumer spending. The project was emblematic of the broad-based economic and social phenomena that James Beniger classifies as a 'control revolution' – a series of communications and information-processing developments spawned in the wake of America's mass production revolution with the goal of greater control and administrative accountability of economic, social, and governmental processes.[32] For market researchers, the promise of consumer surveying was twofold: it was a centralized, cost-effective method to gauge and anticipate aggregate consumer demand; and it was a strategic technique to dissect the amorphous entity known as 'purchasing power,' the winning quotient of people, pocketbooks, and proclivity to spend specific to each marketed good and service.

Canada's main academic centre for consumer survey research was the Department of Business Administration (DBA) at the University of Western Ontario, established in 1927. The department's close ties with the Harvard Business School – many of its faculty were Harvard MBA graduates and, like Harvard, it used the business case study method of instruction – proved important in establishing its market research capacity.[33] In 1930 Harvard MBA alumnus Walter A. Thompson joined the DBA as a marketing professor, and within a short time he had made a significant imprint on the department. A 1938 list of departmental undergraduate theses completed since 1929 contained thirty-one in the marketing field, the largest single group, along with twenty-two in advertising.[34] A number of these studies employed consumer survey methods, many of which were reported in the DBA journal, *Quarterly Review of Commerce*, which appeared in 1933. In the journal's inaugural issue, Thompson supplied an article detailing two of his students' survey work on London-area consumer 'brand habits.' Food and other dry goods purchases were investigated, and about 70 per cent of respondents favoured brand goods over generic ones. The reporting of survey methodology left much to be desired; there was no information on survey method or sample size, and very little on sample composition.[35]

Again, in Walter Tamblyn's 1934 article on consumer opinions of retail store clerks, there was scant mention of survey methods. Sample size, interviewing method, and respondent make-up were not identified. Respondents identified 'efficient store clerks' as being more important than merchandise quality, prompt deliveries, or a good exchange policy. Women more than men were 'very particular' about their treatment by store clerks, and the affluent, shopping in higher-end stores, were, not surprisingly, generally more pleased with the service received.[36]

A more thorough reporting of interview procedures characterizes DBA student Gilbert Clarke's 1934 survey of gasoline purchasing and service station use. A total of 130 drivers completed questionnaires, probably while at the pump buying fuel. All but ten of the sample were men, since 'female drivers do not ordinarily buy gasoline or oil' and when they did they were 'conditioned' by their husbands. Age breakdowns were also provided, and socio-economic class was a function of car model: 'A' drivers were those with recent makes 'above the Buick type'; the 'B' pool comprised the 'Buick class but not below the Pontiac'; and 'C' respondents fell under the Pontiac benchmark or drove any other pre-1928 model. Drivers indicated a strong preference for brand-name gasoline, especially high among 'A' drivers, who cited quality and dependability.[37]

The reporting of survey methods was further advanced with Walter Thompson's 1935 article on Londoners' consumer spending outside the city. The sample contained 140 persons who were interviewed by the DBA's sales management class. Respondents were divided into four 'purchasing power' classes in proportion to their London-area population. Importantly, for the first time the entire questionnaire was reprinted. Indeed, the impulse for scientific 'accuracy' was overzealous, as evidenced by the reporting of survey results to the decimal point. For example, '29.41%' of lower-class shoppers selected price as the main reason for out-of-town shopping. While the total number of respondents for this subgroup was not provided, assuming it comprised one-quarter of the 140-person sample, or about 35 cases, then the margin of error would be about 25 per cent, rendering any decimal point reporting utterly gratuitous. Toronto was the most frequent out-of-town shopping destination, and, characteristically, upper-income groups were most likely to partake.[38]

The DBA's most methodologically advanced pre-war consumer survey reported in the *Quarterly* was Kenneth Murray's thesis-based article, 'Radio Listening Habits,' appearing in 1938. With help from London's postmaster, Murray designed a 170–person representative quota sample of London radio listeners broken down into five class categories, ranging from the 'A' group of 'those able to have most luxuries without stinting their pocketbooks,' down to the 'E' group, comprising 'those on "relief" or [in] the poorest type of dwelling that could be seen.' Again, reflecting the 'scientific' authority of quantitative precision, Murray reported that '87.468%' of London homes owned radios in 1937; on average, Londoners listened for 5.7 hours daily. Subsequent questions probed program preferences – variety, dance orchestras, and classical music topped the list of favourites – and listeners were asked about their likes and dislikes in Canadian broadcasting. A general consensus cutting across class lines held that 'better announcers' would most improve radio programming. Interestingly, Murray's study was undertaken, in part, to 'test the results of radio advertising,' but listeners countered this assumption with their assessment of the CBC: its 'non-advertising' format, according to Murray, was 'very heartily endorsed in most cases,' and was 'appreciated as a contrast to the influx of advertising from the United States.'[39]

Some observations can be drawn from these DBA surveys.[40] They were modest in scope: sample sizes were all under two hundred, surveying was limited to the London area, and interviewing was generally done by the students themselves. Reporting of survey methodology was erratic, notably so early on. Significantly, the wide margin of error characterizing small sample sizes, and especially subgroup breakdowns, went undetected, or at least unreported. While they were commendable undergraduate and graduate undertakings, the studies' impact on the wider market research community was probably limited, as Thompson himself inferred in 1939: 'most of the progress made in connection with [market] surveys, in which the sampling technique is used, may be attributed to advertising agencies.'[41]

As noted above, Cockfield, Brown and Company was Canada's first advertising agency to acquire an extensive market research capacity. The Montreal firm, which later developed close ties with the Liberal party (see chapter 5), was formed in early 1929 when Warren Brown of National Publicity merged operations with Harry Cockfield's Advertising Service. In the late 1920s, Brown became concerned about the paucity of available statistics for advertising research. Most DBS data dealt with manufacturing and population demographics, and Brown championed the need for a 'self-contained operation,' capable not only of analysing data, but collecting them too.[42] In late 1928, just before the merger, he hired William Goforth of McGill's Economics and Political Science Department as a part-time adviser on 'commercial research.' As Goforth was not available on a full-time basis until the end of the 1928–9 academic year, Henry King, an Oxford-educated classicist with prior advertising experience, was hired in January 1929 to oversee the firm's research operations. Cockfield, Brown quickly became a 'university of advertising' in its own right, employing and drawing on the assistance of many university-trained professionals. Hubert Kemp, a marketing professor in the political economy department at the University of Toronto, worked in the Montreal office during teaching breaks. Other economists offering their consulting services included Gilbert Jackson of the University of Toronto, Burton Hurd of the University of Manitoba, and McGill's John Culliton. Of the four full-time staff members of the recently formed Commercial Research and Economic Investigation Department in 1930, outside of King and Goforth, two were Harvard MBA graduates and another had an MA in economics. By 1930, the department was conducting a wide range of market studies for advertising clients.[43]

The extent of this research work is revealed in a June 1930 memo from Goforth to Cockfield, Brown executive H.E. Kidd, who in 1949 became the national secretary of the Liberal party.[44] The recently formed commercial research department functioned 'to transform advertising from a haphazard adjunct of high-pressure salesmanship into a scientific and essential function of modern business.' Along with its in-house employees, it oversaw an external organization of eighty-three 'research representatives' from British Columbia to Nova Scotia. The 'core' of this group were fifteen professional economists and statisticians, 'selected for youth, and progressive and aggressive thinking.' The remainder were 'men of professional, economic training,' prominent in their local business communities. Their contractual relationship with Cockfield, Brown was not spelled out, but they were presumably paid on a per job basis. The department's research process combined elements of 'desk' and 'field' work and included any number of the following steps with each assignment. Initially, the commissioning firm's executives and key clients were interviewed to determine the exact nature of the problem. A cost-accounting analysis of production and sales systems was performed to isolate any 'waste and inefficiency.' Next, questionnaires for 'all classes to be interviewed,' including consumers, retailers, and wholesalers, were prepared and then administered by research representatives in the field. The survey results were combined with extant studies and theses, including those from the Harvard Bureau of Business Research, to draft a final report listing recommendations.

Judging by the rapid growth of research clientele, Cockfield, Brown had struck a resonant chord in the business community. In 1929 the firm conducted six major and eighty minor research assignments; during the first six months of 1930 alone it contracted for thirty major research commissions.[45] A cumulative list of completed market research studies, circa 1936, lists sixty-eight major surveys spanning a broad range of fields, including such titles as 'Canadian Market for Surgical Dressings and Kindred Products,' 'Rubber Footwear and Tire Market,' 'Canadian Market for Canned Soup, Beans and Spaghetti,' and 'Canadian Market for Swimming Suits and Other Knit Goods.' Such firms as the Campbell Soup Company, Molson's Brewery, Kenwood Mills, Imperial Oil, and the Dominion Rubber Company counted among the many research clients of Cockfield, Brown.[46] One of its most thorough studies was done in 1932 for the soda maker Orange Crush. It investigated potential retail outlets by analysing local business and weather conditions, and included a consumer sample survey of beverage preferences and drinking habits. Unfortunately, the latter's methodology was not discussed. Cockfield, Brown's extensive research program, broadening the advertiser's traditional role beyond that of space buyer and copywriter, was championed by Harry Cockfield as early as 1931 as a 'highly important and even essential factor in effective agency work.' Relying on 'pretty pictures and clever copy' at the expense of research was a 'fundamentally unsound' advertising practice. In 1939, Henry King, now director of research at Cockfield, Brown, reinforced this message: 'what the advertisers and the agencies are crying out for today is FACTS. Bright ideas, hunches, and smart selling schemes by themselves are not enough; if you make a recommendation, you must be able to give a scientific reason (or as scientific as you can) for it.'[47]

Unfortunately, none of Cockfield, Brown's market research reports survive, since the firm's records were lost when it became insolvent in 1983.[48] Hence, information on detailed survey methods is not available.[49] The company conducted both desk and field research, maintaining a far-flung contingent of 'research representatives' in a system that loosely parallelled the Psychological Corporation. At Cockfield, Brown, economists far outnumbered psychologists, and its research associates were not company shareholders as in the Psychological Corporation. But both operations relied on campus-based or university-trained experts to conduct and coordinate research in multiple, distant locales to provide the capacity for 'national' research. Indeed, Kidd's personal files contain extracts of 'Psychological Brand Barometer' reports.[50] While such specialized research programs were touted by Cockfield, Brown executives as the *sine qua non* of modern advertising, there was no guarantee that research clients would become advertising ones. Many firms listed among Cockfield, Brown's market research patrons were absent from the company's advertising clientele list. The point was sorely brought home in 1936 with a market survey done for the British Columbia Tree Fruit Board. While appreciative of the survey, which 'must have cost you considerably more than the amount charged us,' the board, nonetheless, awarded its advertising account to another firm.[51]

In contrast to Cockfield, Brown, many consumer research survey reports done in the 1930s by J. Walter Thompson's Canadian office have been preserved. From yeast-cake to ammonia use, from garment tag reading to newspaper browsing, JWT consumer surveys probed intently the thoughts and behaviour of the buying public. Taken together, they provide the most concerted and systematic Canadian effort to penetrate and harness consumer opinions for advertising purposes. In the late autumn of 1929, JWT opened an office in Montreal, which soon after adopted the market research ethos of its American parent. Office manager Robert Flood, during a briefing of branch operations to JWT executives in New York, described how the firm had conducted 'the first Dominion-wide market survey' for the food manufacturer Standard Brands in December 1929 and January 1930. Although few methodological details were revealed, the survey covered seven food products sold in twenty-nine cities and some twelve thousand retail outlets. Flood reported that 'three out of every four women' bought Magic brand baking powder and that subsequent advertising had increased its sales by 5 per cent. As well, one of four 'housewives' made coffee in 'old-fashioned' pots, the rest in percolators. Sample size, survey method, and field interview systems were not discussed.[52]

While the above survey, probably JWT's first, was only mentioned, more than a dozen consumer surveys exist in the company's archives, documenting the range and increasing sophistication of the firm's research program.[53] A December 1930 report on magazine readership was based on a nation-wide sample survey of 1,688 people, comprising a 'representative cross-section of the urban population.'[54] Interviews were 'divided among families of different economic classes in relation to the estimated proportion of population in each class.' The report did not disclose sex distribution, how class stratification was determined, or how interviewing was conducted, but it did reveal a tidy amount about Canadians' magazine tastes and reading habits. Fifty-eight per cent read American magazines regularly, 7 per cent more than did Canadian magazines, with *Maclean's* and *Canadian Home Journal* being the two most popular of the latter. Thirty-eight per cent read both Canadian and American publications, and reader 'duplication' rates for Canadian magazines were highlighted, information that could help advertisers more efficiently target reader–consumer markets.

Again, with a January 1931 report on household ammonia use by '1,040 housewives in 21 representative cities across Canada,' there was little reporting of survey operation. 'Proportionate numbers from all economic classes' were said to make up the sample, and in Quebec both English and French speakers were 'given adequate representation.'[55] The focus here, as with the earlier Standard Brands survey, on urban, married women was typical of many JWT consumer surveys and those of other organizations. During the 1920s and 1930s, women were thought to control 80 per cent or more of consumer spending; the wife was typically constructed by marketers and advertisers as the family's 'purchasing agent.'[56] City dwellers on average were more affluent than town or rural residents, who were also more expensive to interview owing to greater travel time. The result was a polled preponderance of urban, married women, and the frequent conflation of homemaker, consumer, and respondent.

Accompanying this bias towards urban wives was a class one. The first JWT report to provide class breakdown figures was a 1933 survey for Standard Brands on the use of baking powder by Toronto, Kingston, Montreal, and Sherbrooke housewives.[57] The sample was divided into three economic groups, of which the upper- and middle-income sections constituted 81 per cent of the 832 respondents. A more pronounced class bias was found with a 1938 survey of the consumption of breakfast cereal in Ontario and Quebec.[58] A JWT analysis of occupational statistics indicated that in a survey divided into four income groups, the top two – 'A' and 'B' – should not exceed 30 per cent of the sample. However, 'to permit an adequate upper class sample for tabulation,' it was decided to use the following income quotas: 10 per cent for the 'A' homes (annual income above $5,000); 25 per cent for 'B' ($3,500 to 5,000); 50 per cent for 'C' ($1,500 to 3,500); and 15 per cent for 'D' (under $1,500). These categories, however, grossly inflated the top end of Canada's income distribution. Listed below are the average annual salaries by occupation group for 1931, the most recent census year: labourer ($480); semi-skilled ($791); skilled ($1,042); clerical-commercial-financial ($1,192); professional ($1,924); and managerial ($2,468).[59] Without significant sources of secondary income, none of these average wage earning families even came close to the 'B' range. All but professionals and managers would fall into the 'D' group, which made up just 15 per cent of the survey. Presumably, only plutocrats filled the 'A' quota. Of course, breakfast cereal consumption, like that of many other commodities, was not a democratic phenomenon; 'A' cupboards on average contained three times the cereal as 'D' ones. Understandably, market researchers here and on other occasions targeted consumer markets or 'universes' with disproportionate numbers of the 'buying' public, while simultaneously underrepresenting other groups among the 'general' public.

Witness the unorthodox 1938 survey of adolescent newspaper reading habits which deliberately oversampled upper-income children. Some 495 Toronto youths aged eight to sixteen were given questionnaires to complete in small groups at Sunday Schools, Settlement Houses, and Boy Scout meetings. Boys and girls, at 54 and 46 per cent respectively, were included in near-proportionate numbers. But the sampling framework fixed the 'A-B' group ('those whose fathers earn $3,000 a year or over') at 30 per cent, even though JWT officials estimated 'that only 15% of the population [came] under the AB classification.' Class determination was 'judged by the neighbourhood in which the interviews took place.' Two-thirds of respondents were twelve years or older, which 'correspond[ed] roughly to the potential appeal advertising can make on the adolescent,' since older children were thought more receptive to advertising. The twenty-five-question survey probed reading interests and routines for various Toronto daily and weekly newspapers. Part of the questionnaire adopted a fact-quiz format for comic-strip, editorial, and advertising items, including questions like 'where did Donald Duck try to take a bath in last Sunday's *Telegram*?' and 'what product in the *Star* was advertised by an umbrella and the headline "Under the Weather?"' Comic-strips proved the hands-down reading favourite; nearly three-quarters of children could recall and describe the plot of interviewer-selected strips in their previous day's paper. Only 39 per cent remembered the front page headline. While just 15 per cent recognized prominently displayed ads from yesterday's paper, a remarkable 59 per cent identified products promoted by comic-strip advertising. The implications of such findings for youth-directed advertising were obvious.[60]

JWT's most far-reaching and methodologically advanced consumer surveys were two done in 1938 and 1939 for the soap manufacturer Lever Brothers. The first, a 2,776–person sample of Ontario and Quebec women, included age, geographic, and socio-economic quotas. The same 'A-B-C-D' income divisions seen above were used, although the 'A-B' pool was limited to 15 per cent of the sample and not 30. Notably, 'working women' constituted 21 per cent of respondents, and rural residents 28 per cent. The large sample size allowed for statistically reliable demographic breakdowns, and dozens of pages of cross-tabulations illuminated the relationship between the above-cited variables and the use of soap, cream, and cosmetics, along with general washing habits. Ninety-five per cent of Ontario women regularly washed their faces in the morning, while 73 per cent of Quebec women did so; 66 per cent in Ontario but only 31 per cent in Quebec used soap twice or more daily. Employed women were slightly more frequent washers than homemakers. There was a negative correlation between age and soap use, and rural women lathered less often than their urban counterparts. Surprisingly, in what may account for the sample's pared-down 'A-B' quota, 'lower income groups in Ontario and Quebec appear[ed] to use soap more frequently than the higher brackets.'[61] Here, seemingly, was the unusual case in which consumption related inversely to income.

Perhaps reflecting soap consumption's more democratic nature, JWT's follow-up survey a year later contained a radically revamped income quota structure.[62] Where before 'A' income homes had an annual income above $5,000, the starting-point was now $3,000, and this group constituted only 6 per cent of the sample. The following 'downgraded' income-class categories, with sample percentages in parentheses, far more closely mirrored Canadian society: 'B,' $1,850 to $3,000 (17 per cent); 'C,' $1,150 to 1,850 (25 per cent); 'D,' $700 to 1,150 (28 per cent); and 'E,' under $700 (23 per cent). This survey, conducted in the fall of 1939, was a milestone, both methodologically and conceptually, of consumer research in Canada. More than any other, it was a testimonial to the market research doctrine of scientific empiricism – centred increasingly on the representative sample survey – as the most effective means to forecast consumer demand, formulate advertising, and, ultimately, boost sales.[63] The Dominion-wide survey of 5,162 housewives (the largest sample of any 1930s survey) examined families' laundry and bathing habits, along with their newspaper and magazine reading and radio listening. Patterned on the Lever Brothers' 'General Soap Survey' done annually in the United States, field workers, supervised by JWT New York and Montreal staff, conducted half-hour 'searching discussion' interviews on representative doorsteps across the country. Significantly, 29 per cent of respondents were on farms, 25 per cent were French speakers, and all regions of Canada – including the Maritimes, the area with the lowest per-capita income – were proportionately sampled. Harvard professor Theodore Brown's table of sample size and random error was reprinted, pointing to a low 2 per cent sampling error for a 5,100-person survey.

As important as the survey's methodological rigour were its conceptual underpinnings. The study's purpose was to provide a 'basic fund of information' about soap use and media interaction 'to serve as a guide in advertising and marketing plans and to serve as a base from which trends could be determined through future consumer surveys.' The following section from the report underscores the enduring strength of Stanley Resor's positivist and John Watson's[64] behaviourist principles:

Surveys showing only the percentage of families using a product give an incomplete picture of the market since two users of the same brand have widely different consumption rates. In this survey, therefore, a list of 18 representative items covering the regular wash and fine things was made the basis of careful quantitative analysis in each home. A current week's washing of each item was reconstructed by the housewife giving the number of pieces washed by or for all members of the family, the method and frequency of washing and the soap used. These detailed week's case histories secured from over 5,000 families covered the laundry requirements of approximately 23,000 persons and supplied data on 284,057 pieces of clothing or household items laundered during the week ... The value of users secured in different income groups or different city size groups could be measured and this information could be related to media coverage.

In similar fashion, 'the number of baths per week by each member of the family was secured to measure the relative importance of different users of bath soaps.' Urban English-speaking women bathed on average 3.3 times weekly, compared to only 1.1 times for rural, French-speaking women. Just 3 per cent of all housewives took 'shower baths.' Of course, such figures pointed to a bathing soap market in urban English Canada potentially three times as lucrative as in rural Quebec. Lux and Palmolive were the most popular toilet soaps, with 'good for skin or complexion' being the most-cited reason for their appeal. Information gleaned from newspaper and magazine reading coupled with radio listening routines could be matched against soap usage to determine the most effective advertising venues. (A slogan like 'good for skin or complexion' might very well anchor an ad campaign.) For example, two-thirds of the market for fine-fabric laundry soaps resided with families in the top half of income earners. These families also formed 76 per cent of *Le Film* readers and 63 per cent of *Canadian Home Journal* and *Maclean's* buyers, but only 43 per cent of the readers of agricultural and religious publications, obviously the least appealing advertising vehicles for fine-fabric cleaners. The report contained dozens of cross-tabulations highlighting the relationship between class, region, sex, age, mass media consumption, and soap use, providing an unlimited range of information for future marketing campaigns.[65] Maritime sales quotas might be readjusted, an advertising blitz promoting bathing in rural Quebec could be considered, recommendations to production staff about changing the fragrance of toilet or laundry soaps might be made. The high-water mark of 1930s consumer research, the survey illustrated graphically (literally so) the marketer's scientific impulse to control and rationalize consumption and enhance the effectiveness of corresponding advertising.[66]

Along with J. Walter Thompson and Cockfield, Brown, another firm assumed prominence in the consumer surveying field. Founded in 1932, Canadian Facts was not an advertising agency but a 'research house' which performed specialized market research services for corporate, and later government, clients. Still operating today, it endures as Canada's oldest market research firm. Its origins date back to a 1932 meeting between Cockfield, Brown executive Frank Ryan and Ethel Fulford, a supervisor of Bell Telephone operators. Ryan sought a telephone-based survey method to measure the size and composition of radio program audiences in order to develop advertising strategies for this new medium. Fulford recruited some of her operators into a newly formed business which conducted telephone surveys of Toronto residents to gauge their radio listening. Using what was known as the 'coincidental telephone method,' surveyors asked respondents which if any station they were tuned to when called. Demographic information was also solicited. Canada's pioneer radio 'ratings' service (or 'audience research,'[67] as it later was known), it counted Procter and Gamble and Lever Brothers among its early clients, both major sponsors of daytime radio 'soap' operas.[68]

The firm's early operations focused on radio audiences, but by the late 1930s it had moved into other areas of market research. A December 1938 company advertisement proclaimed the firm's research capacity in retail distribution, consumer interviewing, advertising copy testing, radio listening, and even pantry counts – in which researchers visited homes and recorded numbers of stocked brands. The company claimed, somewhat unrealistically, an interviewing force of twelve hundred part-time 'trained investigators' in sixty-five markets country-wide. To 'eliminate guesswork' it was necessary to 'get the facts' quickly and economically, another ad boasted.[69] In a 1939 sales pitch to a prospective client, Canadian Facts boasted an even broader research network. Ninety-nine 'regional supervisors' oversaw a national field force of two thousand interviewers, 'each one a trained field psychologist, capable of interviewing a banker or a ditch-digger with equal facility.' Among its list of clients were Lever Brothers, Imperial Oil, Ford Motor Company, Kellogg Company of Canada, Bell Telephone Company, and Imperial Tobacco.[70] Unfortunately, since none of Canadian Facts' financial records from the 1930s survive, it is difficult to validate these claims.

The earliest consumer survey in the company's holdings is a 1939 report on the attitudes of parents and non-parents towards children's radio programs in a half-dozen cities in eastern Canada. The 203 respondents, divided into 'A-B-C-D' classes (the 'A-B' pool totalled 38 per cent, though no corresponding dollar figures were provided), were queried about children's programming and breakfast cereal use. Views were solicited on the suitability for children of shows like 'Dick Tracy' and 'Howie Wing.' Three-quarters thought all the selected programs were fine for kids' listening, but dissenters thought 'The Shadow' and 'Speed Gibson' the least beneficial for young minds. As well, respondents disclosed cereal preferences and whether or not these purchases resulted from broadcast advertising. Breakfast food advertisers were no doubt pleased to learn that 'no families ... reported discontinuing a cereal because of broadcasting.' The interviewer also made an in-home pantry count of cereals. Here was another illustration of the youth market's perceived importance to advertisers, highlighting children's influence on the decision-making process for cereal buying. Studies like this, when 'properly conducted' by trained professionals, asserted Canadian Facts general manager N.P. Colwell, could handle 'any given problem in the marketing of any product or service from the time it is available for sale until its ultimate use by the consumer.'[71]

Of extant Canadian Facts surveys, the most ambitious was a December 1940 readership poll for *Maclean's* magazine.[72] A 1,438-person sample of magazine readers were shown two recent issues and asked to select editorial items they had read. Interviewing was restricted to cities and, significantly, targeted upscale readers: 'No attempt was made to match proportionate income levels in the various cities, calls being concentrated primarily in middle and high income areas.' The 'A-B' income group ($1,800 and up) formed 60 per cent of the sample. Among occupational categories, executives and professionals totalled 40 per cent, unskilled labourers just 3 per cent. The survey was highly unusual in one respect: men made up 53 per cent of the sample, one of the few instances in which they outnumbered women. A public affairs magazine with a sizeable male readership, the survey conferred 'consumer' status on this characteristically (and ironically) underrepresented group. Indeed, many of the survey's findings highlighted male-female reading differences. Of the 46 editorial items listed, men on average read (or claimed to have read) 18.2, women 15.3. Men preferred articles and editorials over fiction, women generally the reverse; more women than men tackled crossword puzzles. Both groups judged 'topical subjects' to be better cover photos than 'pretty girls.' A surprise finding, no doubt reassuring to *Maclean's* officials, was the fact that the average number of readers – 4.03 – for each copy sold was higher than had been thought. The report included more than a hundred pages of cross-tabulations by age, sex, class, region, city, and item reading. Such data, according to *Maclean's* associate editor Arthur Irwin, could serve as a guidepost to 'market demand, i.e. the interest and tastes of our reader constituency,' and 'the degree to which our editorial contents meet that demand.' While editorial decisions could not be made 'solely on the basis of a chart,' survey data could be 'extremely useful to a good editor.'[73]

It was also 'extremely useful' for advertisers to learn of survey findings revealing greater than expected readership rates, especially among upper-income audiences. On 15 April 1941, the Maclean Publishing Company hosted a reception for advertising executives, during which presentations were made on the Canadian Facts survey. *Maclean's* editor H. Napier Moore called it the first time that a 'publication [had] revealed the result of a factual test showing each and every [editorial] item' and corresponding reader interest. The data, Moore stated, were 'going to be a guide to us in our editorial planning and they either confirm or revise our editorial judgement.' Irwin, who had earlier corresponded with American magazine publishers about their reader survey experiences, was more lukewarm to this numerative standard: surveys allowed 'scientific methods' to become a planning feature of the editorial process, but the editor's job still remained more an art than a systematic technique. But advertisers, who for over a decade had been exposed to the research doctrine of statistics and scientific investigation,[74] were perhaps more receptive to president Horace Hunter's concluding comments: survey research should function as an 'external audit' of business or marketing practices, mirroring the 'intelligence departments of any army' seeking to 'get at the real facts.'[75] Besieged by advertising competition from American magazines and radio, the company promoted the survey's findings to win back lost advertising dollars.[76] Throughout the war years, Canadian Facts continued to poll *Maclean's* and *Chatelaine* readers annually, and in 1943 Maclean Publishing established its own research department.[77]

Indeed, the links between magazine publishers, advertisers, and survey research ran deep. In 1912, the women's monthly *Canadian Home Journal* printed a questionnaire in the August issue, promising readers who completed and returned it a small recompense. Typical of most mail-back polls, it was a highly unscientific and unrepresentative survey; the response rate was a low 4 per cent. However, the survey's *raison d'être* was thoroughly modern, as suggested by the report's opening sentence: 'There is a growing demand on the part of advertisers to obtain information as to the class of persons reading a publication that they may know that the class of readers is one among which they can profitably advertise their goods.' Illustrating readers' 'purchasing power' (buying habits, property values, etc.) for magazine advertisers was the survey's sole purpose, and no questions gauged views on editorial content. The survey placed a 'scientific' *imprimatur* on publishers' preconceptions: *Canadian Home Journal* subscribers 'represented the great middle class of buyers,' a lucrative market for advertisers.[78] In 1937, the

Western Producer sent out questionnaires to subscribers, receiving 2,556 replies providing details on toothpaste and other consumer goods purchases by 'farmer's wives.' An Association of Canadian Advertisers quantitative analysis of six magazines' editorial content in 1938 also reflected this preoccupation with the reader-consumer. The report offered 'a sounder knowledge of magazine readers' habits, giving factual data so that advertising may be placed where it will appeal most to, and be in harmony with, the thoughts and habits of readers.'[79]

Canadian newspaper owners similarly strove to take the pulse of reader-consumers to bolster advertising revenue, which by the 1930s was the financial cornerstone of the daily press. Mirroring related trends in other industries, newspaper publishing was transformed by mergers and economies-of-scale production, beginning in the 1910s. The number of Canadian dailies peaked at 138 in 1913, but by 1931 this had dropped to 111, and by 1941 only 90 remained. Meanwhile, average circulation rates rose from 5,000 in 1901 to over 25,000 in 1940. In the same period, spurred on by higher rates of literacy and urbanization, total daily newspaper circulation grew from 600,000 to 2,165,000.[80] By the late 1930s, two newspaper chains, Southam and Sifton, controlled nearly 20 per cent of the Canadian market. Whereas Victorian-era newspaper publishers required moderate financial outlays and derived much of their revenue from subscriptions or political patronage, the typical postwar daily was a heavily capitalized, advertising-dependent operation. Subscription and newsstand revenues lagged well behind the large sums needed to meet burgeoning payrolls or operate the photoengraving plants and faster presses of the 'mass' dailies. By 1918, most profitable newspapers required 60 to 65 per cent of their space to be filled by advertising.[81] A key consequence of 'the industrialization of the press and its dependence upon advertising,' according to Carlton McNaught, was the emphasis on broadening circulation, 'not primarily to enlarge a newspaper's influence upon the minds of its public, but to enhance the value of its space to advertisers,' without whom accelerating production costs could not be met.[82]

As noted earlier, American newspapers in the late 1910s began conducting reader surveys to generate 'scientific' data for advertisers. The earliest known Canadian example was a *Toronto Star*–commissioned survey in 1930, the results of which were trumpeted in a *Star* promotional. The poll, done by a little-known organization, the Library Bureau of Canada, comprised a cross-section of the 'newspaper reading habits' of 87,964 Toronto homes. Sample size and survey methodology were not disclosed. Claiming that the *Star* was read in 50,110 Toronto homes (and disproportionately so among home and car owners), the survey constituted 'proof' of the *Star*'s advertising superiority over the *Telegram* and the *Mail and Empire*: 'The mass of buying in Toronto is done by families of the kind who were found to be readers of the *Star*.' Its publishers would later claim in 1934 that 'repeated surveys' had confirmed the *Star*'s widespread penetration of 'the homes of people of means, or those able to buy the produce or service advertised.'[83] In 1938 the *Winnipeg Free Press* released the results of its 'Independent Survey of the Winnipeg Market.' According to the advertising trade magazine *Marketing*, the questionnaire survey revealed not only the number of *Free Press* readers, but also 'how many of these families [owned] automobiles, radios, electric refrigerators,' and homes. Copies of the report were distributed among consumer goods advertisers and ad agencies.[84]

A more centralized and systematic program of newspaper market research was launched in the mid-1930s by the Canadian Daily Newspapers Association (CDNA). Here again, the primary objective was to augment advertising revenue, which the Depression and magazine and radio competition had rendered more tenuous. In 1936, the CDNA established a Research Committee, which worked closely with the Dominion Bureau of Statistics to compile data on newspaper buying and consumer markets. The following year the committee released *The Canadian Market*, a compilation of census and marketing statistics elucidating consumer purchasing power in regional and local markets served by newspapers. Its promotional campaign stressed the strengths of the daily newspaper as an advertising vehicle. As well, the committee conducted a study of the food industry, a sector making up one-quarter of total retail sales and a heavy print advertiser.[85] In 1939 CDNA researchers published *The Consumer Survey*, a statistical overview of consumer brand buying in newspaper markets based on the results of questionnaires printed in 70 CDNA member dailies. Respondents who completed and mailed back the surveys were eligible for gifts and prize money, and some twenty thousand questionnaires were reportedly returned. National advertisers and ad agencies were also involved with the project.[86]

While none of this research incorporated sample survey interviews, this would change with the activities of the Bureau of Advertising, which succeeded the Research Committee in late 1938. Possessing a larger budget and broader mandate than its predecessor, the bureau also benefited from formal affiliation with an American partner, the

Bureau of Advertising of the American Newspaper Publishers Association (ANPA). Ties to the American bureau, CDNA officials asserted, would grant Canadian publishers access to American head-office executives who made advertising decisions for their Canadian branches. As well, the ANPA since 1935 had been spearheading a 'United Front' campaign among newspaper owners seeking to win back advertising lost to radio, magazine, and billboard advertising.[87]

Consumer and advertising research figured prominently in the United Front campaign, best exemplified by 'The Continuing Study of Newspaper Reading.' Launched in July 1939 in cooperation with the Association of National Advertisers and the American Association of Advertising Agencies, the Continuing Study encompassed a series of newspaper reader surveys conducted by the Publication Research Service, formerly the Gallup Research Service. The supervisor of field operations was Harold Anderson, a partner of George Gallup and co-founder of the American Institute of Public Opinion. The survey method used was pioneered by Gallup in the 1920s and was known among market researchers as the 'Gallup method' (see chapter 2). Selected samples of individuals were presented copies of the previous day's newspaper and asked to mark editorial, advertising, and other items they had read. By 1941 such surveys had been done for some two dozen American newspapers, and in Canada *Hamilton Spectator*, *Windsor Star*, and *Montreal Star* readers were similarly polled.[88] The combined survey results revealed that 75 per cent of men and 93 per cent of women read advertisements, excluding the classifieds. Countering conventional wisdom, left-page ads were read more often than right-page ones. Local ads registered more with readers than national ones, a fact which privileged newspaper advertising, as one speaker at the 1940 CDNA annual meeting highlighted: 'Each individual man or woman is most interested in the things that immediately concern him, his neighbour, his town, his county ... the newspaper is the only medium which is hand-tailored to fit exactly this interest in every market.'[89]

Though the study's composite data were mostly American, CDNA officials actively publicized its findings to Canadian advertisers. In 1940 and 1941, the Advertising Bureau gave presentations on Continuing Study results to nineteen different groups of advertisers and ad agency executives. Firms like General Foods, Campbell Soup Company, Kellogg's, and Pepsi-Cola were supplied with survey results. Large companies seen as underemploying newspaper advertising, or those which had recently curtailed print advertising, were specifically targeted. Indeed, promotional work for the Continuing Study was deemed the bureau's 'foremost activity' in 1941. The research program, in the words of bureau executive Duncan MacInnes, worked to foster a 'new and more constructive concept of media.' Newspapers could now advance beyond a preoccupation with circulation figures and concentrate on 'the potentialities of the markets reached ... [and] the manner in which people read.'[90] Such research secured fact-based assessments of reader-consumer habits and functioned, asserted one newspaper market researcher in 1940, to 'make the newspaper an adviser, friend, and counsellor to [ad] agencies and manufacturers, rather than the space-chaser it largely is today.'[91]

No doubt, some corporate advertisers and ad firm executives cast sceptical glances on newspaper-sponsored surveys trumpeting the merits of daily press advertising. Any claims of 'objectivity' were obviously compromised by economic self-interest. But the significance of the CDNA research program lies less in its impartial credibility than in its very presence. Aware that magazine publishers and radio owners were using sample surveys to shore up advertising revenue, newspaper publishers followed suit, believing quantitative analyses were necessary to maintain or boost ad dollars – the *sine qua non* of the modern daily. By 1941 the Advertising Bureau's research activities had grown considerably from their mid-1930s origins; procuring newspaper advertising and conducting market research were increasingly coterminous.

Significantly, a publisher – Maclean Publishing – was the backer of the first known attempt at national public opinion polling in Canada. Since the mid-1930s in the United States, Gallup, Roper, and Link had been regularly polling the public on political, social, and economic issues employing survey techniques honed in consumer research (see chapter 2). As Link would later remark in 1947, the marriage of 'consumer' and 'public' polling was not unusual: 'The fact that much of this early [market] research was devoted to the study of people's opinions about magazines, about food products, about soaps and many other things of everyday life should not obscure its great importance to the field of public opinion research. After all, opinions are opinions.'[92] Maclean officials, however, when contemplating public opinion polling, were less interested in expanding the scope of consumer surveying than in securing a public relations tool in the wake of controversy surrounding the Bren Gun Scandal.

On 1 September 1938 *Maclean's* published an article by Ontario Conservative leader George Drew alleging government incompetence and profiteering in the awarding of a defence contract to a Toronto industrialist to manufacture Bren machine guns.[93] The accompanying publicity prompted the King government to establish a royal commission to investigate the affair. Its report, tabled in late 1938, indicated no corruption or other government improprieties, but did recommend that a Defence Purchasing Board be created to oversee the awarding of military contracts. The principal targets of the Drew piece, national defence minister Ian Mackenzie and L.R. LaFlèche, his deputy minister, were not singled out for criticism by the report. Although Ottawa soon agreed to establish the purchasing board as recommended, Maclean officials remained unsatisfied and continued to press the matter. *Maclean's* was then attacked by parliamentarians and other public officials for carrying out a vendetta against Mackenzie and LaFlèche. The company remained steadfast, even defiant: 'we must answer that propaganda,' president Horace Hunter affirmed on 25 March, 'or sacrifice absolutely the whole position we have taken.' Two lines of attack were drawn up. Arthur Irwin would conduct an intensive investigation of other defence department contracts, and the possibility of a public opinion survey on the Bren Gun affair and Mackenzie's performance as defence minister would be explored.[94]

In late May, Irwin conferred with Canadian Facts general manager N.P. Colwell about the cost of a national opinion poll, though he avoided mention of the Bren Gun issue. Canadian Facts, according to Colwell, had the capacity to survey a national cross-section of public opinion through a ten-thousand-person sample controlled by sex, income, age, religion, language, political affiliation, home ownership, and geographical quotas. This coast-to-coast operation could collect 'pertinent data concerning buying habits, political tendency, in fact public opinion on any subject with absolute freedom from bias, in the quickest possible time.' Irwin seemed impressed, and a couple of weeks later he presented the idea to H.V. Tyrrell, general manager for *Maclean's*. In late July, the company struck a deal with Canadian Facts for a 5,250–person poll on the Bren Gun issue and Mackenzie's record as defence minister. Pre-testing of questions would occur in Hamilton and small towns surrounding Toronto. Geographical, occupational, age, sex, and language quotas would be used to ensure a representative cross-section of Canada's voting population. The cost was $420, with the stipulation that Canadian Facts be credited in the event of publication of poll results.[95]

But the poll never took place. Maclean officials cancelled the contract in late August 1939, citing delays in the survey's start date and the changed political climate brought on by the deteriorating 'war situation.' Not for another two years would Maclean executives again broach the issue of opinion polling. In April 1941, Hunter wrote Irwin about the prospect of running American Gallup Poll results in *Maclean's* magazine once a month, but nothing came of the initiative.[96] Six months later, Canada's first public opinion polling firm began conducting national surveys. The results, however, would not go to magazine publishers but to a consortium of daily newspapers. Nor was this enterprise an outgrowth of Canadian market research operations; rather, it was the imported handiwork of George Gallup.

By 1941, consumer surveys were a familiar, if not ubiquitous, feature of Canadian marketing and advertising. The advance of this commercial technique was a manifestation of a deeper drive for rationalization and efficiency characterizing large-scale manufacturing in the United States and Canada. In Canada since the early 1900s, census manufacturing statistics had helped facilitate economies-of-scale production systems. The Census of Merchandising and Service Establishments of 1931, along with other DBS marketing data, were conceived and championed as statistical tools to replicate this feat for distribution and sales. Such data, however, fell short of procuring 'facts' about consumer attitudes and the purchasing decision-making process. Consequently, following the lead of American predecessors, firms like Cockfield, Brown, J. Walter Thompson, and Canadian Facts turned to quota sample surveys in order, in the words of one contemporary, to determine 'the *what* of manufacturing, the *where* of advertising and the *how* of selling.'[97] That academics, like those at the University of Western Ontario's Department of Business Administration and others in the employ of Cockfield, Brown, played no small role in this project highlights both the greater technical complexity of this research genre and the blurring of the traditional boundaries between academe and business. The market researcher's frequent invocation of 'science' to distinguish the consumer survey from rule-of-thumb practices served more as an appropriation of an authoritative symbol than as a *bona fide* display of experimentally derived predictive 'proof.'[98] But market research polling, nonetheless, remained a powerful and singular technique for quantifying and correlating consumer opinions, tastes, and behaviours, a fact supported by the ready adoption of consumer surveys by advertising-dependent newspaper and magazine publishers.

It is useful to reiterate James Beniger's by now self-evident point that specific business interests were the impetus and locomotion for early American market research surveys, which were definitely not the result of 'consumers looking for new ways to "speak their minds."' Empowering consumers or expanding 'consumer sovereignty' via opinion surveys did not factor into the market researcher's schema in either the United States or Canada. [The goal was to penetrate, and exploit for profit, consumers' worries, fancies, and longings.]But not necessarily all consumers. While, as Susan Strasser observes, 'twentieth-century rhetoric has conflated democracy with an abundance of consumer goods,' business decision making operated mainly on a 'one dollar–one vote basis.' The poor were and are effectively disenfranchised. Converse similarly underscores that early American market research samples were predominantly 'cross sections of the prosperous.'[99] The JWT soap surveys notwithstanding, the same was also true for most Canadian consumer polls before 1941. As the poor went largely undetected, so too did most men. 'Woman is a shopper,' pioneer marketer Charles Parlin proclaimed in 1912,[100] and in interwar Canadian consumer surveys so she largely remained, most likely married, a city dweller, and drawn from middle-to-upper-income ranks. The conceptual model in use here – drawing samples from a variable-delineated universe of preferred or 'ideal' consumers – fitted well in a society with contrasting income levels, where products were often marketed to specific social groups defined by age, sex, location, educational level, or any number of variables. But this model's differentiated design would also carry over to public opinion polling. As market researchers regarded one's capacity to spend as a prime factor in gaining inclusion in a sample, opinion pollsters privileged propensity to vote as the litmus test for including the citizen in a poll. As we shall soon see with Gallup polling in the United States and Canada, the sampled polity was often a distorted facsimile of the adult 'general public.'

2

'Selling Toothpaste and Plumbing the Public Mind': George Gallup and American Democracy

In the summer of 1936 the *Literary Digest* began work on its presidential straw poll. Starting in August and continuing until mid-October, millions of voter 'ballots' would be mailed to Americans across the country asking them to return the postage-paid cards indicating their choice between Franklin Roosevelt and Alfred Landon. The 1936 election was but the latest chapter in the magazine's long involvement with straw votes. Since the 1890s, the *Digest*'s publishers had been amassing names and addresses of likely magazine subscribers. By the 1920s, the mailing list had grown to over twenty million entries, thanks largely to the inclusion of nation-wide telephone and automobile owners.[1] The *Digest*'s owners saw a great marketing opportunity in straw polling. These massive prospective buyers' lists could become a voter 'sample' and the magazine would reap the publicity from being the country's largest straw-polling operation.[2] In 1916 it completed its first presidential poll, which it repeated every four years, and this strategy had helped the *Digest* become the nation's largest news magazine by the 1920s, with a circulation of nearly two million. While the magazine's fortunes had slipped during the Depression, its 1932 presidential poll had been its best effort yet – a 1 per cent prediction error – and 1936, the editors promised, would match that performance.[3]

In light of the sizeable financial and editorial stakes invested in the poll, the *Digest* editors were understandably piqued when over a month before the survey's start date a young market researcher proclaimed that the poll would be a bust. George Gallup's 12 July salvo was a double-edged blow; not only would the *Digest* mistakenly point to a Landon win, but he even forecast the poll's erroneous final results three months in advance.[4] Undeterred, the *Digest* pushed ahead with its survey method, imperiously confident of its 'uncanny accuracy' in pointing to a Landon victory.[5] Of course, in what has become the classic example of sample bias in survey research history, Gallup was right. The lists of telephone and car owners making up the bulk of the *Digest* sample, though numbering in the millions, were heavily weighted towards upper-income groups; the 1936 vote divided along class lines, with lower socio-economic groups favouring the Democratic ticket and the more affluent siding with Landon. Consequently, the myopic *Digest* poll entered an electoral minefield and emerged battered with a 20 per cent prediction error.[6] Roosevelt's overwhelming victory so discredited the straw-polling Goliath, and in the process compounded its recent financial problems, that six months later the magazine was sold to new buyers. Soon after, it ceased publishing altogether.

The void of authority left in the wake of the *Digest* débâcle was filled by the cadre of market researchers whose survey techniques had detected the electorate's deepening class cleavages, thus enabling them to forecast a Roosevelt victory. Gallup, Elmo Roper, and Archibald Crossley had independently applied their consumer research expertise to construct national samples of representative voters. The coup of 1936, reaffirmed by subsequent generations of public opinion researchers, confirmed the arrival of these 'paragons of the new scientific survey method'[7] and ushered American democracy into the modern electoral age. The representative sample survey would over time discredit or supplant outright such rule-of-thumb methods of gauging public opinion as newspaper editorials, poll captain reports, man-on-the-street interviews, congressional mail, public demonstrations, and straw polls. More important for Gallup and his confrères, however, the promise of scientific polling transcended its technical capacity to provide prompt and accurate readings of the public mood; opinion polls would restore grassroots democratic practices in an increasingly corporatist age. The voices of the masses, 'The People,' could now finally be heard over those of the powerful few, 'The Interests.' The 1936 election, both for how the people voted and for the new-found credibility it conferred on those who would decipher their future votes and opinions, suggested a confluence of forces promoting popular democracy.

The most ardent champion of polling's democratizing function was George Gallup, the profession's most prominent and successful representative. Throughout the 1930s and 1940s, in many articles and countless speeches, Gallup expounded his populist gospel that the representative sample survey promoted democratic expression because it registered opinions from the entire social and economic spectrum. His apologia for polling rested on two key assumptions: surveying the general public was a necessary counterbalance to the inordinate influence of organized lobbies and pressure groups; and, because ordinary Americans exhibited a 'remarkably high degree of common sense,' their views were valid and useful to governments. 'The plain people,' as Theodore Roosevelt had said and Gallup often repeated, 'will make fewer mistakes in governing themselves than any smaller group will make in trying to govern them.'[8] Gallup's 'sampling referenda' would halt the trend towards elite-brokered government by providing elected leaders with a clear idea of where the people stood on public issues. It was an ideological justification for the social and political utility of polling, a project whose authority, however, derived in large measure from its association with the 'value-free' science of survey research.

But did Gallup's promise of polling correspond with its practice? While promoted rhetorically as a disinterested scientific technique reporting on the body politic, Gallup's opinion polls operated in a business and ideological context that undercut this value-neutral claim. The Gallup Poll was a commercial enterprise whose revenues derived from the sale of surveys to subscribing newspapers. Gallup was also a leading figure in market research and advertising circles, one who pioneered innovative methods to measure the opinions and behaviour of consumers. His empirical assessment of consumers' intelligence, however, contradicted his portrayal of the commonsensical citizen, even though the survey methods used for both groups were virtually identical: consumers were more persuaded by emotional and sensationalist appeals than by reason. Accompanying this paradox was an irony spawned also, in part, by business considerations. Because election forecasts were the principal yardsticks to determine the overall reliability of the early opinion polls, Gallup's sampling framework targeted probable voters and conflated them with the 'general public.' Gallup's polls, while heralded as a democratic leveller of state and private power, incorporated a sampling design which underrepresented the very constituencies most marginalized in American public life: women, African Americans, and low socio-economic groups.[9]

George Horace Gallup was born in 1901 in Jefferson, a community of some three thousand typical of many small towns in early 1900s Iowa. Religiously and racially, it was largely homogeneous; Protestants outnumbered Roman Catholics nine to one, and the 1920 census for Jefferson and its surrounding county listed only sixteen 'non-white' residents in a total population of 16,467. Since the 1870s, the town had voted solidly Republican. The bulk of the labour force worked in agriculture, commerce, and small manufacturing. There were no large industries and few unionized workers.[10] Gallup's family, like many in the town, had migrated from New England after the Civil War, and he later recalled how Jefferson 'was more New England than any New England town that [he] ever knew.'[11] His point of reference was not Lowell or Woonsocket, where industrialization and immigrant work-forces were long-standing social facts, but rather the mythic 'New England' of thrift, self-reliance, education, and civic-mindedness, what Jefferson's historian described as the 'Yankee moral standard that served as a measure of righteousness.'[12] Self-reliance and entrepreneurship came early to Gallup; when he was nine years old his parents gave him and his brother six cows for a small dairy operation, from which they were to use the money to buy clothes and school supplies. In high school, Gallup served as managing editor of the school newspaper and president of his senior class, but he was probably most remembered for using his milk profits to equip the school football team when its budget was cut during the First World War.[13]

Following the route of many Jefferson High graduates, Gallup proceeded to college, studying journalism and editing the college newspaper at the State University of Iowa. His first contact with survey research was in the summer of 1922 when he worked for the *St. Louis Post-Dispatch* interviewing householders about their newspaper reading habits. The subject piqued his interest and in 1923 he enrolled in the graduate program of psychology at the University of Iowa. His master's thesis, completed two years later, used survey research methods to ascertain the optimal personal attributes of successful department store sales clerks. In 1928 he defended his PhD dissertation, 'An Objective Method for Determining Reader Interest in the Content of a Newspaper,' which employed a technique later known in market research and advertising circles as the 'Gallup Method.' To a one-thousand–person sample of *Des Moines Tribune and Register* readers, Gallup and his interviewers presented copies of the previous day's newspaper and had people indicate, column by column, what items they had read. Upon graduating, Gallup conducted similar readership surveys for the *Cleveland Plain Dealer* and *Liberty* magazine, and after brief teaching stints in the journalism departments of his alma mater and Drake and Northwestern universities, he moved to New York in 1932 to become vice-president and director of research for the advertising firm of Young and Rubicam.[14]

Gallup's interest in journalism, market research, and applied psychology coalesced around the idea of creating a systematic and scientifically verifiable method of gauging public opinion. At Young and Rubicam he conducted studies on consumer preferences and purchasing habits, but the potential for survey research seemed far greater. 'I had the idea of polling on every major issue,' Gallup later recalled, a 'continuing poll' of the *vox populi* that would become a central feature of the political landscape. His early efforts in this regard, begun in 1933, were in hindsight rather crude. During weekends and evenings he sent penny postcard opinion ballots to people listed in a variety of voters' and subscribers' lists. Unlike the *Literary Digest*, however, Gallup employed rudimentary control measures (i.e. questions on past voting or demographic characteristics) in order to ensure that the returned ballots reflected an approximate cross-section of the voting public. He also began to experiment with personal interviewing. This low-budget operation, nonetheless, was able to predict the Democrats' electoral gains of 1934, despite the prevailing political wisdom that the party in power traditionally lost seats in mid-term elections. This feat enabled Gallup to convince fellow midwesterner Harry Anderson of the Publishers' Syndicate that a newspaper column reporting the results of his fledgling polls was viable and potentially profitable. In the summer of 1935 they established the American Institute of Public Opinion (AIPO); Gallup handled the operation's surveying end and Anderson secured newspaper buyers for the column. An office was set up in Princeton, New Jersey (where Gallup had recently bought a house), a dozen staff were retained, and approximately two hundred part-time interviewers from across the country were hired by post. Helped along by the backing of *Washington Post* publisher Eugene Meyer, the first AIPO 'America Speaks' column appeared on 20 October 1935 in some sixty newspapers nationwide, including the *Post*.[15] The first question put to Americans was 'Do you think expenditures by the Government for relief and recovery are too little, too great, or just about right?' Sixty per cent said 'too great.'[16] The AIPO column embodied two postwar trends in newspaper journalism: the proliferation of syndicated features and columns, and the enhanced ideal of 'objectivity' in news reporting. The column's tables, graphs, charts, and accompanying commentary soon became the journalistic standard bearer of quantitative authority, seeking to render public opinion more tactile (more 'scientific') and less amorphous.[17]

Gallup's initial involvement with the AIPO was on a part-time basis. He remained full-time at Young and Rubicam (as he would until 1947), and consequently his work at the AIPO Princeton office was confined largely to evenings and weekends. Each week Gallup and his editorial staff selected questions for the weekly survey. Although postcard ballots were still in use until shortly after the 1936 election, they were increasingly replaced by the more reliable technique of face-to-face interviewing. The survey method employed was known as purposive design quota sampling. Interviewing locations across the country were chosen to reflect proper proportions of state and rural, town, and city dwellers. Within these zones, interviewers selected predetermined 'quotas' of individuals usually from the following categories: age, sex, socioeconomic status, and political affiliation. The aggregate totals formed a microcosm, usually around three thousand respondents, of the geographical, social, and political landscape as determined by recent census figures and electoral returns.[18]

Collecting this data were the roughly six hundred part-time interviewers who had joined the AIPO by 1938, although not all were used for each survey. Most were college educated, since Gallup used educational directories and professionals' lists to recruit field workers. If a listee lived where an AIPO interviewer was needed, he or she (women formed at least 60 per cent of the total by the late 1930s) was contacted by post. Those interested in this new line of work were sent a manual outlining interviewing procedures and a trial questionnaire. No personal training or staff supervision was provided. When the interviews were completed, the questionnaires were mailed to the Princeton office and tabulated by machine on IBM punch cards. The editorial staff, working in New York, completed the process by writing the column, which usually focused on one surveyed issue, and sending it to the subscribing newspapers. The column appeared weekly until January 1938, and thereafter three times a week.[19] While additional newspapers picked up the column after the 1936 election, high operating costs and the ongoing Depression made the AIPO less a money maker than a 'labor of love,' Gallup confided to a colleague in November 1937.[20]

By the early 1940s, however, the AIPO had achieved a good measure of fiscal success and public recognition. Gallup's finances were secure enough in 1939 that he could donate $2,500 to Princeton University to assist its debt-troubled journal, Public Opinion Quarterly. In March 1940, a New Yorker piece on Gallup described the AIPO, or the 'Gallup Poll' as it was now commonly called, as being 'certainly in a healthy financial state.' Thirty people worked in the Princeton office, making it the largest non-university enterprise in town, and 106 newspapers carried the poll.

By 1944 this number had grown to 130, over double the original 60.[21] By the mid-1940s, Gallup affiliates had been established in Britain, France, Australia, Sweden, and Canada. Gallup even formed a partnership with a film company to 'reflect on the screen and to visualize public opinion as reflected by the Gallup Polls.' One of these short films, showing a cross-section of people answering the question 'If Hitler should win abroad, would he invade the United States?,' was screened in the White House for the Roosevelts in 1941.[22] During its initial years of operation, the Gallup Poll queried Americans on hundreds of issues, including Roosevelt's popularity, the sterilization of habitual criminals and the insane, the merits of women jurors, jail sentences for drunk drivers, sit-down strikes, New Deal legislation, the humaneness of modern warfare, and birth control. 'That man Gallup,' one observer remarked in 1942, 'has become the arbiter of social change to the man in the street – and to many in the offices looking out on the street.'[23] The subject of many press stories,[24] Gallup was 'almost a household word'[25] in the early 1940s, by which point his name was synonymous with polling itself.

Not just the recipient of press attention, Gallup wrote numerous popular and scholarly articles on the representative sample survey, trumpeting its ability to reveal the collective wisdom of average Americans and to promote grassroots democratic expression.[26] Gallup's most-cited political philosopher was James Bryce, who a half-century earlier had exalted the advanced state of American democracy, lamenting only that it could not progress to a higher plateau where the will of the majority would be 'ascertainable at all times.' The scientific opinion poll, Gallup argued, would realize this 'fourth stage' of democracy by continuously transporting the views of ordinary citizens into the corridors of power. As described in Gallup's co-authored polling opus, *The Pulse of Democracy*, published in 1940, the project was decidedly progressive and pluralistic: 'If government with the consent of the governed is to be preserved and strengthened, then the common man, the farmer, the industrial worker, the stenographer, the clerk, the factory hand must become as politically articulate as the professional man, the businessman, and the banker.'[27] In addition, polling, in conjunction with existing technologies, promised to rekindle the immediacy and vibrancy of civic debate from an earlier 'golden age.' Reflecting, perhaps, on his Jefferson years, Gallup wrote in 1939:

Today, the New England town meeting idea has, in a sense, been restored. The wide distribution of daily newspapers reporting the views of statesmen on issues of the day, the almost universal ownership of radios which bring the whole nation within the hearing of any voice, and now the advent of the sampling referendum which provides a means of determining quickly the response of the public to debate on issues of the day, have in effect created a town meeting on a national scale.[28]

Nor should one worry about the people's aggregate 'responses,' for generally they proved thoughtful and reasoned. 'Their minds are active, not dull,' Gallup noted: 'Talking with the people is a good cure for any one who has been gloomy about America.'[29] And many in the 1920s and 1930s, like Walter Lippmann and Thurman Arnold, were 'gloomy' about the prospects of an informed and intelligent citizenry playing a meaningful role in a complex, industrialized society.[30] To such critics, Gallup offered up a kind of Deweyian social scientific praxis (the term 'fact-finding' appears throughout Gallup's writings, though he never acknowledges Dewey by name) that presented 'empirical' evidence of the popular will and of the people's collective acumen, thus serving the public interest.[31]

On one level, Gallup embodied aspects of the fusion of social science and democratic idealism characteristic of public-spirited reformers, especially during the Progressive era.[32] He signed his newspaper columns and popular articles as 'Dr' Gallup; the name 'Institute' was chosen over 'Company' or 'Organization' because of its more august, disinterested association; the AIPO trademark logo was a picture of the Capitol Dome. When explaining the principles of population sampling, Gallup adopted the metaphorical language of the doctor extracting a blood sample or of the bacteriologist taking water samples from a river.[33] But Gallup, though the holder of a psychology PhD, was largely absent from the social scientific debate taking place in the academy.[34] Instead, it is to the matrix of commerce that one turns to assess Gallup's claims of polling's democratizing function. While he was known internationally by the early 1940s for his public opinion surveys, throughout Gallup's career he was far more involved in consumer research, both for other firms and with the many market research companies he established during his lifetime.

Market research surveys traced their origin to the early 1910s. At that time, such developments as improved distribution and communication infrastructures along with the spread of name-brand products, coast-to-coast chain and department stores, and mail-order shopping demonstrated the need for increased advertising in the emerging national mass market. Total advertising volume jumped from $256 million in 1900 to $2,987 million in 1929. To ensure that these dollars reached their optimal buyer markets and that advertisers employed the most persuasive selling tactics, studies on consumer preference and the purchasing decision-making process took on additional importance. By 1916 house-to-house interviewing had begun and consumer surveys proliferated by the late 1920s.[35] Well before the public opinion surveys of the 1930s, market researchers used quota sampling methods, and their adaptation to the measurement of opinion on political and social issues was, from a technical standpoint, an easy transition.[36] Indeed, the editorial accompanying the first-ever published scientific opinion poll in July 1935 noted approvingly that the technique for the 'selling of toothpaste' would now be applied to the 'plumbing of the public mind.'[37]

Gallup was the quintessential market researcher-cum-pollster. In an early book, which he co-authored with University of Iowa colleagues in 1927, Gallup's biographical note listed him as 'formerly connected with advertising agencies.'[38] His newspaper and magazine readership studies covered advertising as well as editorial items, and it was the importance of the former that led the soap manufacturer Lever Brothers to hire him as a consultant in 1931.[39] He also caught the attention of executives at J. Walter Thompson, America's largest advertising firm, who spent most of a November 1931 staff meeting discussing the 'Gallup method' and corresponding advertising strategies.[40] Indeed, Gallup's readership studies are described in numerous advertising works of the 1930s and early 1940s.[41] This fact was not overlooked by one journalist of the period: 'Mr. Gallup, having worked out a system of tests to help advertisers know whether to sink their money in full pages on the virtues of brushless shaving cream or the old-fashioned soapy lather, transferred his technique to politics.'[42] Gallup pursued additional market research ventures even while working at Young and Rubicam and the AIPO. In 1937, he and David Ogilvy founded Audience Research Inc., which conducted market research for the feature film industry. In 1941, the firm had completed 194 surveys probing the demographics and habits of movie-goers, along with their preferences for story lines and star billings. In 1938, Gallup teamed up with Claude Robinson to establish another market research company, the Opinion Research Corporation, which conducted a wide array of consumer studies. A year later, a Gallup affiliate oversaw research for the *Continuing Study of Newspaper Reading*, a series of readership surveys which by 1941 encompassed some two dozen dailies, many of them Gallup Poll subscribers.[43]

On the surface, it seems hard to imagine how Gallup could have managed so many different and concurrent business interests. In fact, however, they complemented one another nicely. John Maloney, who worked in the AIPO's Princeton office between 1935 and 1941, recounted how Gallup's market research and public opinion polling operations effectively merged. The far-reaching AIPO contingent of interviewers were conducting consumer surveys in addition to their public opinion assignments by the late 1930s, and 'omnibus' surveys, comprising consumer and public opinion questions, were in use soon after. The publicity generated by the AIPO, especially during election campaigns, served as a 'builder-upper of clientele for market research.' Business clients of Young and Rubicam who wanted more extensive market surveys sought out Gallup's services. Early on, newspaper subscriptions barely covered the AIPO's costs, and it was largely thanks to market research revenues that 'Gallup managed to keep the thing alive financially,' according to Maloney.[44] One journalist, writing in 1940, commented on this when noting that Gallup's consumer research employed 'the same tactics, and sometimes the same staff of [Princeton] assistants, he uses for gathering his [AIPO] material.'[45] It is symbolic – if owing only to convenience on Gallup's part – that the AIPO New York editorial office was originally located in the same Madison Avenue building as Young and Rubicam.[46]

Considering the close interconnection between Gallup's market research and public opinion operations and his strong faith in the intelligence of the common citizenry, one might ask what views of consumer thought and behaviour prevailed among market researchers and advertisers in the interwar period. The psychology profession's rejection of a rational, 'instinctual' paradigm for a behaviourist one did not go unnoticed. The 'Psychological Corporation,' established in the early 1920s by social scientists who conducted market research for the business community, made extensive use of behaviourist studies, particularly within its Market Survey Division. The division's first director, applied psychologist Henry Link, sought to expunge from market research any structural theories of introspection concerning the mind and thought processes. The focus now was on how total organisms acted, or rather 'reacted,' to advertising and other stimuli, with the primary task being to elucidate the relationship between opinions and behaviour.[47] The market research community's embrace of behaviourism, coupled with the swelling number of psychologists on Madison Avenue payrolls – including John Watson, the 'father' of behaviourism[48] – contributed to advertising's becoming 'truly an applied science of persuasion' by the late 1920s.[49]

The most effective means of 'persuasion' was that which targeted the psyche and the emotions, not the intellect. During the late nineteenth and early twentieth centuries, most advertising copy consisted of factual descriptions of products, appealing rationally to the prospective buyer. By the 1920s, however, as Merle Curti has documented, advertising copy had completed a transition from an emphasis on the dominance of reason and will over the emotions to one assuming the exact opposite. The average consumer was a malleable, impulsive being, swayed easily by emotions and sensual experiences and highly susceptible to manipulative techniques.[50] Advertising, according to one 1938 publication, had evolved into 'a powerful medium for influencing public opinion or belief' that operated outside of logical processes.[51]

Gallup shared the assumption that the thoughts and actions of consumers lacked a rational basis. His dissertation study of *Des Moines Register and Tribune* readers revealed that comic strips and photographs were the most popular features of the paper, far ahead of front-page news and other editorial content. The *Register* heeded Gallup's findings, and by 1937 it was ranked first among fifty-two major newspapers in frequency of photographs.[52] By the early 1930s, Gallup's readership surveys had contributed to the rapid increase of comic-strip style advertisements in newspapers and magazines. Writing in April 1932 in the advertising trade journal *Printers' Ink*, J.D. Tarcher cited the importance of Gallup's work in the rise of the comic-strip genre, a phenomenon which was 'a startling commentary on our national tastes and mentality.' He was careful to add, however, that while 'as citizens we may despair that it should be so ... as advertising men we must objectively note the fact that comic-strips ... provide an extraordinarily potent means of attracting reader attention.'[53] Another advertising writer described Gallup as the 'father' of 'picture magazines and the picture-and-caption advertising technique.' Gallup was also the author of a study of the effectiveness of magazine advertising that yielded unexpected results. While some advertisers continued to emphasize economy and efficiency in their sales pitches, the most influential selling technique from the readers' perspective was the one least used – sex appeal.[54]

Similarly, in a study for Young and Rubicam, Gallup expressed frustration with the many 'stupid women' whose newspaper reading leaned towards lurid sex scandals, comic strips, and sensational crime stories and away from the news pages. The success of the lowbrow *New York Daily News*, according to him, sprang from the predilection of 'whole legions of women to read only the headlines except in the case of a juicy crime story where their interest overc[ame] their mental inertia.'[55] Gallup was by no means alone in his singling out of women as plebeian and dim-witted. It was estimated that women controlled more than 80 per cent of consumer spending in the 1930s; most market research and advertising professionals were men. The latter's assessment of the thoroughly 'feminized' consumerate, as Roland Marchand shows, stressed the 'well-authenticated greater emotionality,' the 'natural inferiority complexes,' and the fickle, 'inarticulate longings' of unrefined female shoppers.[56]

How then could Gallup reconcile this vision of the quixotic and vapid consumer with that of the common-sense-wielding citizen when they were ostensibly one and the same? Were not these women consumers just as likely to be polled on public issues as were men? In actual fact they were deliberately underrepresented in Gallup's sampling design, partly because of a perceived business consideration. During its early years, the accuracy of the Gallup Poll in the eyes of the general public, subscribing newspapers, and businessmen interested in Gallup's market research services was measured against its success in predicting elections. Between 1936 and 1940 the AIPO conducted pre-election polls in eleven state and national contests. 'The election was the criterion,' recalled Paul Perry, who worked for Gallup from 1935 to the early 1970s, 'because at that time there was a lot of doubt about the validity and reliability of surveys.'[57] For this reason Gallup sought a 'representative' sample that would reflect the likely voting public and not the general adult population.

The point is brought home in *The Pulse of Democracy* in the chapter discussing his sample survey design and aptly entitled 'Building the Miniature Electorate.' The distinction is made between a 'social' cross-section of the population and the AIPO-employed 'political' one, determined 'on the basis of estimates of probable voting participation.' How did women rate as likely voters? 'Since the advent of women's suffrage,' Gallup wrote, 'women have neither registered nor, according to the [AIPO's] experience, voted to the same extent as men.' Nor were women thought to be interested in public issues. In a later chapter, two general types of survey respondents are contrasted. The thoughtful and serious 'average American ... will take up the questions slowly and carefully, like a man pondering his next move in a game of checkers.' Not all respondents, however, were as deliberate and civic-minded. On the next page, part of a report is reprinted from an interviewer who had classified survey respondents into three categories: the 'positive class' (those with immediate and firm responses); the 'pondering class' (similar to Gallup's checkers player) and the 'parasite class':

The parasite class is composed of those to whom a genuine opinion is unknown. The nearest they come to conviction is 'Well, yes, I guess so.' Their usual answer is 'Well, I just don't know. I can't say as to that ...' If it is a woman (and unfortunately, the bulk of this class is made up of women), she will look for her husband and say with an explanatory air, 'Ask him. I always think like he does.' ... Many of these 'I don't knows' are women well up in the economic level who 'just don't believe women have any place in politics.' They don't want to be bothered with answering a lot of questions. 'What difference does it make what I think anyway?' How will they vote on election day? Just as exactly as they were told the night before.[58]

The extent of AIPO undersampling of women is revealed in an analysis of a data set of twenty-one Gallup surveys conducted in 1936–7. Of the total number of respondents in these polls, men on average made up 66 per cent of samples, women only 34 per cent.[59] Women were undersampled for both voting and issue questions. Voting questions were not weighted to reflect women's 50 per cent population share, but among the half-dozen issue questions examined, the reported results were weighted by sex, though they did not completely compensate for female undersampling.[60] The data also suggest that women were not as politically indifferent as commonly believed. To attain a rough indicator of political apathy, the number of 'no opinion' answers was tabulated as a percentage of total male and female responses. Among men the 'no opinion' response rate was 11 per cent; among women it was 15.5. In other words, 89 per cent of male responses and 84.5 per cent female responses offered opinions. This 4.5 per cent discrepancy would hardly justify a 'parasitic' labelling of women's civic interest as defined by the polls.[61]

How accurate were Gallup's claims that women voted infrequently and that when they did they merely replicated the ballots of their male relations? No statistical evidence of female voter turnout is cited in *The Pulse of Democracy,* but there are passing references to the electoral studies of Charles Merriam and Harold Gosnell. Their highly influential analysis of the 1923 Chicago mayoralty election found that women made up 63 per cent of all non-voters, and that among this group was 'an unduly large proportion' of women of German, Italian, and Polish back-grounds.[62] Illinois was also the only state in 1916 and 1920 where men and women voted in separate ballot boxes, and thus it was the only juris-diction that could report actual and not estimated male-female voter rates. In 1920, 47 per cent of women cast ballots compared to 74 per cent of men.[63] The Merriam-Gosnell study and the Illinois figures were soon cited by social commentators as proof that women throughout the United States were lukewarm towards their newly won franchise.[64] Charles Russell, writing in *Century* in 1924, argued that female suffrage had not lived up to its advanced billing because most women 'did not care enough about any public duty to vote.' The end result was a dou-bling of the 'number of docile ballot-droppers' and the development among men of a 'half-contemptuous attitude' towards women voters.[65] A common truism took hold that female suffrage was to blame for the abysmally low voter turnout rates of the 1920s and that women voters merely emulated the choices of their husbands, brothers, and fathers.[66]

By the 1930s, however, there was a mounting body of evidence which refuted this view of women as ill-informed citizens and lacklustre vot-ers. In a study of 'political intelligence' conducted in the mid-1920s in Kansas, Seba Eldridge found that the 'women slightly outclassed the men on all measures' of political knowledge. Sophinisba Breckinridge's 1933 study of American women in public life examined rates of female voter registration where these records were codified by sex. By the early 1930s, women constituted 45 per cent or more of all registered voters in many jurisdictions, including Los Angeles, Pennsylvania, Rhode Island, and Vermont. Charles Titus, in his 1935 examination of American voting habits, was careful to note that, while female suffrage and low voter turnout in the late 1910s and 1920s were parallel phenomena, there 'was no attempt to suggest that one necessarily accompanies the other or that one is the cause of the other.'[67] Indeed, the voter participation rate in 1936 (61 per cent) was higher than that of 1912 (58.8 per cent) when only a marginal proportion of American women were eligible to vote in national elections.[68] Women and men scored equally on an intensity of voter interest test conducted by Princeton University researchers before the 1942 mid-term election.[69] Incredibly, information reported in an AIPO publication confirms these findings. The male proportion of regis-tered voters in 1940 for selected cities and states was listed as ranging from a low of 51 per cent in Boston to a high of 56 per cent in Pennsylva-nia. As well, the AIPO, in an early example of exit polling, gauged voter sex differences more directly: 'A sample of the voting places in this survey revealed that in 1942, 53 percent of the voters were women and 47 percent men.[70] While wartime enlistment probably accounted for some of the reduction in male voter turnout, the results, nonetheless, reflected the growing impact of women's suffrage.[71]

Gallup's opinion polls, however, failed to reflect women's accelerated presence at the polls. In a report done for the Roper Center for Public Opinion Research, Norval Glenn analysed AIPO data and found that women generally made up less than 40 per cent of the samples in the early 1940s. The first AIPO survey with roughly 50 per cent female representation did not occur until November 1944, but women did not consistently constitute half of all respondents until 1948. Significantly, Gallup's underrepresentation of women was not a polling industry standard. Both the Roper Poll and the National Opinion Research Center (NORC), a non-profit polling organization established in 1941 at the University of Denver, included women at or near the 50 per cent mark throughout the 1940s.[72]

How then do we account for Gallup's continued diminution of female respondents in the face of substantial empirical evidence pointing to increasing rates of female voting? The answer, perhaps, lies in Gallup's views on the proper role of women in public life. While editing the University of Iowa student newspaper in 1921, Gallup wrote a controversial column in the form of a dialogue between two male students entitled 'Unattractive Women.' It was the 'duty' of female students to 'make themselves as attractive as they can,' for no proper varsity man would marry a women who was little more than 'a bone, a rag, and a hank of hair.'[73] Later, in 1942, Gallup discussed Eleanor Roosevelt's public activities with a colleague. Her pronouncements on 'family life have brought her many friends and have helped the Democratic cause,' he stated, but 'her views on political matters have not been received with much enthusiasm.'[74] This despite Gallup's own polls, which showed that two-thirds of Americans in December 1938 and February 1940 approved of the First Lady's performance.[75] American women, while enfranchised since 1920 (excluding, of course, African American women in the South), were still regarded by many as ill-suited for public life, thanks in part to a western philosophical tradition which defined reason as a male characteristic and its counterpart, 'emotionality,' as a female one.[76] Women's involvement in civic affairs, even in the passive form of answering polling questions, arguably challenged the 'rational' characterization of the citizenry that Gallup saw as vital in maintaining the polls' social utility and commercial viability.

African Americans were another constituency which failed to meet Gallup's criteria for proportional representation in his opinion polls. In the 1936–7 Gallup data set, they formed 1.9 per cent of respondents,[77] well below their approximate 10 per cent share of the 1930 and 1940 censuses.[78] Glenn's statistical analysis also reveals that African Americans averaged less than 5 per cent of AIPO samples until the mid-1950s, at which point their numbers began to correspond with census levels.[79] Because the majority of African Americans lived in the South, where they were mostly disenfranchised by Jim Crow laws and practices, Gallup justified the virtual exclusion of all southern blacks from his sampling design in order to ensure reliable election forecasts.[80] Of course, black voting did occur in outer southern states like Tennessee, Texas, and North Carolina, particularly in urban areas.[81] And African Americans outside the South were by no means indifferent voters. Harold Gosnell's 1935 political study noted that Chicago blacks exhibited a 'higher participation in elections than [did] most of the whites.' This point was reconfirmed by the Myrdal report's conclusion that blacks 'vote[d] almost as much, or more, in most Northern cities than whites,' and that available data did 'not support ... the common stereotype that Negroes [were] politically apathetic.'[82]

Fully three-quarters of African Americans in 1940, though, lived in the South, the bulk of whom were barred from voting. But it was this very fact, the negation of this fundamental democratic right, that should have warranted the proportional representation of African Americans in Gallup's samples. For if indeed his polls' lauded purpose was to serve as an emancipatory vehicle for popular expression traditionally muted or thwarted, then no greater imperative existed than of providing a political voice for African Americans denied that opportunity at the ballot box. In such a scenario, regular polling in the South, highlighting black as well as white opinion, could have served to undermine the 'democratic' authority of whites-only government. Working against this prospect, however, were bottom-line considerations: a good number of Gallup's newspaper subscribers were southern,[83] a fact which may also explain the paucity of race-related topics in AIPO surveys during the period.[84] Symbolically, the first survey (August 1943) with the subject heading 'Negroes' in the Gallup Poll compendium is a poll of white southerners' opinions on Washington's handling of 'the Negro problem.'[85] As seen earlier, this time with skewed racial samples, the AIPO was unique; the proportion of African Americans in NORC and Roper polls during the 1940s approximated that of the 1940 census.[86]

The underrepresentation of African Americans, according to AIPO staffer John Maloney, was also a function of the perceived difficulty of hiring qualified black interviewers: 'a lot of [blacks] just weren't well enough educated or interested for that matter to come forward,' and thus 'the vast majority' of interviewers were white.[87] AIPO officials were unaware of or chose to ignore Charles Johnson's 1937 study, *The Negro College and Professional Graduate*, which reported on the 37,700 African Americans who had graduated from college between 1900 and 1936, and who might have served as interviewers for Gallup. Inquiries at Howard, Fisk, or Atlanta universities, for example, could have provided the names and addresses of many of these graduates. In the late 1930s, there were notable black social scientists – Johnson, E. Franklin Frazier, and Ralph Bunche, among others – who were experienced in personal interviewing and who had trained other black students in the practice. Indeed, a generation earlier, W.E.B. Du Bois had been a pioneer in the development of the social survey in America.[88]

Election forecasting and interviewer recruitment were acknowledged justifications for Gallup's undersampling of African Americans, but another less overt factor is also noteworthy – the prevailing climate of opinion among whites impugning the civic competence, political independence, and general intelligence of African Americans. Here, one finds similarities with popular attitudes towards women. As female voters were deemed to be under the sway of male relatives, black voters in northern cities were regarded as tractable election fodder for party machines.[89] Women were ill suited for public life because of their 'emotional' endowments and less-than-serious interests, while adjectives like 'irrational,' 'apathetic,' and 'docile' were regularly affixed to African Americans. Gunnar Myrdal was so struck by the two groups' analogous situation that he included an appendix in *An American Dilemma* on this 'parallel to the Negro problem':

The arguments, when arguments were used, have been about the same: smaller brains, scarcity of geniuses and so on. The study of women's intelligence and personality has had broadly the same history as the one we record for Negroes. As in the case of the Negro, women themselves have often been brought to believe in their inferiority of endowment. As the Negro was awarded his 'place' in society, so there was a 'women's place.'

Racist stereotyping was ubiquitous in the South, but was not confined to the region, as Myrdal observed: 'most Northerners seem also to be convinced of the mental and moral inferiority of Negroes.'[90] Jefferson, Iowa, was apparently no exception. Although only a handful of African Americans lived in the town during Gallup's youth, racial doctrines, wrote Morain, fostered a world view in which 'to be a white Anglo-Saxon meant that one was among the most highly advanced people in human history.' In local parlance, a con man was a 'nigger in a wood-pile,' and when the town code banned slingshots, it labelled them 'nig-ger shooters.'[91] By the 1930s most U.S. social scientists had abandoned biological theories linking intelligence to race,[92] but this realization was not yet firmly rooted in the general population. In 1942, a NORC survey asked if 'Negroes are as intelligent as white people – that is, can they learn things just as well if they are given the same education (and train-ing)?' Fifty-three per cent of decided opinion said no.[93]

It must be emphasized that nowhere in Gallup's published work or private correspondence is there any evidence of support for race-based assessments of intelligence or responsible citizenship. On the few occa-sions he broached the race question, it was to address the problem of election forecasting in a country with a sizeable number of disenfran-chised blacks. Undersampling African Americans, for Gallup, was a pragmatic response to an existing political situation, one made neces-sary by the importance of election prognostication to the commercial success of his consumer research and opinion-polling operations. But such a practice may also have performed a latent function; the accep-tance of polling as a technique to register the 'people's' collective intelli-gence – at a time when many doubted its existence – was arguably promoted by the sampling shortfall of 'irrational' and 'apathetic' groups like African Americans and women.

Gallup's samples also contained notable class biases. In a study exam-ining AIPO survey procedures during the early 1940s, Hadley Cantril, director of Princeton University's Office of Public Opinion Research and a close colleague of Gallup's (his book is dedicated to Gallup), high-lighted systematic sampling biases in occupational categories. Profes-sionals and semi-professionals made up 11.4 per cent of AIPO samples, but only 5.6 per cent of the 1940 census. The following job categories, accompanied in parentheses by their census correspondents, were also overrepresented: proprietors, managers and officials, 13.1 per cent (9.8); clerical and sales, 16.2 per cent (12.9); and service workers, 11.5 per cent (6.9). Those underreported were mainly in the industrial sector: skilled workers, 9.5 per cent (14.6); semi-skilled, 10.9 per cent (18.4); and unskilled labourers, 7.1 per cent (8.8). Compounding this occupational bias was an educational one. Respondents with grade 8 education or less – 60.4 per cent of the 1940 census – constituted only 38.5 per cent of Gallup's sampled polity. Those with more than grade 12 education formed 26.6 per cent of the AIPO 'public,' but made up just 10.1 per cent of the population as a whole.[94]

These discrepancies occurred because occupation and education were not directly controlled variables, as were, for example, age or urban-rural distribution. The standard measure of economic status was instead determined by the interviewer's estimation of a respondent's income within five categories ranging from 'wealthy' to 'on relief.' As interviewers were free to fill their assigned quotas wherever suitable respondents might be found (i.e. parks, bus stops, doorsteps), and since these college-trained questioners were drawn largely from middle- and upper-class ranks, there was a tendency, Cantril observed, for them to 'choose respondents whose whole frame of reference [was] like their own.'[95] Gallup, in 1944, also commented on this form of sampling bias favouring higher socio-economic groups: 'In all forms of interviewing ... the problem always is to reach the very lowest level. When you get down to the foreign-born, and so on, you have one devil of a problem interviewing. Interviewers are always loath to interview those people ... And that is why you always have to fight in this business to get the lower groups, especially with a quota sampling system.'[96]

On another occasion, Gallup offered business and ideological reasons for why this 'fight' may not have been pursued vigorously. It was 'axiomatic,' he wrote in 1944, that 'no opinion' responses predominated among the low educated, a group generally 'uninterested' and 'uninformed' about most national issues.[97] High 'no opinion' response rates required additional interviewing – and added expenditures – to ensure a statistically reliable sample of 'decided' opinion. Of course, 'uninformed' respondents also tainted an otherwise intelligent citizenry. And indeed, Glenn's study demonstrates that the AIPO continued throughout the 1940s and 1950s to underreport those with less than grade 12 education.[98]

Even when the 'very lowest level' was reached, other forms of bias could affect a poll's reliability. In a 1941 study, Princeton psychologist Daniel Katz analysed the effect of the interviewer's social class on the opinions of working-class respondents. Katz recruited and trained eleven working-class interviewers, who, along with a group of AIPO white-collar interviewers, conducted a survey in a low-rental district of Pittsburgh. The responses obtained by the blue-collar interviewers were consistently more liberal than those of their middle-class counterparts. This was especially so for labour issues. For instance, among white-collar interviewers, 61 per cent of respondents supported a law prohibiting sit-down strikes, 26 per cent opposed it, and 13 per cent were undecided. Among working-class interviewers, the respective figures were 47, 34, and 19 per cent. A similar, if less pronounced, pattern prevailed for other labour-related questions, and the discrepancy was most striking among trade unionist respondents. Katz had found what later survey researchers would define as 'interviewer effects' – in this case, that certain people, mostly unconsciously, tend to give the responses they believe their questioners prefer to hear. Katz's advice to commercial polling firms like the AIPO was to reduce their 'exclusive reliance upon white-collar interviewers' and hire more field workers of working-class origin who were better able 'to discover the true opinions of the labour voter.'[99]

A 1946 study by Arthur Kornhauser, a member of Columbia's Bureau of Social Research, uncovered further evidence of the polls' anti-union bias. Kornhauser examined all labour-related polls conducted by seven survey organizations between 1940 and 1945. Sixty of the 155 total were AIPO questions. Only 8 questions dealt with topics judged 'positive' for unions (i.e., improved working conditions), 66 were categorized as 'neutral,' but 81 questions concerned 'negative' issues – for example, wartime strikes. Three-quarters of AIPO questions, but only one-third of those of other polling organizations, fell into the negative category. The Gallup Poll was also criticized for slanted, anti-union wording of questions and for survey reporting which exaggerated the extent of anti-labour popular sentiment. The primary cause of this pervasive bias, Kornhauser contended, was a structural feature of commercial polling. Firms like the AIPO worked first and foremost to serve their principal 'markets' – newspaper publishers, subscribers, and business clients – and were successful 'because the men who built them and who run them are effective executives whose own views are acceptable to the business world.'[100]

Mindful of the Cantril, Katz, and Kornhauser findings, we turn to Gallup's treatment of class. Gallup was particularly interested in attitudes on organized labour, as evidenced by the many dozens of AIPO polls on sit-down strikes, government regulation of unions, the closed shop, John L. Lewis, and similar topics throughout the 1930s and early 1940s.[101] The results of these polls, Gallup argued, suggested little popular support for labour's agenda: two-thirds of voters in March and July

1937 favoured making sit-down strikes illegal; similar majorities in April and November 1937 advocated force to remove such strikers;[102] nearly three-quarters of Americans in June 1939 opposed closed-shop and union-shop practices; 81 per cent in January 1943 favoured the legal prohibition of strikes in wartime industries.[103] What made these findings especially compelling, Gallup contended, was that they derived from a 'careful measurement of opinion at each social and economic level,' one that 'reflect[ed] both the wage-earners and the employers of America in their approximate proportions.'[104]

Less prevalent was AIPO polling on the activities of business and its influence on public policy, a point also made by Kornhauser and David Thelen.[105] For example, only twice between 1935 and 1944 did the AIPO ask directly about corporate taxation, and one of these questions in May 1939 was so slanted as to be humorous: 'Do you think that conditions in this country would be more prosperous if taxes on business were reduced?' Not surprisingly, public opinion ran three to one in favour.[106] In a similar vein, the AIPO asked Americans in April 1938: 'In your opinion, which will do more to get us out of the depression – increased government spending for relief and public works or helping business by reducing taxes?' The phrase, 'helping business by reducing taxes,' in the words of journalist J.J. O'Malley, resembled 'something that, in a lovely dream, an angel would say to J.P. Morgan.' Here again, not surprisingly, respondents sided solidly with this option. In fact, O'Malley ventured, business considerations were foremost in Gallup's mind when he took his inaugural poll showing that the public did not favour high levels of New Deal government spending: 'Many publishers were dourly pleased with this survey, which bore out their own notions,' and consequently signed on with the institute.[107] Despite Gallup's first-hand knowledge of class-based voting in 1936, he denied that Americans were forming 'self-conscious class blocs'; such a phenomenon belied the people's overall 'strong sympathies for business,' and their conviction that Washington 'should pay more attention to "the business man's point of view."'[108]

Gallup similarly denied a common criticism made of his surveys – that they contributed to a 'bandwagon' effect among electors. This phenomenon, occurring when undecided voters sided mainly with disclosed majority opinion, was thought inimical to the workings of a sound polity, in which citizens made independent use of reasoned judgment to assess civic issues and voting decisions. Not surprisingly, Gallup often dismissed the bandwagon theory, even once asserting that 'not one bit of scientific evidence' could support it.[109] This was a clear overstatement. Yale psychologist Leonard Doob described how by the late 1930s there were 'experimental studies galore' illustrating the causal effect of revealed majority opinion on the formation of attitudes and opinions.[110] Of particular note was a 1939 study detailing how 'planted' AIPO poll results consistently swayed people towards the majority view. Opinion polls were a 'potent force' for influencing individual decision making, Winston Allard concluded, and if placed in 'unscrupulous hands [they] might become effective propaganda weapons.'[111] In a similar vein, Princeton political scientist Harwood Childs expressed concerns about these 'instruments of power.' The selection, timing, and wording of questions, along with the reporting of data, afforded an 'infinite number of ways, some of them very subtle, for using these techniques for private rather than public advantage.'[112] Bandwagon concerns were behind congressional attempts to restrict election polls. As early as February 1935, Oregon congressman Walter Pierce proposed a bill to prohibit the use of the postal system for election straw polls. A similar bill was reintroduced in the House in 1937, though it, like its predecessor, went nowhere. Pierce attacked polling for serving to 'create rather than measure' opinion and for opening the door to 'uncontrolled, private manipulation of public opinion for financial profit.' Fifty per cent of congressmen surveyed in 1939 believed polling propelled the bandwagon effect.[113]

The Gallup Poll's ability to 'create rather than measure' the public mood was reported on by other Washington insiders. Roosevelt cabinet member James Farley recalled how Robert Wagner referred to him half-jokingly as 'Mr President' when a 1940 Gallup Poll of preferred Democratic party nominees gave him strong public support. When a poll the same year showed secretary of state Cordell Hull running stronger than FDR, the response was less lighthearted. Roosevelt was apparently dismayed by the results, and Hull, who claimed no presidential ambitions, maintained that after the poll's release 'every effort [was] made to destroy' him.[114] The president even worried during the 1940 campaign that Gallup might try to profit financially by manipulating poll results to the Democrats' detriment.[115] One journalist ventured, with obvious embellishment, that AIPO poll results came 'a lot closer to telling Congress what to do' than did Roosevelt. Gallup's numerative offerings prompted another observer to bemoan the 'propagandist possibilities of such devices' and to hope that a 'Congressional investigation may one day prod into their uses.'[116]

That day came in late 1944. Since it had begun polling, the AIPO had regularly underforecast Roosevelt's presidential vote (a prediction error ranging from 2 to 7 per cent in 1936, 1940, and 1944), although it always picked FDR as the winner.[117] This steady pattern contributed to rumours, all unfounded, that Gallup was in the pay of Wall Street interests or in league with the GOP. Though an acquaintance of Thomas Dewey, Nelson Rockefeller, and other Republicans, Gallup, for obvious reasons, never declared any party affiliation.[118] He did, however, according to Maloney, 'tend to lean a little more toward the Republican side,' reflecting the fact that his business dealings 'were mostly [with] people with a lot of money.'[119] This was true of his contacts through market research and newspaper publishers.

After the 1944 contest, congressional Democrats became concerned about the prospect of partisan tampering with AIPO election polls, and the House Committee to Investigate Campaign Expenditures launched a probe of the Gallup Poll. Committee members visited the AIPO in Princeton, and on 28 December Gallup appeared before them in Washington. Gallup attributed the Democratic undercount in 1944 to higher rates of migrant voting and the better-than-expected efforts of Democratic party machines to mobilize their vote in large cities. A technical report from the committee, written by Louis Bean, Philip Hauser, Morris Hansen, and Rensis Likert (all renowned authorities on survey sampling), countered, however, that Gallup's problem in part owed to his use of quota sampling, a methodology which 'did not provide insurance that the sample drawn [was] a completely representative cross-section of the population eligible to vote.' Even though interviewers may 'obtain the proper quota of persons of a given age or income level, [they] may unwittingly obtain persons who are not representative with respect to education, church affiliation, employment, attitude toward the war, or other characteristics.'[120] The report suggested that Gallup make greater use of area probability sampling (in which interviewers called at fixed-interval residences and had little say in the selection of respondents), a statistically more reliable, if more expensive, method employed by most government and academic survey researchers.[121] The advice went mainly unheeded. Gallup carried on with quota sampling, and in the 1948 presidential contest, nearly as confident as the *Literary Digest* had been in 1936, he forecast a Dewey victory.[122]

In his analysis of American popular culture in the 1930s, Warren Susman underscored polling's importance in affirming cultural hegemony:

'It was easier now to find the core of values and opinions that united Americans, the symbols that tied them together, that helped define the American Way.'[123] Polls became numerative benchmarks of popular sanction for a variety of ideas and ideologies, programs of reform or reaction, codes of social conduct and moral belief. That opinion surveys, construed rhetorically as the voice of 'The People,' came to command both political and moral authority in a country whose progressive tradition embodied strong democratic and scientific currents was foreseeable.[124] As Susan Herbst has argued, polling's symbolic power was (and is) a function of its scientific and representative claims: 'Sampling itself is a democratic notion.'[125] Less foreseeable, and certainly less desirable from an egalitarian standpoint, were Gallup's survey and business practices, which undermined his assertion that polling rendered the 'industrial worker and the stenographer' as politically articulate as the 'businessman and the banker.' While Gallup promoted polling as a new chapter in the advance of American democracy, the AIPO's early years resonated more with irony than grassroots resurgence. Sampling bias, which toppled the *Digest* survey, became a methodological feature of its 'scientific' successor, albeit less pronounced, which in turn damaged the polls' credibility after the 1948 election. Gallup, the champion of the public's collective wisdom, was simultaneously a leader in marketing thought and advertising techniques like the comic-strip genre which debased consumers' rationality, a fact which may have worked to weaken his populist and egalitarian message. It was the 1936 election – the victory of the New Deal Coalition over the Roosevelt-derided 'economic royalists' – that established Gallup's polling credentials, enabling him to proceed with a survey design that undercounted African Americans, women, and low socio-economic groups. While Gallup's polls, as Susman observed, may have served symbolically to help 'define the American Way,' this should not mask the realization that certain surveyed voices were heard more than others. The mass citizenry and the AIPO-polled 'public' were not synonymous.

The democratic promise of Gallup polling collided with commercial imperatives. The AIPO was one of a number of Gallup-run enterprises that operated to 'sell toothpaste' and 'plumb the public mind.'[And it is in probing the business practices and resultant contradictions brought on by his dual capacity as consumer researcher and opinion pollster that a broader contextual understanding of the AIPO's origins and early years is gained – one which also illustrates its severe limitations as a purported quasi-public service.]The AIPO's commercial viability hinged on selling survey results to other private interests, namely newspapers. Its professional credibility, and to a lesser extent that of Gallup's other market research ventures, derived largely from election forecasting. These facts, along with the concomitant ideological biases drawn from Gallup's business setting, worked to narrow the field of social inquiry, skew his samples, and affect the interpretation of poll results. The many salvos aimed at the AIPO decrying 'propagandistic' or 'private interest' manipulation also underscore that hand-wringing over polling's civic merits long predates recent jeremiads on the modern sampled polity.[126]

3

Polling Citizens: Gallup in Canada

After years of research, it is possible to construct a nation in miniature – a sample of the population which has all of the political, social and economic characteristics of the total population. Division of opinion among a scientifically selected sample of people proves to be almost exactly the same as that of the whole voting population of the country.

CIPO pamphlet, circa 1945[1]

As in the United States, Gallup polling in Canada promised democratic regeneration. The voices of ordinary citizens would now compete with those of pols and special interest groups. 'The People,' as constituted by the polls, could finally assume their rightful, central place in the body politic. Scientific expertise helped facilitate and legitimate this exercise in grassroots rejuvenation; time and time again, Canadian Gallup officials would claim, accurate election forecasts 'proved' the representative (and hence democratic) nature of the sample survey. But in Canada, as in the United States, Gallup polling constructed a composite portrait of 'voting' Canadians which differed fundamentally from the adult population. Women and low socio-economic groups were again underreported, and French Canadians, owing to French-language interviewing problems, were also inadequately polled. The sampled 'public,' both as defined rhetorically in Gallup Poll columns and statistically in the sample design, constituted a disproportionate domain of white-collar, English-speaking males. As well, reminiscent of the American Gallup experience, market research surveys were soon operating in close tandem with public opinion polling. While numerous American–Canadian parallels existed, Gallup polling in Canada differed on at least one level. When the American Institute of Public Opinion was disparaged publicly it was usually for threatening to subvert, through private-interest manipulation, the popular will. Canada's Tory political tradition, however, blunted the appeal of Gallup's populist evangelizing of polling; conversely, criticisms of Canadian Gallup polling levied by journalists and public officials more often stressed the deleterious effects of unrestrained popular expression unleashed by the sample survey.

By the summer of 1940, AIPO affiliates had been established in Great Britain and France. Under the directorship of Henry Durant, the British Institute of Public Opinion (BIPO) was launched in 1936, and two years later the London *News Chronicle* began publishing its survey results. It was even claimed, perhaps apocryphally, that BIPO field workers, wearing tin helmets, carried on interviewing during blitz bombing raids. The French survey counterpart, L'Institut Français d'Opinion Publique (IFOP), organized by Jean Stoetzel in 1938, ran its poll results in the newspaper *Paris-Soir* until the start of the Second World War. Following the German occupation, the IFOP was shut down.[2] Australia was also slated for Gallup-style polling. Roy Morgan of the *Melbourne Herald* spent part of the summer of 1940 in the Princeton AIPO office learning the commercial and methodological rigours of survey work. When the Australian Public Opinion Polls organization, underwritten by six newspapers including the *Herald*, began operating in October 1941, Morgan was its general manager. While the exact contractual relationship between the AIPO and its overseas partners was never disclosed, the foreign affiliates, according to Gallup, all used 'the same basic survey methods as those of' the AIPO.[3]

Also in 1940, Gallup turned his attention to polling north of the border. Their work on the *Pulse of Democracy* complete by June, Gallup asked Saul Rae to help organize and manage an AIPO affiliate in Canada. Rae declined, preferring a career more closely tied to Canada's war effort. Poor vision kept him out of the armed forces but not the civil service, and, soon after, he joined the Department of External Affairs.[4] In September, Gallup travelled to Toronto and Montreal to meet with newspaper and advertising officials. A story in *Saturday Night* magazine covering his visit lavished praise on Gallup's sampling achievements: 'The results of his polls are usually within three per cent of being dead right,' and Gallup's solid grounding in 'research and horse-sense' ensured the scientific soundness and political utility of AIPO surveys.

Characteristically, Gallup did not miss the chance to expound his democratic creed: '[Gallup] is a tremendous believer in democracy and in the solid sense of the people and thinks that the "sampling" of public opinion ... may become a big factor in bringing about better government.'[5] Gallup's fame prompted Nathaniel Benson, president of the Canadian Literature Club and an executive in Young and Rubicam's Toronto office, to ask Prime Minister King if he wished to meet the polling maestro during his Canadian visit. Gallup 'might, no doubt, be able to give you statistical information of certain matters of present importance.'[6] King did not pursue the matter.

Not until mid-1941 did concrete plans to bring Gallup polling to Canada take shape. During the summer, two AIPO executives, Arthur Porter and John Tibby, traversed Canada, sounding out newspaper publishers on the idea of sponsoring a Canadian poll modelled on the AIPO. Support was especially forthcoming from *Toronto Star* publisher J.E. Atkinson.[7] By September, fourteen papers had been lined up, and later that month Gallup and a half-dozen colleagues arrived in Toronto to begin organizing a Canadian polling operation. Their stay, however, was unexpectedly cut short. Their requests for temporary immigration visas, which they thought would be granted *pro forma*, were being held up by none other than immigration minister T.A. Crerar, who was 'doubtful of the wisdom of such an organization in Canada.' Consequently, Gallup and his officials were forced to return to the United States. The impasse prompted *Toronto Star* executive H.R. Armstrong to appeal directly to Prime Minister King on 14 October. The AIPO officials, he emphasized, would be in Canada no longer than six months, at which point the 'Canadian institute would be operated entirely by Canadians, with the fourteen newspapers listed as a Board of Advisors.' Armstrong urged King to take the matter up with Crerar, reiterating that the *Star* and the thirteen other dailies strongly backed the AIPO venture: 'Government action to prohibit such an organization, which apparently Mr. Crerar thinks possible, might be widely misinterpreted and possibly resented by the newspapers in the movement.'[8] The ultra-cautious King, fearful of incurring editorial enmity, especially from a Liberal supporter like the *Star*, no doubt took the admonition seriously. Soon after, AIPO officials were back in Toronto.

Why did Gallup launch a Canadian operation at this time? According to Saul Rae, who met with his former AIPO colleagues in Toronto in late November, it was in part a response to newspaper publishers seeking to boost circulation levels via the column. But the foremost reason involved commercial considerations south of the border. The AIPO had lost some newspaper subscribers following the 1940 election, and 'in order to regain this market,' Rae asserted, 'it became necessary for the Gallup people to impress upon their editors in the United States that this newspaper feature would shortly provide information concerning opinion in other democratic countries.'[9] The Canadian venture was projected to be a break-even affair at best.

Not surprisingly, when established in November 1941, the Canadian Institute of Public Opinion (CIPO) mirrored in many ways its American parent. As the AIPO had chosen the Capitol Dome for its company logo, the CIPO adopted the Peace Tower. Some two hundred part-time interviewers from across the country were hired by mail. By 1945, this number had reached four hundred. Field workers earned sixty cents an hour, with the average assignment lasting four hours. Paralleling the AIPO model, a quota sampling system was devised whereby field workers were assigned ten interviews per survey, the total number averaging between 1,500 and 2,000. Dominion Bureau of Statistics (DBS) data were used to select interviewing locations and to construct representative samples reflecting the nation's geographical, age, sex, socio-economic, and language composition. Interviewing was conducted on average every six weeks, and anywhere from about ten to twenty-five issues were probed with each survey.[10] The completed questionnaires were mailed to the Toronto office, but statistical tabulating was done by the International Business Machine Corporation in Toronto. CIPO press releases, usually focusing on one issue, were forwarded twice a week to subscribing newspapers. In addition, a third column highlighting poll results from other Gallup affiliates, usually the AIPO or BIPO, was provided weekly. The CIPO charged newspapers a sliding-scale fee based on circulation levels. For instance, the weekly rate for the *Prince Albert Herald* would run about $10, while that for larger circulation dailies like the *Toronto Star* could reach $150. By late November the number of affiliated newspapers totalled twenty-seven, including all the Southam papers and two French-language dailies, *La Presse* and *L'Action Catholique*.[11] Their combined national readership was about four million. Porter, a long-time Gallup associate,[12] was made general manager, and Tibby assumed the editorial job of writing the poll columns. Samuel Northcross oversaw the interviewing staff. O.J. Morris, a fourth American from the Princeton office, was installed as chief statistician.[13]

The all-American composition of CIPO senior ranks was a sensitive issue for the fledgling organization, particularly in light of its recent immigration difficulties. Gallup and CIPO officials stressed from the outset their intention to train Canadians for key positions as soon as possible. Unlike the American operation, the CIPO was established as a non-profit enterprise, with revenues coming mainly from sponsoring newspapers, whose representatives also sat on the institute's board of directors. The terms of agreement barred the CIPO from performing commercial surveys, the member papers believing this would give an unfair competitive advantage to the Gallup group over other market research firms.[14] However, as we shall see, this restriction proved short-lived, and within a year the CIPO was conducting market research surveys. Word-of-mouth accounts at the time of the CIPO's formation hinted of this later eventuality. Arthur Irwin of *Maclean's* magazine had heard from a contact that Gallup hoped to 'use the working force which will handle the newspaper surveys [for] commercial surveys for Young and Rubicam.'[15] While in Toronto to establish the Canadian affiliate, Gallup took the opportunity to address the annual meeting of the Association of Canadian Advertisers (ACA) on 31 October 1941. Gallup's visit was especially anticipated by ACA organizers: 'the importance of market research in wartime should ensure a keen interest among Canadian advertisers [for the speech] by this well-known specialist.'[16]

The first CIPO poll results hit the newsstands on 29 November, reporting on a topic that would preoccupy the polling firm and the Canadian government for months to come – conscription. The open-ended question 'In your opinion, what is the most important problem the Canadian government must solve in the next few months?' did not mention conscription specifically, but Canadians' responses revealed it was uppermost in many minds. Thirty-five per cent of all Canadians, but only 23 per cent in Quebec, chose conscription as the nation's single most important issue. (The next largest group, at 23 per cent, were those wanting 'increased production' and additional efforts to 'win the war.') Among English Canadians the problem was how to implement conscription; among French Canadians, how to avoid it.

The inaugural column also underlined the scientific, disinterested, and democratic nature of opinion surveying. CIPO polls were 'impartial, fact-finding' tools, enabling an 'objective, scientific reporting of public opinion.' Institute samples comprised 'the correct proportions of farmers and city-dwellers, Liberals, Conservatives and members of other parties, persons of average, above-average and below-average income, young and old, men and women, in each province.' As well, English and French speakers were 'included in proportion to their numbers.'[17] In a

Toronto Star article the same day, covering a speech by Gallup to representatives of subscriber newspapers that was also broadcast on CBC radio, the pollster oracle reaffirmed his egalitarian-populist ethos: the 'vast mechanism of modern government cannot afford to lose touch with the people'; opinion polling served the public good as it strengthened the 'process of democratic government by making the will of the people known.' Moreover, the average citizen could be trusted to choose wisely on most public issues.[18]

Gallup's democratic championing of opinion surveys in Canada replicated his apologia south of the border, but important differences separated American and Canadian democratic traditions. Gallup's populist-egalitarian pronouncements were deeply rooted in American political culture. Beginning in the 1820s, American politics became progressively defined by widening popular participation in civic affairs. In the 1840s, with the removal of remaining property qualifications, the United States became the first nation to achieve universal white manhood suffrage. The sixteenth amendment allowed for the popular election of senators. Other nineteenth- and early twentieth-century democratizing trends included the primary system, voting for judges and public administrators, the initiative, and the referendum. Whether in the form of Jacksonian Democracy or Populism, these movements shared, in varying degrees, the animating belief that the popular will possessed the moral and political authority to supersede the interests of professional, business, or governmental elites.[19] The magnitude of this democratic-populist creed, if not always realized in practice, was such that Lord Bryce could conclude in 1921, as he had almost thirty years earlier, that in America 'Public Opinion is, more fully than elsewhere, the ruling power.'[20]

Canada, on the other hand, possessed a much weaker tradition of popular sovereignty. The United Empire Loyalists who fled north to British North America laid the foundation for a conservative political culture rooted in deferential respect for authority, a hierarchical social order, and, perhaps most of all, a deep distrust of unfettered democracy, the dreaded 'mobocracy.' While the influence of Toryism waned by the mid-1800s, most Reform opponents steered clear of outright republicanism. Liberty and democracy, as defined by the British parliamentary and monarchical tradition, ensured the protection of minority rights by curbing the popular excesses of majoritarianism. This was all the more important in a country with a sizeable minority of French-speaking Catholics. In nineteenth-century Canada, the saying went, 'freedom wears a crown.' Judges, senators, and most government officials were appointed, not elected. Outside of the western provinces, referendum and plebiscite votes were rare.[21] In 1885, six of seven provinces maintained property qualifications for voting. As W.L. Morton observed, democracy, as determined by the franchise, 'came to Canada almost by stealth, certainly not as an army with banners' as in America. Bryce concurred, noting that while Americans possessed an 'almost superstitious devotion to the idea of popular sovereignty,' in Canada 'neither the idea in theory nor its application in the incessant exercise of voting power has possessed any special fascination.'[22]

While populist ideas occasionally surfaced in Canada,[23] they did not form the centre-piece of the country's political creed as in the United States. Homilies extolling the 'equality of all men' and the 'will of the People' peppered Americans' civic vocabulary, becoming part of the national belief system, even if, as the treatment of African Americans confirms, there was often a wide gulf between democratic ideals and actual practices. For Americans, the hallowed concept of popular sovereignty constituted a 'self-assertive, obtrusive, gesticulative part of the national consciousness,'[24] but in Canada its influence was far less an animating presence.[25] In the Dominion, democratic legitimacy sprang from Parliament and the Crown, not 'the People.' As C.G. Power counselled his House of Commons colleagues in 1939, the parliamentarian's principal duty was to nation, not riding constituents. Governing decisions should not be 'based upon instruction he may have received from people thousands of miles away who know nothing of the question under discussion ... I do not believe in that kind of democracy.'[26] This Burkean principle was also evident in Mackenzie King's governing mantra, 'Parliament will decide.' Decide it would, but after November 1941 it did so in the presence of an alien, sometimes prickly, competing source of democratic authority: the CIPO's thrice-weekly 'sampling referendum.' As we shall later see, for some pols and pundits, polling proved more politically disconcerting than it did democratically inspiring.

The Japanese attack on Pearl Harbor in early December 1941 brought America into the war and, soon after, a Canadian into the CIPO senior ranks. John Tibby, who held a naval commission, was recalled to active service on 8 December, and the CIPO began a search for his editorial replacement. Their choice, Wilfrid Sanders, would remain with the Gallup Poll for over a decade, writing many CIPO-related articles and later becoming a managing director.[27] Born in South Africa in 1907, he emigrated with his family four years later to southwestern Ontario, where his father practised law, mostly unsuccessfully, in Woodstock, Paris, and Norwich. Sanders entered the University of Toronto in 1926, writing and editing for the *Varsity*, and completed a Bachelor of Arts degree in 1930. Soon after, he landed a cub reporter position with the *Toronto Star*. Capitalizing on a capacity for hard work and an engaging personality, Sanders advanced remarkably well in his journalistic career during the Depression. Lured by a higher salary, he joined the *Financial Post* in 1934, serving as features writer and mining editor, positions which saw him travel widely across the country. In 1938, he became the Toronto office manager of the Dow Jones news bureau, writing articles for the *Wall Street Journal* and *Barron's Weekly*. A year later he returned to the *Post* as a features writer. When the CIPO position opened up, *Toronto Star* president Harry Hindmarsh recommended him, and in early January he took over as editorial director.[28] What he brought to the job, along with his nationality, was a solid background in newspaper writing and editing, most notably with the business press.

America's entry into the war, Gallup asserted, heralded a more vitalized role for opinion polling. In a 19 December CIPO column, he emphasized polling's utility in improving the 'efficiency of the democracies' to surmount wartime problems. Polling would 'speed up' the democratic process, thus 'compet[ing] with the swiftness of action possible in dictator countries.' In the United States, Gallup surveys would tackle problems of civilian morale. What amount of personal sacrifice would people endure for the war effort? What kinds of social and economic controls would they accept? How much additional tax would they pay? Commenting on the recent addition of Canadian and Australian polling affiliates, Gallup noted that 'public opinion news' was no longer 'limited by national horizons,' but was now truly an international phenomenon.[29]

And indeed, during December and the early months of 1942, numerous CIPO polls documented Canadians' willingness to accept wartime controls and endure personal sacrifice. By a three-to-one margin, Canadians approved of wage and price ceilings in early December. Seventy-eight per cent of decided voters agreed that the federal government should have unrestricted power to allocate manpower in industry, farming, and the armed forces.[30] An overwhelming majority, nearly 95 per cent of decided respondents, thought Ottawa should have unlimited authority to determine production in the nation's factories. A proposed plan to 'draft' single women between twenty-one and thirty-five years of age for training in war-related jobs was favoured by 54 per cent, opposed by 38 per cent, with 8 per cent undecided. On 28 January, the

Gallup Poll reported that nearly half of all Canadians not engaged in civil defence work were willing to spend three evenings a week in training for such positions. When asked to choose between an honour system and rationing to reduce sugar consumption, nearly 70 per cent of decided voters chose the latter. During the March tax-filing season, Canadians were asked what amount a family of four earning $1,500, $2,500, or $5,000 *should* pay in income taxes. These were then compared with actual tax amounts, included in parentheses. For the $1,500 group, the suggested rate was $23 (zero); for the $2,500 group it was $191 ($30), and for the $5,000 family it was $875 ($525). Moreover, the figures varied little between lower-, middle-, and upper-income respondents. Canadians, however, balked at one sacrificial measure; by a four-to-one margin they opposed a ban on the sale of beer, wine, and spirits.[31]

The most contentious issue involving wartime sacrifice was, of course, conscription for overseas service. Prime Minister King, having witnessed first-hand the issue's deleterious effect on the country and the Liberal party during the Great War, directed much of his political energy to shoring up the middle ground between conscriptionists like minister of national defence J.L. Ralston and equally staunch opponents like public works and transport minister P.J.A. Cardin. When King announced on 22 January 1942 his intent to hold a plebiscite asking Canadians to release his government from its pledge not to send conscripts overseas, he thought this half-way measure would forestall the pro- and anti-conscriptionist hard-liners.[32]

For the neophyte CIPO, the conscription issue was similarly a source of consternation, but also one of opportunity. After only a few months in the field, the Gallup Poll faced its first voter prediction test. Not just any forecasting test, the conscription plebiscite was the first *national* referendum-style vote in any Gallup-polled country.[33] It was also the first time that voter-forecast Gallup polling would take place in two languages. Polling, the CIPO argued, promised to do more than merely predict the vote results; it would dissect them too, revealing the relationship between conscription sentiment and variables like age, sex, or socio-economic status. More important, as the institute optimistically asserted soon after King's announcement, the plebiscite would serve to validate the accuracy of Gallup polling, which in turn would diminish the future need for such votes: 'a plebiscite involving the entire electorate takes weeks to prepare, and costs hundreds of thousands of dollars at the very least. Scientific surveys of public opinion make possible the rapid measurement of Canadian sentiment on scores of issues in a year's time.'[34]

Not surprisingly, given the issue's paramountcy, the Gallup Poll surveyed repeatedly on conscription and the plebiscite question during the run-up to the 27 April vote, a total of thirteen of thirty-four CIPO columns in February, March, and April. Its task was not made easier by divisions concerning the plebiscite's overall meaning. Forty-five per cent maintained it was about freeing Ottawa from a prior commitment; 42 per cent believed it was a vote for or against conscription, with the remaining 13 per cent citing miscellaneous reasons. Forty-nine per cent in Quebec, but only 39 per cent in other provinces, pegged conscription as the central issue. King's bid to disassociate conscription as much as possible from the plebiscite was failing in the one province viscerally opposed to compulsory overseas service. In English-speaking Canada, support for conscription ran deep, but some constituencies remained less enthusiastic than others; three-quarters of decided urban respondents favoured freeing King from his pledge, compared to 66 per cent of farm residents. Seventy-eight per cent of middle- and upper-income voters supported the Yes side, compared to 61 per cent of lower-class respondents.[35]

Plebiscite polling enhanced the CIPO's profile, but without an accurate forecast such publicity promised only ignominy. During the campaign's final month, the CIPO polled weekly, instead of at the usual six-week intervals, and interviewers were in the field up to a week before voting day. As well, supplementary 'secret' ballots were mailed to voters, according to Sanders, as 'a double check on our resident interviewers.' The CIPO issued two plebiscite forecasts, one for members of the armed forces in Canada and abroad (the BIPO interviewed Canadian servicemen in Britain), and the other for the civilian population. On 18 April, the institute released its first ever vote forecast: 86 per cent of armed forces personnel would vote Yes. On 25 April, two days before voting, the CIPO projected the Yes side would take 68 per cent of the civilian vote. Forecasts for individual provinces were also issued, showing all but Quebec siding heavily with the Yes side.[36]

The margin of random error for CIPO surveys was repeatedly given by Gallup officials as 4 per cent.[37] Any forecast wide of this mark pointed to problems of sampling bias, or deficiencies in survey design or interviewing. Accordingly, Gallup officials viewed the 4 per cent band as the yardstick of polling accuracy. And, seemingly, when the CIPO announced the plebiscite vote results in its 28 April column, the Gallup Poll had narrowly passed the test. 'Early returns' showed 64.5 per cent Yes support among civilians, 3.5 per cent below the Gallup forecast. The average error for the provincial predictions, though, was

TABLE 3.1
1942 Conscription Plebiscite

	Forecast	CIPO-listed yes vote	Actual yes vote	Error
National	68	64.5	63.0	+5.0
NS & PEI	79	80	79.2	−0.2
New Brunswick	59	71	69.7	−10.7
Quebec	25	28	27.5	−2.5
Ontario	87	84	83.8	+3.2
Manitoba	86	81	79.9	+6.1
Saskatchewan	79	73	71.6	+7.4
Alberta	76	73	70.4	+5.6
BC	87	81	80.0	+7.0

4.9 per cent, a fact explained in part by smaller provincial sample sizes and corresponding higher margins of random error. The next day, the CIPO proclaimed that 'virtually complete' returns confirmed that its forecast was 'accurate to within three and a half per cent of the actual vote cast.'[38] But this claim was inaccurate. Official vote figures show that only 63.0 per cent of civilians voted Yes, a full 5 per cent below the CIPO projection.[39] Only in Ontario, Quebec, and statistically merged Nova Scotia and PEI were the provincial forecasts within 4 per cent. In New Brunswick, the forecast was off by almost 11 per cent, and in the four western provinces the CIPO overprojected Yes support by an average of 6.5 per cent. (See table 3.1.)

Reasons for this polling miscue are not easily determined, as CIPO survey data prior to 1945 do not survive. The bias favouring the Yes side is likely the result of two factors. First, low-income and rural respondents,[40] as noted above, backed conscription in fewer numbers than their wealthier, urban counterparts. As will be shown later, CIPO samples underrepresented blue-collar families. Second, non-Anglo-Saxon immigrants, many living in western Canada, voted No in greater proportions than Canadians of British origin.[41] As is also discussed below, the CIPO underreported persons whose mother tongue was neither English nor French. Undercounting low-income, 'ethnic,' and rural respondents would have its greatest impact in western Canada, a confluence of sampling biases which may account for the systematic overforecast of Yes support west of Ontario.

The CIPO's forecast for military voters also exceeded the 4 per cent threshold. Only 80.5 per cent of armed forces personnel voted Yes,

5.5 per cent lower than predicted. The error was mostly the result of lower-than-expected Yes support among service personnel overseas, where just 72 per cent backed King, compared to 84 per cent of military voters in Canada. Since the BIPO handled interviewing in Britain, Canadian Gallup officials might have attributed some of the blame to 'outside' factors beyond their control. But making a scapegoat of the BIPO was a short-sighted strategy: the British Institute employed the same survey methods as its Canadian cousin, and BIPO polls appeared regularly in CIPO columns. Instead, the Canadian institute handled the reporting of this forecasting test as it did the civilian plebiscite vote – it misrepresented its achievement. Witness the CIPO's statement of 6 May: 'the accuracy of this survey has been confirmed by results of the vote reported today, which shows the vote of soldiers in Canada at 84 per cent yes and the overseas vote at 72 per cent "yes."'[42] Nowhere does the column mention that the forecast was off by 5.5 per cent. Again, the institute erroneously claimed to have predicted the civilian vote within 4 per cent. Such slanted reporting, however, seemed to have had its desired effect. A memo from Porter to newspaper subscribers on 7 May thanked them for their congratulatory telegrams. It also described how American newspapers had 'widely publicized the accuracy of our prediction,' with some even suggesting 'that this "bull's-eye" is the final proof of the accuracy of the scientific method of selected sampling.'[43]

The CIPO would take up three more forecasting challenges during the war – the Ontario and Quebec elections of 1943 and 1944, and the federal election of 1945.[44] Gallup officials approached the 4 August 1943 Ontario election very cautiously, even nervously. The phenomenal rise of the CCF, which commanded nearly a third of voter support in CIPO polls of 10 July and 24 July, meant the race was a close three-way affair. Nearly all the AIPO's experience in electoral polling was limited to two-party contests. When issuing its final forecast on 3 August (CCF 36 per cent; PC 33 per cent; Liberal 31 per cent), the institute cited a litany of reasons why its prediction might falter: the difficulty of gauging voter turnout; wartime population shifts rendering out of date the CIPO's quota sampling design; the unknown extent of proxy voting among armed services personnel; last-minute campaign developments; and the vagaries of (August?) weather. Considering the many preemptive justifications issued, the election results were no doubt a welcome relief for Gallup executives. Of the three-party vote, the CCF captured 32.2 per cent, the Tories 36.4 per cent, and the Liberals 31.4 per cent. The institute's widest error was 3.8 per cent, and the three-party average error

TABLE 3.2
1944 Quebec Election

Party	Forecast	CIPO-reported 4–party popular vote (91% returns)	Actual 4–party popular vote (100% returns)	Error
Liberal	35	42.4	41.7	−6.7
Union Nationale	32	38.2	40.3	−8.3
Bloc Populaire	27	16.3	15.3	+11.7
CCF	6	3.1	2.7	+3.3

Source: GC, CIPO releases, 5 Aug. 1944, 9 Aug. 1944. Scarrow, *Canada Votes*, 208, 210.

was a low 2.5 per cent.[45] The polling coup was immediately hailed by CIPO officials and subscriber newspapers as evidence of the Gallup Poll's scientific rigour and general reliability. Porter wrote a colleague that the results proved that 'our polling machinery is as adaptable to three-cornered races as it is to those with only two candidates.' George Gallup was especially impressed, and member newspapers had 'been sending orchids regularly.' For example, the *Saskatoon Star-Phoenix* claimed that the Ontario results 'substantially endors[ed] the correctness of the views found by the Gallup Poll in its inquiry into other matters of public interest in Canada. In other words, questions of any public nature which are the subject of sampling may be taken as reflecting the public opinion to a close degree.'[46]

Again with the Quebec election of 8 August 1944, CIPO pollsters projected a close three-party race. Only this time, voters would prove them wrong – very wrong, in fact. The main story of the campaign was the meteoric rise of the Union Nationale, from just 14 per cent support in a 8 July survey to 29 per cent on 29 July. The institute's final forecast on 5 August (Liberal 35 per cent; Union Nationale 32 per cent; Bloc Populaire 27 per cent; CCF 6 per cent) put Maurice Duplessis's forces just three points behind the leading Liberals. Again, the CIPO advised readers of the many eventualities that could upset its prediction: last minute changes of mind, inclement weather, the serviceman vote, actions by the federal government, and the unknown voting rate of Quebec women casting ballots provincially for the first time. As seen in table 3.2, the election results provided disquieting news for Gallup officials.

Once again, CIPO officials put a deceptive gloss on bad tidings. The four-party average error, based on 91 per cent returns and issued 9 August, was reported as 6.8 per cent. The actual error, based on final returns and withheld by the CIPO, was 7.5 per cent; for the three main parties, it was 8.9 per cent. The institute attributed the flawed forecast 'to last minute trends.' The 'unusually mercurial political views of Quebec voters' resulted in almost half of Bloc Populaire supporters abandoning the party in the campaign's final week. This unsupported theory was advanced even though the CIPO's own polls showed support for the Bloc holding steady at between 25 and 29 per cent from late May until early August.[47]

Bruised by the Quebec election, the Gallup Poll approached the 11 June 1945 Dominion vote determined to make a better showing. At considerable expense, six surveys were conducted during the campaign, an average of one per week from late April to early June. In addition to the regular contingent of CIPO field workers, special travelling crews of interviewers worked in Ontario and Quebec to broaden the sample base and cross-check the results of resident interviewers.[48] The institute's efforts were rewarded with its best prediction yet – an average party error of just 1.7 per cent, although error margins in Ontario and Quebec were higher at 3.2 and 3.4 per cent respectively. (The main discrepancy in Ontario was a 5.8 per cent overestimate for the CCF; in Quebec the CIPO again inflated Bloc Populaire support, this time by 6.8 per cent.) The close forecast, the CIPO crowed, confirmed 'once again' the 'accuracy and objectivity of scientific opinion polls.' But the institute's bravado belied its wartime record. Five forecasts had been made since 1942 – the civilian and military plebiscites, and the Ontario, Quebec, and federal elections. The average error for these was 4.5 per cent, just outside the allowable margin of random error. While by no means an apologetic record for a young organization, it paled beside the AIPO's professed 2.5 per cent average forecasting error since 1940.[49]

Like its American parent, the CIPO polled on a wide array of topics during the war. Some forty-five surveys between November 1941 and August 1945 provided material for over four hundred poll columns, in addition to the two hundred or so poll reports coming from foreign Gallup affiliates. Ranging from the silly to the sublime, the sentimental to the serious, CIPO polling traversed the political and social landscape, aggregating the responses of 'average' Canadians to provide tabular readings of the 'public mind.' Among the many offerings were polls on prohibition, rationing, repatriating Japanese Canadians, sex education in high schools, public funding for venereal disease treatment, belief in God, the thirty-hour work week, daylight saving time, favourite Canadian cities, Senate reform, the effects of movies on youngsters, whether Hitler was truly dead, and the merits of women in the factory, the jury box, and the driver's seat.

A detailed documentation and analysis of Canadians' wartime opinions far exceeds this study's scope.[50] Instead, discussion will focus on two general themes which preoccupied government and Liberal party officials and which will be examined in subsequent chapters. First, after the plebiscite's reconfirmation of linguistic schism, CIPO polling in 1942–3 intently probed issues involving French-English opinion differences. Second, from 1943 until early 1945, the institute documented Canadians' move to the left, polling repeatedly on such topics as social security, public ownership, and labour unions.

Jack and Jacques Canuck

In August 1942, the CIPO launched a three-part special series on French Canadian opinion. One of the 'most significant and interesting projects' undertaken by a polling firm, the survey results would 'expose the mind-beat' of French Canada, fostering mutual understanding and national unity. The first column revealed the depth of French Canadian (more properly French Quebecker, as only those francophones were polled) alienation from political and economic affairs. Asked if French Canadians had been well treated in the civil service (neither federal nor provincial was specified), 70 per cent of decided respondents said No. For the army the total was 68 per cent, in war industries 65 per cent, and in business 67 per cent. Lest readers worry that such alienation might spawn 'revolutionary' attempts to change the political or economic status quo, the CIPO offered reassurance: French Canadians were far less 'state conscious' than English Canadians, and were opposed to the continuance of government controls of the economy after the war. The second article contrasted English and French views on Canada and the Empire. Fifty-five per cent of decided anglophones viewed Canada as an 'independent country' and not dependent on Britain, while only 26 per cent of francophones did. Asked if Canada would still have gone to war were she not part of the Empire, more than four-fifths of anglophones said Yes, compared to one-third of francophones. French Canadians also revealed residual ties to France. When polled on whether France should have an 'equal voice' with the Great Powers in the postwar peace process, nine in ten French Canadians agreed, compared to just four in ten in English Canada.[51]

If Gallup officials believed that such polls advanced the cause of national unity, they did so in the face of survey results revealing overwhelming disparities between French and English speakers. With no other demographic variable (i.e., age, sex, or income) were differences of opinion as pronounced as between Canada's two linguistic groups. This was so for a myriad of issues, encompassing domestic politics, social and economic questions, and international affairs. French–English opinion variations were the subject of the institute's most ambitious wartime publication, a forty-five page booklet by Sanders. Written for a popular audience, *Jack and Jacques* (1943) contrasted the opinions and world views of 'Tweedle Jack and Tweedle Jacques,' poll-derived composites of political man and *homme politique* in Canada. According to Sanders, 'The mixed strains in the Tweedles bloodstream make their mental processes a fascinating picture for the student of public opinion – a bit complex, and contradictory at times, but nevertheless sufficiently clear cut to give the lie to those who maintain that Canada, because of her minorities, is incapable of producing cohesive National Opinion.'[52] The claim was a peculiar one, for it prefaced a work that demonstrated decisively the schismatic nature of the bilingual body politic. 'National Opinion' was a chimera; far more often than not, divergent sets of French and English views were merged to form 'national' public sentiment. Of the book's sixty-five tables differentiating French and English opinion, only thirteen contained variations of less than 10 per cent. For the remaining fifty-two, differences of 30 per cent or more were not uncommon, with the widest linguistic chasm (78 per cent) occurring with conscription.[53]

For example, when asked in July 1942 if they would accept a Hitler peace proposal recognizing the geopolitical status quo, 93 per cent of English Canadians said No, compared to 59 per cent of French Canadians. In summer 1942, 50 per cent of francophones chose Mackenzie King as 'the greatest living Canadian,' whereas just 14 per cent of anglophones did. (Among this group, 'don't know' and 'is none' combined to top the list at 47 per cent). A beef rationing proposal in October 1942 was endorsed by half of English Canada, but only one-quarter of French Canada. Three months later, just 13 per cent of those of British origin favoured a closed-door immigration policy after the war, compared to 46 per cent of French Canadians. Two-thirds of anglophones, but just one-third of francophones, believed women should serve on juries. Forty-two per cent of French Canadians in July 1943 thought divorce too easy to come by, compared to 23 per cent of English Canadians.[54] The phrase 'two solitudes' entered the Canadian lexicon in 1945 as the title of Hugh MacLennan's novel, but its thesis embodied a sociological fact.[55]

Social Security and John Public

The centrist King Liberals were also challenged by Canadians' headstrong turn to the political left. Its most obvious manifestation was the surge of support for the Cooperative Commonwealth Federation, which, in a much ballyhooed CIPO poll of September 1943, nosed past the Liberals and Tories to capture first place, albeit within the poll's margin of error.[56] The rising CCF tide was but one feature of the groundswell shift in public opinion away from individualist social values and laissez-faire economics and towards the beneficence of the activist state. From 1942 on, 'security' was the Canadian watchword – security of the hearth, of the workplace, of the postwar social order. 'Social security' (an ambiguous concept, even to its proponents) promised an end to the crippling poverty known during the Depression. It meant insurance against life's calamities – losing a job, falling sick, retiring with insufficient means. The security ethos fostered too a belief that the vicissitudes of the market could be moderated, even eliminated, and Canadians eyed public ownership prospects – factories, banks, insurance companies, even dairies – seldom, if ever, considered before. Ottawa's expanded economic and social presence was helping to win the war, and so too should it work to win the peace, increasing numbers of Canadians believed.[57]

Accordingly, the CIPO polled regularly on themes of social security and nationalization. Paralleling its approach to the 'Jack and Jacques' theme, the institute released a special four-part poll series in May 1943 entitled 'Social Security and John Public,' which examined public opinion on health insurance, minimum living standards, old age pensions, and Canadians' understanding of social security. State-run health insurance proved especially popular with Canadians. Earlier in April 1942, four-fifths of Canadians had said Yes to paying a 'small part' of their income for family medical and hospital coverage, and a year later the same proportion endorsed this plan. Again in April 1944, 83 per cent of decided Canadians backed the proposal, and two-thirds favoured a province-wide health insurance plan.[58] Family allowances were initially less popular; just 54 per cent in October 1943 approved of a $9-per-child monthly payment, but by next August support had climbed to 62 per cent, and in Quebec it stood at 87 per cent. In May 1945, two-thirds of

Canadians believed mothers would 'properly' spend the baby bonus on children's needs.[59] The *vox populi* similarly championed higher pensions. Asked in spring 1943 to set the monthly sum pensioners with no other means of support should receive, over 90 per cent of Canadians listed amounts above $20, the current pension rate. Unemployment insurance registered 76 per cent approval in July 1943. While support for social welfare measures ran high, only 34 per cent of Canadians, the CIPO reported in May 1943, could provide a reasonably correct definition of the term 'social security.'[60]

Support for state-owned enterprise also grew, albeit less dramatically than for social welfare measures. In January 1943, the CIPO asked: 'Do you think that, after the war, it would be a good idea for the government to own all industries that handle and distribute certain necessities of life, like milk, bread, meat and fuel, and sell them to the public without profit?' Incredibly, 44 per cent of respondents backed this radical proposal, while 45 per cent disagreed and 11 per cent were unsure. One-half of Canadians in July 1943 favoured public control of airlines after the war, 31 per cent backed a public-private mixture, and only 19 per cent advocated exclusive private ownership. Three months later, public opinion split evenly on whether government economic controls on business and industry should continue after the war. Forty-three per cent agreed, 45 per cent were opposed, and 11 per cent remained undecided.[61] Canadians were asked in late 1943 if after the war 'workers would be better off if all the industries in Canada were owned and run by the Government, or do you think that workers would be better off if these industries were left under private management?' Forty-five per cent of decided respondents chose the socialist alternative.[62] By a more than two-to-one margin, Canadians in December 1943 preferred public over private ownership of utilities like water, gas, and electricity.[63] Five months later, 38 per cent of decided respondents favoured the nationalization of life insurance companies.[64] Even when responding to a slanted question ('Do you think the government should own and operate all banks in Canada or do you think we should continue with the present system?'), just over a quarter of decided Canadians in spring 1944 rejected 'continuing with the present system' and opted for state banking.[65]

Support for organized labour formed a third pillar of Canadians' wartime embrace of social democracy. The institute's first labour query ('Are you in favour of labour unions?') registered almost three times as many labour supporters as detractors in December 1941.[66] In April 1943,

71 per cent of decided respondents agreed that when a majority of workers in an industry belonged to a union, the employer should 'be compelled to deal with that union.'[67] Later that year, the CIPO asked a forced choice question: 'Most people believe the government should not be controlled by any one group. However, if you had to choose, which would you prefer to have control of the government – big business or labour unions?' Of decided respondents, 65 per cent favoured labour, only 35 per cent big business. In the United States, the results were just the opposite – 63 per cent for big business, 37 per cent for labour. Canadians, however, were not entirely uncritical of labour. Asked in November 1943 if they approved of the way labour unions were 'handling things,' nearly half of respondents said No, 31 said Yes, and 20 per cent were undecided. And Canadians were strongly opposed to wartime strikes. In January 1943, 72 per cent of decided Canadians endorsed the use of force to end strikes in war industries after other methods had failed. And when asked to choose who among labour leaders, management, government, and rank-and-file workers were most responsible for war industry strikes, union leaders topped the list (38 per cent), with management coming a distant second (17 per cent). Canadian attitudes towards wartime strikes were perhaps influenced by American views on the subject. As seen in chapter 2, the AIPO queried repeatedly on labour matters during the early 1940s. From December 1941 to early 1945, nine such polls appeared as CIPO releases, five of which highlighted Americans' opposition to wartime strikes.[68]

Conspicuously absent, especially in light of these labour polls, were CIPO queries on business-related issues. While income taxes came under the institute's purview, not once did it canvass opinion on corporate or profit taxes. Nor did it ask Canadians to rate the wartime service of business executives. Monopolistic and oligopolistic practices went unsurveyed, as did issues involving business leadership and social responsibility. The institute asked once about press censorship, but it avoided any questions on the performance of newspapers as providers of news and commentary. Certainly, the CIPO never broached the subject of corporate concentration in the newspaper industry, which should not surprise, since thirteen of twenty-seven subscriber newspapers in 1944 belonged to the Southam, Sifton, or Thompson chains.[69]

The CIPO's foray into market research further curtailed the likelihood of business-related polling with potentially negative results. As noted earlier, the CIPO, like its American parent, began asking commercial questions alongside its public opinion queries. CIPO surveys in January and February 1942 contained questions on movie-going habits and preferences for leading actors and actresses. Respondents were asked if and how many times they had seen *Gone with the Wind*, and which scenes they remembered most. A July 1942 questionnaire asked French Canadians about their newspaper reading and radio listening habits. In November 1942, the institute asked if theatres should show fewer or more war movies.[70] None of these results were reported in CIPO press releases, and it is probable, in light of George Gallup's work with Audience Research Inc. and Hollywood's tight lock on the Canadian feature film market, that some if not all of this survey data made its way to the Princeton office. In late 1942, CIPO officials, citing higher costs linked to wartime inflation,[71] asked formal permission of the newspaper Board of Advisors to supplement their income with commercial research. The board agreed, provided all commercial survey work was done separately from the Gallup Poll and under a different company name. Consequently, the Canadian Opinion Company (COC) was formed, which soon after offered an omnibus consumer survey service to business clients. According to one account, 'a buyer could now use the vehicle of the Gallup Poll, but not its name, to ask specific questions.'[72] While few COC financial records survive, its launch was an apparent success. Arthur Porter wrote a colleague in January 1943 that the COC was 'such a sterling organization that there are many people who want them to do surveys.' Among its earliest customers were Lever Brothers and Canada Packers.[73] Another major client, discussed in the next chapter, was the Wartime Information Board (WIB), for whom Gallup officials undertook extensive secret polling.

The advisory board proviso that public opinion and commercial polling be done separately was also circumvented. On a number of occasions, COC poll results conducted for the WIB in 1943 were released as CIPO columns after Ottawa's approval was secured. Both COC and CIPO questionnaires used the same format and control questions. Indeed, CIPO interviewers doubled as COC field workers and the CIPO Toronto staff handled COC assignments in addition to their regular work. By 1944 the standard accounting procedure was to transfer 20 per cent of the operating cost of COC commissions to the CIPO ledger as compensation for the newspapers' subsidy of CIPO directors' salaries.[74] To all intents and purposes, the Canadian Opinion Company was a separate organization in letterhead only.

Gallup officials were also not averse to using the CIPO to assist the financial concerns of member newspapers. When in early 1943 advisory board officials became worried about the lack of paper carriers, the CIPO responded, as had the AIPO in the United States, with a special poll on the occupational merits of newspaper delivery. For the question 'If you had a son 12 years old who wanted to deliver newspapers, would you permit him to do so?' the institute reported nearly 80 per cent approval among decided Canadians in March 1943. Almost the same percentage thought delivering papers was 'helpful to a boy.' In an accompanying memo, Sanders noted that the findings should 'merit some rather extensive promotion, particularly for member papers who are experiencing difficulty in obtaining carrier boys.' The poll results were also released to Canadian Press to garner wider publicity.[75] The institute was so intent on securing favourable results that it concealed some of the poll's findings and wrongly reported others. Respondents had also been asked if they would approve of a daughter delivering newspapers. This time, though, nearly four-fifths of decided Canadians were opposed, contrary poll results of sociological significance and certainly newsworthy, but which, owing to commercial considerations, went unreported. More important, the actual survey question had asked if Canadians would permit 'a son *over* twelve years old' to deliver papers, not one twelve years of age, as reported in the poll release. One assumes that support for newspaper delivery would rise with the boy's age. Whether the discrepancy was accidental or deliberate is unknown, but the end result was the dissemination of likely exaggerated levels of support for the idea of twelve-year-old boys managing paper routes, which, in any case, served the newspapers' carrier-seeking goal nicely.[76]

A more systemic shortcoming of the Gallup Poll was the often lengthy interval between interviewing and poll publication. The CIPO promoted itself as an 'opinion news' operation, providing readers with up-to-date opinion tallies on topical issues as compiled by its far-flung crew of 'reporter-interviewers.' Interviewing dates were seldom disclosed in CIPO columns, and the common use of phrases like 'latest' and 'just completed' reinforced the impression that poll results represented a fresh reading of the public mind. In fact, with the exception of election polls, the earliest survey results did not appear until at least two to three weeks after interviewing, and waits of six to eight weeks were commonplace. Even longer delays were not unusual. In a 19 December 1942 column on political party support, the institute, in a rare departure from usual practice, specified that interviewing had finished 'just before' the Tories' Winnipeg convention of 9–11 December. In fact, the survey began on 29 September, nearly three months before 'today's' party standings were revealed in the column. Similarly, a 23 December 1942 column on prohibition with the headline 'Festive Season Does Not Halt Steady Rise of "Dry" Sentiment' was based on findings from the same 29 September questionnaire. A 20 September 1944 column describing 'as of now' opinion on political parties employed polling data from an early July survey. Interviewing completed in early November 1944 on whether politicians should visit the war front provided the statistical grist for a 24 January 1945 column. In accounting for higher support among Tories for such visits, the CIPO pointed to Progressive Conservative leader John Bracken's recent tour of the European battle front. Bracken's trip, however, began 26 December, well over a month after the survey was taken! A 'just completed' poll on mandatory saluting of the flag in high schools released 30 June 1945 was actually conducted three months earlier.[77]

Finally, we turn to the composition of CIPO samples in order to determine their representativeness *vis-à-vis* Canadian society. While numerous pre-1946 AIPO surveys exist in data form, only two CIPO polls prior to 1949 – from May and June 1945 – survive, and both these polls were limited to voting questions on the upcoming federal election. But the sampling design for election and non-election surveys, according to the CIPO, were 'exactly the same,' with the latter surveys reporting, in effect, 'how the public would vote on ... issues if they were made the subject of a national referendum or plebiscite.' The following analysis centres on the May survey, whose sample size was 1880. The most striking underreported group were women, who made up just 33 per cent of the sample, virtually the same percentage they had in the AIPO polls discussed in the last chapter. Evidently, the former AIPO executives designing CIPO samples brought with them the view that Canadian women, like their American counterparts, were infrequent or deferential voters. Election forecasting, as noted above, was a regular feature of CIPO polling, but the Canadian organization did not attempt to ascertain female voting rates in Canada. As the institute wrote in May 1945: 'No scientifically accurate or fool-proof method of measuring in advance what the [voter] turnout will be has yet been discovered.'[78] But even a cursory study of Canadian voting patterns would have seriously challenged the wisdom of a 33 per cent female inclusion rate. In 1911, the last federal election with an exclusively male franchise, the voter participation rate was 70 per cent. In 1921, after complete female suffrage, the rate dipped marginally to 68 per cent, and again in 1925 to 66 per cent.[79] But thereafter voting rates rose, reaching 74 per cent in 1935, four points higher than in 1911.[80] The claim made by some observers that the decline in voting during the 1920s was a consequence of lower voting among newly enfranchised women has not been empirically substantiated.[81] But the incontrovertible fact remains that voting rates for the dual-sex electorate of the 1930s and 1940s were *higher* than those during the final years of manhood suffrage.[82]

However, the Canadian public of the early 1940s, as depicted rhetorically in CIPO columns, remained very much a male preserve. In March 1942, the institute examined the 'wartime habits and expectations of Mr. John Canadian Motorist,' and later 'Jack Canuck's opinion about conscription.' The ordinary respondent was labelled 'Mr. Canadian Citizen' in June 1942, and a year later the institute relayed 'how John Canadian feels about the war as it affects him personally.' In September 1943, 'John Public' favoured a strengthened postwar navy, and a few months later 'your ordinary John Citizen' provided his views on Sunday sports. Tax season polling in 1945 revealed that 'Mr. Taxpayer' was less surprised than last year about amounts owing. A pre-election column of 23 May 1945 discussed 'why John Voter will vote the way he does.' Sanders' aptly titled *Jack and Jacques* described typical survey respondents in this way: 'If we wanted to, we could call them a lot of other names, such as the Average Man, the Man-on-the-Street, the Common Man, or the Little Guy.'[83]

Specific female references generally occurred with topics falling within the traditional 'woman's sphere.' A December 1941 column on inflation and price controls highlighted the opinions of 'Mr. John Public and Mrs. John Housewife.' A poll on Canadians' eating habits and nutritional knowledge was of special interest to 'John Canuck and his wife' in January 1943. Two May 1943 columns on social security measures reported the views of 'Mr. and Mrs. Canadian.' Demand by 'Mr. and Mrs. John Canadian' for postwar consumer goods, a February 1944 column declared, would likely be very strong. Significantly, all these examples referred to married women only, who in each case were accompanied by a husband figure. As well, the institute on occasion adopted patronizing postures towards women. When 10 per cent fewer women than men favoured executing captured spies in October 1942, the institute argued that this was evidence that 'Canada's women folk again conformed to the tradition that women are more tender-hearted and not "more deadly than the male."' A February 1944 column reported survey results on which of the army, navy, or air force uniforms worn by women looked the best. The higher undecided rate among men, the CIPO jocularly quipped, was 'due to the fact that men find it more difficult to be objective in judging women's clothes. As one man put it: "It's hard not to be influenced by the model."[84]

The May CIPO poll also revealed class biases. For example, among survey respondents, 64 per cent claimed to have telephones in their homes, a figure far exceeding the national average. In 1941, some 1,068,000 residential telephones were registered to the country's 2,706,089 households, for an overall total of 40 per cent.[85] Two other variables were used to determine socio-economic status: the interviewer's estimation of the respondent's class, ranging from 'poor' to 'wealthy'; and the solicited occupation of the 'family head,' which almost always meant the principal male breadwinner. On the surface, the former variable suggested solid levels of lower-class representation in the sample. With the percentage totals provided in parentheses, the interviewer-assessed class breakdowns were 'wealthy' (2); 'average-plus' (9); 'average' (38.2); 'poor-plus' (30.7); and 'poor' (20.1). The bottom three groups made up 89 per cent of the sample. But such a subjective 'democratic' categorization, from the mostly middle- and upper-class interviewers, did not correspond with the class structure revealed by occupational responses. The various job replies were coded, with corresponding percentages in brackets, by the CIPO as professional (3.9); business executive (3.6); small-business owners (6.7); white collar (24.5); skilled labour (24.7); unskilled labour (7.9); farmers (22); other (6.7).[86] Dominion Bureau of Statistics (DBS) occupational groupings differed from those used by the institute, thus making a direct comparison of census and CIPO data more difficult. One likely underreported group were agricultural workers, who made up 31.7 per cent of the 1941 male work-force. Combining occupational groups, for both DBS and CIPO data, also reveals striking dissimilarities between white- and blue-collar representation. Among the Canadian male work-force, those in the finance, trade, service, and clerical sectors totalled 23.8 per cent. The comparable group of CIPO respondents (professionals, executives, small business, white collar) were 38.7 per cent of the sample. In the actual male work-force, blue-collar workers (comprising the fishing, trapping, logging, mining, manufacturing, construction, transportation, and labourer sectors) formed 44.2 per cent of the national total. But in the Gallup Poll's sampled public, the skilled and unskilled labourer groups combined for 32.6 per cent.[87] It would seem that Sanders's fabled 'Common Man' and 'Little Guy' were much more likely to be found in the office than on the shop floor.

French Canadians and ethnic minorities were also disproportionately sampled in the May survey. In the 1941 census, 29 per cent of Canadians listed French as their mother tongue; but just 11 per cent of CIPO respondents were unilingual francophones, compared to 71 per cent speaking English only. A third category comprising bilingual respondents totalled 18 per cent.[88] A few observations can be made. First, an obvious underreported group were persons speaking little or no English or French. Fourteen per cent of Canadians listed mother tongues other than English or French, and those whose proficiency in either language could not manage a quarter-hour interview were effectively excluded from the sampled polity.[89] There were no provisions for 'other' language interviewing. Responding in 1945 to a WIB query about systematic CIPO undercounts of prairie non-Anglo-Saxons, O.J. Morris revealed this to be a long-standing practice: 'in comparing our sample directly to the census reports, it is better to have a slightly higher proportion of British stock if we are trying to find a voting cross section.' Interviewers also found Anglo-Saxons 'easier to talk to,' as much a cultural as a linguistic predisposition.[90]

Second, the CIPO's 18 per cent total for bilingual respondents was also out of line; only 13 per cent of Canadians claimed a speaking ability in both English and French. Among these bilingual Canadians, 78 per cent were French Canadian, according to the census.[91] Let us assume that francophones made up a similar proportion of the CIPO bilingual group, in other words 14 of 18 per cent. Combining this 14 per cent with the 11 per cent of unilingual French speakers brings total francophone inclusion up to 25 per cent, four points shy of the French Canadian census population. But such a sample was a skewed cross-section of French Canada; an estimated 56 per cent of the sampled group were bilingual, whereas only 33 per cent of census francophones were. As English was the working language for most large businesses in Quebec during the 1940s, francophones who spoke English had greater economic opportunities than their unilingual counterparts, and were more likely to be found in higher socio-economic strata.[92]

How does one account for a sample design so wide of the mark? One factor was the French language itself. None of the senior CIPO officials spoke French, and thus drafting French questionnaires and managing francophone interviewers presented distinct problems. The institute's corps of French interviewers was initially recruited by an American college student from New Orleans, presumably a Cajun. Saul Rae judged the CIPO's 'chief personnel defect' to be the absence of any 'competent French Canadian adviser.' In February 1944 a government official examining CIPO data expressed concern about the 'number of obviously French-Canadian replies which appear on the English ballot form and written in English.' The reason for this, O.J. Morris responded, was that interviewers were themselves instructed to translate French comments into English, in order 'to save confusion in this office since the interviewer is in a much better position to translate a fine distinction in meaning than we in this office.'[93] Perhaps they were better positioned than unilingual Americans, but such an idiosyncratic, haphazard translation method must surely have affected the reliability of French-language data. Later, in July 1945, the CIPO was again chastised by a WIB official for sloppy questionnaire translation, particularly in one instance when 'Canadien' was used for 'Canadian'; to many (pre-Québécois) French Canadians, the former term did not encompass English Canadians, 'les Anglais.'[94] The CIPO, according to a Gallup employee hired in 1947, sought to alleviate the French interviewing problem by contracting it out; an intermediary was hired in Montreal to oversee questionnaire translation and the hiring and administration of French-speaking field workers. For CIPO officials, though, this approach was far from ideal. French-language interviewing, owing to questionnaire translation and other delays, took longer to complete than English interviewing, and quality control for the French interviews lagged well behind that for English ones.[95] The response by CIPO officials, as reflected in the sample design, was to minimize French-language interviewing, while meeting the francophone quota with 'bilingual' French Canadians interviewed by English-speaking field workers. The practice may have made good business sense, but it provided a distorted portrait of French-speaking Canada, the pitfalls of which were evident in the Quebec election forecast.

Overall CIPO survey methods were also found wanting by another government official. C.H. McDonald, of the Wartime Prices and Trade Board's Statistics Branch, analysed two 1945 Gallup polls done for the board and levied a broadside of criticisms. CIPO reports presented general conclusions that were unsupported by specific data, and which were likely advanced because they were 'favourable conclusion[s] from the point of view of the client.' CIPO samples had not taken into account interprovincial population shifts since the 1941 census, or for that matter rural–urban migration during the war. The CIPO's use of quota sampling, in which interviewers selected respondents, was an unrepresentative procedure which should be replaced by the more reliable method of area probability sampling. In sum, McDonald stated, CIPO polls 'appear to be biased by incomplete information about the total population and by somewhat doubtful statistical procedures.'[96]

Despite continuous reassurances from Gallup and CIPO officials that 'scientific' polling promoted the public interest by articulating the views of ordinary voters,[97] a number of journalists and political commentators remained sceptical, even critical, of polling's democratic pretensions. Writing in *Saturday Night* soon after the CIPO's launch, Lucy Van Gogh warned against adopting Americans' 'rather extravagant faith' in opinion surveys. Public opinion, 'if there is such a thing,' she asserted, was not the result of 'conscious decisions of the mass of the people, but [was] brought about by their feelings towards the *leaders* who take one or the other side.' Canadians should embrace Britain's 'cautious reserve' *vis-à-vis* public opinion and not America's submission to the popular will. To buttress her point, she closed with a memorable missive from Winston Churchill, delivered in the Commons on 4 October 1941: 'Nothing is more dangerous in wartime than to live in the temperamental atmosphere of a Gallup poll, or in feeling one's pulse and taking one's temperature.' There were some who believed that perilous times obligated leaders to 'keep their ear[s] to the ground,' but Churchill retorted sardonically that 'the British nation will find it very hard to look up to leaders who were detected in that somewhat ungainly posture.'[98] H.T. Stanner, in a *Canadian Business* piece in December 1941, though generally approving of the Gallup Poll, added a cautionary note on opinion surveys: 'All too frequently it is found that large numbers of people have little or no specific knowledge of definite problems and, consequently, are in no position to form a guiding opinion.' Clarissa Duff, writing two years later, reiterated this point, noting that while opinion surveys were reliable yardsticks of 'the momentary trend of the national mind,' there was still no method 'to measure the quality' of representative opinions.[99]

Van Gogh's strong and Stanner and Duff's mild disavowal of the doctrine *vox populi vox dei*, contrary to Gallup, might well reflect the status anxiety of journalists fearing the loss of their customary role as both bellwethers and weathervanes of public opinion. However, their criticisms of polling signalled more than professional self-interest; rather, they reflected an ideological outlook shaped by the country's Tory democratic heritage.[100] Given this political tradition, and reminded of Crerar's attempt to stymie the Gallup initiative, we should not be surprised that polling in general and the CIPO in particular were the subject of numerous other attacks during the war. In June 1943, Winnipeg lawyer and Liberal stalwart J.G. Harvey complained to King about the institute. He could not 'understand why this self-appointed and self-elected, and self-named Canadian Institute of Public Opinion, with its claim to "modern scientific opinion polling" and with its "Gallup Poll" is not exposed for what it is,' namely a 'powerful and insidious opponent of the Liberal Party and Government.' A month later, writing to minister of national defence (navy) Angus Macdonald, his tirade escalated:

[The CIPO] is an attempt at *'newspaper rule'* of the nation by some 25 editors and owners of newspapers who would not dare to offer themselves for election by the people ... Instead of the government of the people and the direction of their affairs being carried on by their own duly elected, responsible and legitimate representatives in parliament or legislature, these irresponsible and self-elected 25 newspaper editors and owners are attempting, by the adoption of such a high-sounding name and by the publication of their 'Gallup Polls,' to govern the people insidiously by twisting their minds, using these 'Gallup Polls' for that purpose.[101]

Ironically, while Harvey was berating the CIPO for an anti-Liberal bias, a Tory member of Parliament was busy denouncing the polling house. A 15 June 1943 CIPO poll disclosed that 21 per cent of Canadians favoured joining the United States,[102] and the next day Toronto imperialist T.L. Church rose in the House to admonish 'this mischievous Gallup poll which is causing a great deal of trouble.' Under no circumstances, Church proclaimed, was Canada 'going to be talked out of the British empire.' The following week, he stepped up his attack, lambasting the institute for hindering the war effort: 'In the way it is being conducted throughout Canada, with all these galloping ghosts behind the scenes, [it] is a real source of mischievous propaganda.' A year later, he again maligned the CIPO, targeting its American connection. The institute was 'a fraud on the public and political propaganda in wartime.' It was 'an American fake ... all Gallup and no poll.'[103] Criticism of polling's function in democratic government was even levelled in 1945 by R.H. Coats, the former long-time head of the Dominion Bureau of Statistics, whose data the CIPO employed to design quota samples: 'we can measure Public Opinion today: you and I may wear a poker face, but not Democracy. Yet Democracy can only put her finger in her mouth and watch Dr. Gallup galloping about ... Really we should edit Lincoln and put it that some of the people want to be fooled all the time and all the people some of the time.' The *Ottawa Journal*, rival of the *Ottawa Citizen* which carried the Gallup Poll, similarly rebuked opinion surveys in a not-so-subtly entitled editorial, 'The Nonsense and Danger of the "Gallup Poll."' It was against the 'danger of possibly unscrupulous men using these "polls" to put over a party or a policy' that proponents of sound government had to stand guard. Because voters would jump on the electoral bandwagon of a poll-reported leader, the opinion survey was a potentially 'dangerous weapon which any sinister group may use at will to prosper their own interests.'[104]

The most symbolic, and poignantly ironic, rejection of opinion polling came from newspaper publishers themselves. The Canadian Daily Newspapers Association (CDNA), whose involvement in newspaper market research was discussed in chapter 1, grew concerned during the war about state censorship and other forms of publishing restrictions. To counteract the trend, a Freedom of the Press Committee was struck in 1944, which the following year issued three principal recommendations: sponsorship of an essay contest on the importance of a free press to a democratic society; lobbying for a constitutional amendment guaranteeing press freedom; and the allocation of $4,000 for a confidential opinion poll to 'ascertain the feeling of the public in regard to the press.' The last proposal met resistance at the 1945 CDNA annual meeting, and the committee only gained approval to draft a tentative questionnaire for distribution among members. When the polling issue again arose at the 1946 annual meeting, opposition was immediate. According to the meeting's minutes, two main objections were made: first, the 'poll might be dangerous to newspapers if the results were not favourable and were circulated'; and second, the survey 'would be of no value.' In defending the proposal, committee chairman Wesley McCullagh steered clear of any democratic rationale for polling's utility. 'Research was the order of the day,' and every enterprise striving for profits needed to 'study its market and learn what people think of its product.' The poll would 'be of great assistance in the administration of each newspaper business.' Even such a bottom-line defence failed to carry the day; the CDNA voted narrowly to scupper the survey.[105]

Commenting on polling's early years in Canada, Bothwell and English underscored that it not only permitted public officials to access citizens' thoughts, but 'equally important "the people" themselves [now] knew what they were thinking.'[106] Or they thought they knew, for 'the people' peopling CIPO samples were less a nation in microcosm than a market in miniature – a market of prospective voters. As in America, a chasm separated the rhetoric and the operating reality of Gallup polling. Successful election forecasts remained the principal yardsticks for determining the scientific veracity of the sample survey method. Indeed, despite the CIPO's mediocre (and evasive) record of voter prognostication, Porter and Sanders would still draw parallels between population sampling and blood sampling, in which in only a few drops 'all the components in the entire bloodstream are found, in the correct proportion.'[107] A more fallacious comparison could hardly be imagined. The Gallup Poll had its critics in Canada, but these pundits took aim at the American or perceived *excessive* democratic character of the poll. Its methodological shortcomings were unknown to them. Had they also known of the CIPO's extensive and secretive dealings with the federal government to track and manage wartime public opinion, their missives might well have proliferated.

4

Mobilizing Popular Consent: The Surveyed Home Front

Business long ago learned that it could no longer expect success while dictating to the public the color or size or shape or price of those things which the public purchased. The public now makes those important decisions, and unless a manufacturer can find some way of learning what the public wants, he soon goes out of business. I should like to see the application of the principles of market research and public opinion to government.

Elmo Roper, 1940

[Government] will become more and more a job of engineering.

Brooke Claxton, 1942

The Canadian Institute of Public Opinion ... is a purely fact-finding organization, whose only purpose is to measure and report, through its member newspapers, public sentiment on issues of the day. It has no connection with governments ...

Wilfrid Sanders, 1943[1]

The Second World War was an initiation by fire for opinion polling and those associated with it. Mere months after its formation, the Canadian Institute of Public Opinion took on the weighty responsibility of being the government's *de facto* pollster. Coordinating this polling program in the Wartime Information Board was J.D. Ketchum, the University of Toronto psychologist who only recently had acquired a grounding in survey research. The key government proponents of polling – Walter Turnbull, Brooke Claxton, and John Grierson – had to overcome opposition from cabinet notables like T.A. Crerar and J.L. Ilsley. Despite these initial obstacles, private CIPO polling by 1943 was thriving in the WIB and the Wartime Prices and Trade Board (WPTB). Initially consulted about the 'problem' of Quebec after the 1942 plebiscite, the CIPO would subsequently become an integral feature of WIB propaganda planning. As such, the board's polling operation involved a curious amalgam of market research and social scientific practices and principles. Ketchum was a social scientist who conceived of his propaganda work as an embodiment of applied psychology's wartime utility. Many other psychologists had taken up war-related duties in Ottawa, and this was seen as enhancing the new-found scientific authority of psychology, while also confirming its practical uses as a 'solver' of social or organizational problems. If there were lapses concerning scientific 'objectivity' – and there were with Ketchum – then these were tolerated in the pursuit of the higher cause of service to the wartime state. That WIB polling data would also serve Liberal partisan interests was similarly glossed over. While on a certain level WIB and WPTB polling paralleled market research techniques and concepts, on at least one vital point they differed. Market researchers were largely agnostic when it came to the merits of consumer choice. If consumers preferred blue over green cigarette packaging, then the production department should ideally adopt blue packaging. But WIB and WPTB polling did not follow this premise. Polling was not designed to secure opinions about how best to organize wartime economic and social mobilization and then implement the most popular ones. Policy making involving complex issues was best left in the hands of qualified experts. But polling did provide a versatile and powerful quantitative technique for determining effective promotional strategies for predetermined policies.

Some two weeks before Canada went to war, a Department of External Affairs officer fixed his attention on wartime state propaganda. On 24 August, one day after the Nazi-Soviet Pact, Hugh Keenleyside[2] asked Montreal psychologist Edward C. Webster and some of his colleagues to bring together ideas on the subject. The hasty memo, submitted the next day, affirmed the importance of social science professionals, while drawing on information control principles characteristic of large-scale enterprise. Propaganda during the Great War had been 'clumsy' and unorganized because there had been no principal agency to coordinate the dissemination of information and counteract 'disruptive currents of opinion.' A 'strong Central Information Bureau,' run by specialists who could 'understand, interpret and influence [Canada's] various racial, social, economic and ideological groups,' should, for any future war, direct Ottawa's propaganda efforts. To unify and mobilize Canadians behind prescribed war aims it was necessary to avoid blind, emotion-based appeals to patriotism or vilification of the enemy and instead employ modern techniques and strategies. A comprehensive research program, including regular public opinion polling, would enable Ottawa to anticipate morale problems and better 'reconcile divergent attitudes' threatening a national consensus. Most important, the long view must not be lost; early on, wartime propaganda should confront issues of postwar reconstruction.

Related themes were shortly after taken up by two other psychologists, J.D. Ketchum and D.C. Williams of the University of Toronto. The most comprehensive analysis of civilian morale and state propaganda to appear in the early war months, the twenty-three-page memo sent to the Prime Minister's Office in October extolled the merits of social scientific expertise in wartime, specifically those of the social psychologist. For over twenty years, psychologists had studied propaganda effects, findings that had been of 'considerable service to advertisers [and] public relations counsels,' among others. Ottawa now could draw on this fount of expertise, for, as Ketchum and Williams emphasized, the Canada of 1939 was decidedly more complex than that of 1914. People were more educated. A decade of economic disarray had made them more cynical and less impressionable. The ubiquity of radio, movies, and mass magazines, along with near-saturation levels of advertising, meant Canadians were far less susceptible to the crude, 'white feather' appeals of the Great War.[4] Instead, propaganda in this new era should be 'rational,' 'logical,' and 'objective,' designed by men of 'quite unusual skill and imagination,' harnessing scientific methods to 'discipline the population' and instil a 'willing acceptance of sacrifice.' In this war, unlike the last one, 'grey matter – at least in the case of those in authority' would prove far more beneficial than 'red bloodedness.'

One such 'grey matter' technique was public opinion polling. To ensure that propaganda appeals reached their intended audiences, it was vital to 'secure accurate and periodic reports on the state of public opinion' to serve as a guide for program planning and later as a 'check-up on [its] success.' This was why, Ketchum and Williams argued, national advertisers currently spent 'huge sums' on market research. Such rule-of-thumb means of tapping the public mood as newspaper editorials and letters to elected officials could not match the scientific rigour and predictive success of opinion polls like the American Institute of Public Opinion and the Roper Poll. In wartime, such surveys, in addition to recording opinions on a wide array of issues, could also monitor people's responses to films and radio broadcasts designed by propagandists. ⌊The market researcher's campaign to penetrate and direct consumer wants and behaviour would serve as a useful model for Ottawa's wartime propaganda needs.⌋Success, however, necessitated the presence of skilled professionals; 'for investigations of the Gallup type the statistical procedures are rather intricate; and in any interview procedure the formulation of successful questions presents many difficulties. In both these fields psychologists have had much experience.'[5]

Though Ketchum had some experience with survey methods, neither he nor any other Canadian psychologist in 1940 was an accomplished authority in representative sample surveying. Ketchum earned a psychology MA at the University of Toronto in 1926. In the early 1930s, he completed PhD course work in sociology at the University of Chicago, but never completed the doctorate. In 1934 he was appointed assistant professor in psychology at the University of Toronto, and his early research dealt mostly with adolescent behaviour.[6] In 1936, Webster had helped found the Psychological Institute, a private enterprise performing applied psychological services for government and business clients, which was loosely modelled on the Psychological Corporation. Opinion surveys, however, were not undertaken.[7] In the fall of 1939 Ketchum began conducting surveys of psychology undergraduates, which he repeated every six months until 1942. The samples ranged from 150 to 200 students, with the in-class questionnaires enlisting views on the war effort, confidence in government, conscription, faith in democracy, postwar expectations, and other issues impinging on national morale. These small surveys, limited to a narrow stratum of University of Toronto students, were likely the most systematic, longitudinal readings of war-related opinions until late 1941. Writing in November 1941 just prior to the CIPO's arrival, Ketchum underscored the *sine qua non* nature of polling for scientific determinations of mass opinion: 'This is not a factual report on civilian morale in Canada; there is probably no one in the country able to make such a report. We have no Gallup Poll, nor is any other systematic sampling of public opinion in progress.'[8]

This was not the case in the United States, where by 1940 a select group of psychologists were thoroughly versed in survey research methods. Henry Link's work with the Psychological Corporation's Market Surveys Division was discussed earlier, but other polling projects involving academic psychologists were also noteworthy. Rensis Likert, who pioneered research in attitudinal scaling in the interwar years, was in 1939 named director of the Department of Agriculture's recently formed Division of Program Surveys, which polled farmers on issues like soil conservation, tenant purchases, and domestic allotment.[9] Though Paul Lazarsfeld's 1925 Vienna University PhD was in applied mathematics, his subsequent research dealt mainly with applied psychology. Emigrating to New York in 1933, he soon after established himself as a leading psychological authority on consumer and radio listening research, which he funded with foundation grants and commercial contracts. By the time of his appointment to Columbia University in 1939, he was a renowned authority in such areas of survey research as panel studies, questionnaire design, and interviewing techniques. His seminal 1940 panel survey of voters in Erie County, Pennsylvania, became a watershed in American election studies.[10] Hadley Cantril joined Princeton University's psychology department in 1936, undertaking research on the cultural and psychological dimensions of radio listening, including a book on the mass hysteria spawned by Orson Welles's 'War of the Worlds' broadcast. With Rockefeller Foundation support, he established the Office of Public Opinion Research (OPOR) at Princeton in 1940. Between 1937 and 1950, Cantril was the most prolific contributor to *Public Opinion Quarterly*.

Though current or former academics, all three psychologists had close ties with commercial pollsters and the marketplace. Likert was a prior shareholder in the Psychological Corporation, had worked for an advertising firm, and in 1935 had taken a market research job with a Hartford insurance institute. While still in Vienna, Lazarsfeld had conducted market research surveys. He continued this line of work in the United States, and was commissioned by the American Marketing Society to write four chapters in its 1937 handbook, *The Technique of Market Research*. Indeed, Lazarsfeld argued – much to the consternation of more conventional colleagues – that applied consumer research was often more theoretically and methodologically illuminating than basic research.[11] A contributing factor in Cantril's acceptance of the Princeton appointment was its proximity to Gallup's AIPO, based in Princeton, New Jersey. Cantril proved especially adept at navigating the divide between commercial polling and academic social science. He developed close ties with Gallup, who forwarded raw AIPO data to him for methodological and policy analysis. In turn, Cantril provided Gallup with suggestions for improved question wording and interviewing methods. This commercial-academic partnership in 1940–1 secretly funnelled war-related polling data to President Roosevelt, at a time when the White House lacked the discretionary funds for such ventures.[12] As the early careers of Likert, Lazarsfeld, and Cantril attest, the flowering of American survey research occurred not in the 'interstices of academic disciplines but developed in cross-fertilization of research conducted in the realms of business, government, and the academy.'[13] A similar three-cornered symbiosis later became the governing paradigm for Ottawa's wartime use of polling.

Canada counted no polling-literate psychologists comparable to Link, Likert, Lazarsfeld, or Cantril, but by 1940 the country's psychological profession had made notable strides towards establishing the academic authority and social utility of the 'science of the mind.' In Canadian universities before the Great War, psychology came under the aegis of departments of philosophy, and was usually taught as mental or moral philosophy, though some work was done in experimental psychology from the 1890s onward. It was in the 1920s that Canadian universities began forming separate psychology departments. By the late 1930s, about thirty-five professional psychologists were teaching in Canadian universities and some twenty others worked outside the academy.[14] The interwar years also saw an upswing in applied research, as psychologists sought to combine their new-found scholastic standing with the social recognition and financial rewards derived from solving 'practical problems.' Hence, University of Toronto psychologists conducted research for the Canadian National Committee for Mental Hygiene, and their McGill counterparts received federal contracts to study the psychological effects of unemployment. Vocational and educational testing for business and governments was also undertaken.[15] The threat of war in 1938 prompted psychologists to consider more coordinated means of professional response to 'human problems' associated with war mobilization. In December 1938, Canadian psychologists assumed control of one program section of the American Association for the Advancement of Sciences when it met in Ottawa, and the following spring this group organized itself as the Canadian Psychological Association (CPA). After the outbreak of war, the CPA's primary goals, Mary J. Wright argues, were 'to identify and marshall the psychological resources of the nation, to coordinate the efforts of psychologists to demonstrate what psychologists could and should do for the war effort, and to negotiate with the government to see that in the event of war these were, in fact, the things that they did do.'[16] An October 1939 conference, 'The Use of Psychological Methods in Wartime,' sponsored by the National Research Council, saw its president, Major-General A.G.L. McNaughton,[17] back the use of psychological techniques to select and classify military recruits. Within a year, the CPA and a number of psychologists were working closely with armed forces personnel to develop aptitude and intelligence tests for enlistees.[18]

On the home front, applied psychology was a comparative latecomer. More than two years after the CPA's formation and the Ketchum-Williams discussion paper on civilian morale, federal officials first approached psychologists for counsel. In November 1941, G.H. Lash, director of the Bureau of Public Information (BPI) – predecessor of the Wartime Information Board – asked Ketchum and two other psychologists to serve on an informal advisory committee.[19] Meetings began in early 1942, and soon after committee members opted to create a larger, more formal body. In June, the Committee on Civilian Morale was established, composed mostly of psychologists and public relations officers, to 'study and advise the Government on all subjects relating to the maintenance and improvement of the wartime morale of the civilian population.'[20]

Why did over two years elapse before Ottawa solicited the counsel of psychologists for propaganda and civilian morale matters? Ketchum attributed the delay to the preponderance of 'publicity men' in the BPI and government departments, who exhibited 'considerable prejudice' towards university psychologists. What social scientists offered Ottawa, and publicists could not, were effective means to gauge and manage public opinion, techniques which in part sprang from 'scientific' developments in advertising and market research. 'The continuing study of public attitudes coupled with efforts to measure the effects of the propaganda issued,' Ketchum argued, 'would seem indispensable to any publicity organization.' While 'commercial advertisers have long accepted this view,' Ottawa, unfortunately, had 'in general disregarded it.'[21] In early committee meetings, techniques gleaned from market research were taken up. Before posters and leaflets were distributed, pre-testing should be done to ensure that key messages were properly received by readers. Plans for a 'survey of public opinion throughout Canada' were discussed.[22] J.A. Irving, a University of British Columbia psychologist and the committee's research secretary, visited the United States to assess social science techniques used by Washington to gauge public opinion.[23] Psychologists also offered theoretical assessments, some drawn from the Ketchum-Williams memo, on the impact of social structure, culture, and individual motivation on civilian morale and propaganda reception. While Ketchum dismissed the publicists' earlier information efforts as crude hucksterism ('to them we owe the vicious assumption ... that the war must be "sold" to the people like a new brand of toothpaste'),[24] a number of the proposed social science techniques continued, paradoxically, to derive from research methods honed in the marketplace, notably by marketers and advertisers.

Prime Minister King and other government officials grew progressively displeased with the BPI, and in August 1942 they moved to replace it with the Wartime Information Board (WIB). The new organization, similar to the BPI, emphasized the role of disseminating information to the press, still viewed as the most credible and effective means of conveying war news and government information to the public. But the work of the Committee on Civilian Morale was not cast aside. Charles Vining, the WIB's architect and its first chairman and chief executive officer, was said to be 'wholly in sympathy' with the committee's work. A Reports Branch in the WIB to 'collect, analyze and report on all information relating to Canada's war effort' would allow for the continuation of research work initiated by the morale committee. Davidson Dunton, editor of the Montreal *Standard*, was made the branch's first director, and its research section was put under the charge of Ketchum, Vining's 'only real innovation in staffing,' according to William Young.[25] For Ketchum, the appointment and subsequent move to Ottawa culminated three years of research, writing, and public speaking on propaganda and morale, including a four-part address on CBC radio in early 1942 that garnered far-ranging attention. Indeed, Stuart Rice, the assistant director in charge of statistical standards in the White House, wrote Ketchum requesting copies of his speeches on national morale. During an address to the Royal Canadian Institute in January 1942, Ketchum lamented that the Gallup Poll had not operated in Canada since the outbreak of war, in contrast with the United States, where AIPO-based studies by psychologists 'had added enormously to our knowledge of how public opinion behaves.'[26] Gallup polling, however, would soon perform a similar function north of the border.

In fact, well before Ketchum's appointment to the board in September 1942, government officials were tapping the resources of the CIPO. External affairs officer Saul Rae visited the CIPO office in November 1941, before it had even issued its first poll results. Rae received advance numbers for the inaugural column, and took the opportunity to advise his former AIPO colleagues not to lose sight of Canada's 'complex racial, religious, and political structure' when polling, notably on conscription. It was imperative that no poll results 'should be supplied in Canada for the use of the Hitler propaganda machine.'[27] In February 1942, Arthur Porter, the former AIPO executive and transplanted American director of the CIPO, met with King to discuss poll findings on conscription. King, as he would remain in subsequent years, was unmoved by polling's instrumental or partisan potential,[28] but not so Walter Turnbull, King's principal secretary. After some preliminary correspondence in March, Turnbull wrote Porter on 3 June about the 'much vexed question of opinion in Quebec.' He inquired how Ottawa might learn 'why the Quebec people think as they do' and thus be better situated to 'make plans to provide the answers.' Turnbull's comments three days later illustrate poignantly the conflation of political, advertising, and polling discourses. Ottawa had done a 'very poor job of selling the war' to Quebec, as most speeches and printed material were 'almost entirely prepared for the Anglo-Saxon mind.' Discovering French Canadian views on the war via opinion polling would enable the government to determine 'what target to shoot at in preparing propaganda instead of sending it out in haphazard fashion as at present.' Porter responded with recent breakdowns of opinion in Quebec and the rest of Canada, along with accompanying analysis. He expressed an eagerness to work closely with Ottawa to remedy the fact 'that not only the war but the plebiscite was not "sold" to Quebec as well as it might have been.'[29]

Alongside Turnbull, another policy maker pushed for the use of opinion polls. Brooke Claxton, the Montreal Liberal MP first elected in 1940, had cultivated, in addition to his many other pursuits, a strong interest in government information services. Earlier, in May 1941, he had prepared a seventeen-page memo on government publicity for King, recommending the creation of a ministry of information to supervise the work of the National Film Board, the Canadian Broadcasting Corporation, and a bureau of information.[30] King thought the proposal too radical, and Claxton was jettisoned as a possible replacement for minister of agriculture Jimmy Gardiner, who had recently quit his other portfolio as minister of national war services. Had the ultra-cautious King heard Claxton's address to the Canadian Political Science Association later that month, his concerns might well have mounted. While government information work in the form of disseminating facts and figures was important, Claxton argued, there was also a dire need for outright 'propaganda,' an activity encompassing 'everything from the nasty, effective product of Dr. Goebbels, to the spreading of the Christian faith.' The purpose of propaganda was 'to influence opinion and conduct' and was 'different from education in that the educational process has as its aim the good of the person subjected to it, while propaganda is designed to serve the ends of the propagandist, in this case the nation.' The primacy of democracy, 'the freedom we are fighting for,' Claxton asserted, 'must be made a reality' to Canadians from all walks of life through effective propaganda employing modern techniques. In the aftermath of the plebiscite vote, government officials focused their attention on anti-war sentiment in Quebec, most notably the conscription dilemma. Writing King on 29 May 1942, Claxton outlined a number of initiatives to reverse the government's sagging fortunes in French Canada, including having a 'survey made by Gallop [sic] or someone else to see what Quebec is thinking, why it voted the way it did, [and] what "line" should be taken.'[31]

Turnbull and Claxton then approached Saul Rae about the merits of a CIPO poll of Quebec opinion. By far Ottawa's most knowledgeable authority on polling procedures, Rae was also sensitive to the potential political damage resulting from government-sponsored surveys. While the CIPO had performed assignments for the Wartime Prices and Trade Board (discussed below), there were sharp differences in kind between polling on generally accepted matters like price controls and polling on contentious issues like conscription. State-initiated surveys on the latter, should they become public, might expose the government to attack, if critics portrayed them as subverting the democratic will of Quebeckers. Should officials decide to proceed with such polling, Rae recommended that they 'quietly' solicit Hadley Cantril to perform the post-interview analysis, since he was already doing similar work with AIPO data for American government agencies. This would provide Ottawa with useful information, and would go a long way towards leaving 'the poll free from the charge that it is Government inspired.'[32] Soon after, Cantril, at Ottawa's expense, visited Montreal and the nation's capital to meet with Claxton and Turnbull, but he subsequently played only a minor role in the federal government's polling designs.[33] Instead, government officials turned to the CIPO.

The next institute survey, which entered the field in early July, bore the imprint of Turnbull and Claxton.[34] The French questionnaire contained seven more questions than the English one, covering the following topics: the perceived effect of an Axis victory on Quebec; who among Pierre Laval, General de Gaulle, and Marshall Pétain had done the most for the French people; whether a majority of local able-bodied men would enlist if Canada were invaded; listening habits for Paris or

Vichy broadcasts; the Nazis' treatment of the Catholic Church in con-
quered countries; the treatment of French Canadians in the civil service,
war industries, the army, and business; and views on René Chalout, the
nationalist Quebec MLA. Turnbull had earlier discussed with Porter
whether French Canadians understood the dangers to Canada presented by the war and whether they knew about Nazi oppression of the
Catholic Church in invaded lands. In the 29 May memo to King, Claxton
had advocated some heavy-handed measures to mute anti-war criticism
in Quebec, including surveillance by 'plainsclothesmen' of nationalist
speakers and the offices of La Ligue pour la Défense du Canada, the
possible prosecution of Le Devoir, and the expedition of Chalout's prosecution under the Defence of Canada Regulations.[35] The survey, parts of
which formed the CIPO's 'Jack and Jacques Canuck' series discussed in
the previous chapter, assumes a new meaning in light of its association
with Ottawa officialdom. It was also the first institute poll to probe
newspaper reading and radio listening habits, specifically asking which
media people received their 'war news' from and which they deemed
most objective and credible. Such data, when combined with demographic breakdowns and cross-tabulations of 'unfavourable' opinions,
could, in theory, allow information strategists to identify social groups
most opposed to war measures, devise corrective publicity campaigns,
and feature them in the media most used by the targeted groups. As
Turnbull acknowledged when thanking Porter for the advance results,
the survey uncovered 'an amazingly important mass of material which,
if properly related, can be most useful in dealing with our immediate
problems.' The poll's worth was enhanced by the institute's decision to
keep under wraps controversial results 'which would not tend to further
Canadian unity if published.'[36]

The 'much vexed question' of French Canadian opinion kindled
Ottawa's interest in two other pulse-taking ventures, though neither
constituted sample surveys of the Gallup Poll type. In 1941, author and
publisher Albert Lévesque formed a non-profit organization, 'Les Informations Albert Lévesque,' to conduct social research in French Canada.
In April 1942, he supervised a questionnaire survey of francophone
youth across Canada, comprising some 2,200 mostly teenage boys and
young men attending classical and technical colleges.[37] More reminiscent of a social survey[38] than a scientific opinion poll, the investigation
provided a social and cultural portrait of family life among 'l'élite canadienne de langue française,' quantifying such behaviour as recreational
activities, religious practices, and family interaction.[39] Of particular

interest to the Committee on Civilian Morale when it discussed part of Lévesque's study on 19 June were newspaper reading patterns. Committee member and psychologist J.S.A. Bois pointed to the benefits of a content analysis of French newspapers coupled with research 'to identify the process of change that has occurred in people of different classes from Nationalism to Canadianism.' Subsequently, Lévesque forwarded to the committee additional material on reading habits of the daily, weekly, and monthly press, broken down by area, occupational group, and sex variables. As well, he provided an editorial content analysis of leading French-language dailies concerning war themes. Ketchum's later 'misgivings' about Lévesque's research methods, however, ended the latter's involvement with government information planners.[40]

Similarly, a July survey of Quebec public opinion coordinated by Saul Rae and fellow external affairs officers Marcel Cadieux and Paul Tremblay also illuminated newspaper reading habits. The survey of eighty-four francophones (seventy-seven men and seven women, drawn from Quebec cities, towns, and villages) was not made on the 'basis of the regular Gallup Poll,' despite the authors' claims. The sample was very small,[41] only two (unidentified, but presumably Cadieux and Tremblay) interviewers were used, and the data derived not from standardized questionnaires but from conversations with people in which the interviewer attempted 'to gauge their feelings about various questions listed in a guide questionnaire.' In most cases, respondents were unaware they were being interviewed. The survey explored five general themes, with the results cross-tabulated by area, sex, and social class. The first section dealt with the 'sources of opinion,' mainly newspaper and magazine reading and radio listening patterns. Subsequent sections solicited opinions on economic conditions in Quebec and Canada; the treatment of francophones in Canada; the Allied Powers; and the postwar world. Though the survey's statistical shortcomings must be kept in mind, it nonetheless suggested severe levels of francophone alienation and discontent. Ninety-five per cent believed French Canadians received unequal treatment in Canada; 70 per cent thought Canada should have stayed out of the war in 1939; a majority regarded rationing as unnecessary; nearly two-thirds favoured annexation to the United States, despite the near-unanimous sentiment that Quebec was being 'exploited by Anglo-Canadian and American capital.' French Canadians were highly sceptical of and increasingly immune to government propaganda, and none of the standard appeals for supporting the war – preserving democracy, assisting Great Britain and France, defending

Canada – registered in any serious way. In this context, conscription was more symbolic of past and ongoing conflicts, a lightning rod for long-standing national grievances and collective frustrations felt within Canada. In sum, French Canadians did not think 'the present regime' was 'so satisfactory that they [were] bound to accept conscription for overseas service.' Though the authors provided an informed analysis of the structure of Quebec opinion, they offered little in the way of prescriptive measures, and no attempt was made to draw on the relationship between opinions, demographic variables, and media use in order to devise remedial information programs. Had they tried, the eighty-four-person sample would have rendered the effort statistically unreliable.[42]

After completing the 'Jack and Jacques' report, Porter circulated it beyond Turnbull and Claxton in a bid to promote the CIPO's wartime utility. Copies went to Lash and later Vining when he took over the WIB in late August. Along with 'gather[ing] the facts that are necessary in directing Canada's war effort,' as Porter wrote the WIB chairman, the CIPO could secure polling data on American opinion about Canada through its links with the AIPO. To illustrate, Porter enclosed recent AIPO polls on Canada's war effort and Americans' general knowledge of Canada. That only 8 per cent of Porter's compatriots could roughly estimate Canada's population was 'appalling,' Porter contended, but this nonetheless underscored Ottawa's need for enhanced publicity in the United States. Vining was 'extremely interested' in Porter's suggestion, later meeting him and a visiting George Gallup in Ottawa to discuss how the CIPO and AIPO could assist the WIB. As Porter underlined on 8 October following the meeting, both American and Canadian Gallup executives were 'standing ready' to carry out their twofold mission: 'service for the member newspapers' and 'cooperat[ion] with the various departments of our national governments.' Serving newspaper readers and the state, presumably, were wholly compatible enterprises.[43]

The WIB's polling point man – indeed, a guiding force behind many social science innovations in information policy – was J.D. Ketchum. Soon after assuming his WIB duties, he struck up what would become a close relationship with Porter and other CIPO officials. In fact, the following year Ketchum rented out his Toronto house to Porter, and their subsequent correspondence touched on faulty water heaters and leaky roofs along with the pitfalls of question wording and population sampling. Ketchum's initial interest in the CIPO centred on combating the destabilizing effects of rumours on public morale. He asked Porter if

CIPO interviewers could keep a tally of circulating rumours, and for the late September 1942 survey field workers compiled rumours heard privately and those heard while interviewing. A list of these was forwarded to Ketchum, who, impressed with them, suggested that Porter carry on with this line of intelligence gathering, billing the WIB for tabulating expenses for material the CIPO did not publish. The CIPO's rumour checking also impressed Gallup, and the AIPO began considering similar work in the United States. In late October, Porter proposed that a 'rumour ballot' be drawn up for regular interviewing of Canadians, performed by the CIPO at an 'extremely reasonable' cost. Ketchum expressed interest, and some preliminary questions were drafted. But the 'risk of having interviewers relate [dangerous rumours] to people, even if they denied their truth later,' along with other problems effectively shelved the proposed survey.[44] Moreover, CIPO interviewers were only in the field every six weeks or so, far too infrequently to track fast-breaking rumours. As well, by late fall, Ketchum was far along in securing a cross-country network of correspondents to provide weekly rumour reports via a private group, the Canadian Column.[45]

Ketchum held out larger ambitions for Gallup polling. In late November he began drafting 'general morale' questions, which he envisioned asking at regular intervals. The questions were brought together in a mid-December survey, the first entire CIPO poll commissioned by the WIB and conducted separately from the regular newspaper survey. Most of the twenty-one non-control questions can be grouped under five general areas: Ottawa's handling of the war effort; views of the war itself; reception of war news via newspapers and radio; foreign affairs; and postwar reconstruction. The survey was also noteworthy for its nine open-ended questions, which, while hiking the poll's cost owing to extra coding, secured valuable subjective responses. Thus, after the question 'Do you feel more confident or less confident than you did three months ago about the way our government is running the war effort?' respondents were asked to state reasons for feeling this way. When asked if they thought postwar unemployment would be high, those in the affirmative (66 per cent of decided respondents) were requested to list ways to avoid this outcome. The two-thirds of decided respondents wanting 'great change in our way of life after the war' similarly cited examples of desired changes.[46] The potential political applications of the last two questions were not lost on Ketchum, who wrote Porter on 17 December about response coding: '[it was important] to keep together those comments which imply governmental measures as against those which seem to rely on free enterprise and ordinary economic factors. With respect to government intervention, a clear difference is emerging between state control of the socialistic type and the extension of social insurance, as in the Beveridge report.' The overall survey results, according to Reports Branch chief Davidson Dunton, proved 'extremely useful,' and the board, even in early January, was 'already incorporating some [of the findings] in our reports, on which we have had very favourable comment from people in high places.'[47]

Polling revealed levels of public support for any number of issues among the national populace or for smaller subgroups, but it could also elucidate correlations between opinions. For example, 35 per cent of decided respondents in the December survey wanted Canada to join the United States after the war. In attempting to account for this sentiment, Ketchum examined correlations between annexationists, those who thought the American war effort more concerted than Canada's, and those maintaining that domestic war news 'was made to look better than it is.' While Ketchum's correspondence does not reveal whether his statistical analysis properly accounted for annexationism (if the desire to join the United States was conditioned by the other two independent variables), it does illustrate the application of social science techniques to dissect public opinion in search of causal relationships.[48] To perform additional analyses, steady access to CIPO data was needed, and in subsequent months and years, especially after March 1943, Ketchum regularly tapped Gallup officials for opinion breakdowns, cross-tabulations, and other statistics on numerous issues, mostly from the regular newspaper surveys. Indeed, this practice would continue until war's end.[49] In early 1943, the CIPO began making arrangements for continued WIB collaboration. The board survey had netted the firm almost $2,000, and Porter now contemplated hiring an employee to assist with WIB assignments. A survey of industrial workers for Ottawa was also being considered.[50]

Both organizations' plans for government polling were temporarily derailed by two events on 27 January: Vining's resignation from the board, and the War Cabinet Committee's move to ban the use of Gallup polls. Plans for another WIB opinion survey in February were put on hold as the Reports Branch became engulfed in an 'atmosphere of crisis.' Ketchum was unsure if Vining's replacement as general manager, John Grierson, the head of the National Film Board, would similarly back the use of opinion polls.[51] Of course, the more pressing concern was cabinet opposition. On 21 January, cabinet endorsed the WIB's use of Gallup surveys. Just six days later, however, it revoked this decision in response to concerns, particularly from finance minister J.L. Ilsley, that employing an outside group like the CIPO might expose the government to opposition criticism that it secured the polls for partisan purposes. Ketchum and Grierson, who soon revealed himself as a polling advocate, lobbied to reverse the decision. Ketchum drafted a memo for WIB board members on polling's importance, and Grierson presented his case to Arnold Heeney, secretary to the cabinet.[52] Heeney's subsequent memo to King laid out Grierson's arguments for the reinstatement of Gallup surveys. Polling's only drawback concerned not the 'conduct of enquiry' but the publication of results, which might 'crystallize opinion at the point of questioning.' Its instrumental advantages were many: polls revealed 'gaps and confusion in popular information'; they accurately gauged the views of ordinary citizens; the Wartime Prices and Trade Board already used them, as did the American and British governments. Finally, Heeney mentioned, more as an afterthought, that polls were 'essentially democratic' (presumably so even when the results remained secret). The government should not fear possible criticism that the polls served partisan ends, for elected officials 'need have nothing to say about the questions asked, nor obtain the actual poll results.' Opinion surveys were vital to the WIB in securing the 'inward flow' of information, which Grierson envisioned would later form the basis for a 'series of reports for the various government departments, [containing] conclusions of particular concern to them.' Heeney was unaware or did not reveal that officials like Claxton had already showed a first-hand aptitude for polling's political merits. The appeal was successful, and on 3 March the cabinet again cleared the way for WIB polling, though it cautioned the board to 'exercise careful judgement and discretion ... particularly as regards the nature of the questions asked.'[53]

Grierson's arrival at the WIB, Young notes, reinforced the presence of academics and social scientists in information work, and his theories on propaganda and education also permeated the board.[54] Born in Scotland in 1898, Grierson received a master's degree in philosophy from Glasgow University in 1923. A Rockefeller Foundation Fellowship brought him to the University of Chicago in 1924, where for three years he studied under such luminaries as Charles Merriam, Harold Lasswell, and Walter Lippmann. At Chicago, Grierson became interested in the psychology of propaganda, probing the influence of film and newspapers on popular belief systems, and related problems in education and government information.[55] Lippmann, whose 1922 classic, *Public Opinion*, would influence a generation of political theorists, exerted the strongest pull on Grierson. Modern society and mass communications, Lippmann wrote, had created communities where cultural and political messages so inundated average citizens that they could no longer filter out useful information to make rational decisions about public affairs. The typical voter's comprehension of society transpired within a 'pseudo-environment,' composed of mental 'pictures' of events and issues, where distorted stereotypes, fictions, and facts intermeshed. Lippmann's hope for salvaging popular democracy – an elite-managed government information agency to advance informed opinion – itself gave way three years later to a more pessimistic outlook. The general public, now a 'phantom public,' should, in the interests of efficiency and practicality, cede authority to social scientists and special interest groups operating with the 'least possible interference from ignorant and meddlesome outsiders.'[56]

While embracing Lippmann's repudiation of the nineteenth-century ideal of the all-competent citizen, Grierson recoiled from his abject pessimism. Grierson's subsequent involvement in documentary filmmaking and educational theory strove, in Gary Evans's words, to 'reveal to the ordinary voter the pattern of the twentieth century so that those who were part of it could feel that they had a stake in the future their leaders were planning.'[57] Film and purposeful education could endow citizens with a regimen of thought and feeling, allowing them to secure meaningful reference points amid social upheaval and political uncertainty. Reanimating public life, in this mould, was premised in large measure on the skilful directives of civic-minded, state-centred experts, as Grierson indicated in a 1941 address: 'the key to education in the modern complex world no longer lies in what we have known as education but in what we have known as propaganda. By the same token, propaganda, so far from being the denial of the democratic principle of education, becomes the necessary instrument for its practical fulfilment.' If the state was 'the machinery by which the best interests of the people are secured,'[58] it followed that any means to enhance its knowledge, to improve its capacity for effective governance, would also serve the public good. Polling proved one such technique for Canada's 'propaganda maestro.' In subsequent months, it figured prominently in the Research Branch's reporting on the public mood, notably so in *Information Briefs,* a publication distributed throughout the government; 'WIB Survey,' a confidential, semi-monthly report; and regular memoranda prepared for cabinet.[59]

Even while the cabinet polling ban was in effect from 27 January to

3 March, Ketchum kept open the CIPO pipeline. On 9 February he requested the above-cited survey data on U.S. annexationism. Four days later he told Porter of the 'little trouble about the use of polling methods' affecting Reports Branch, but this did not detour him from soliciting and receiving breakdowns for a recent institute poll on Canadians' willingness to endure wartime sacrifices. On 1 March, Ketchum met with CIPO statistician O.J. Morris in Ottawa about a possible poll of war-industry workers. The next day, Ketchum requested additional survey breakdowns, assuring Porter that there would 'be no difficulty about meeting the small expenses involved; [they] will come under our last poll.' To help the board overcome opposition to the CIPO, Porter forwarded copies of the institute's post-plebiscite release praising the survey's accuracy.[60]

Once the formal ban was lifted, Ketchum moved quickly on two sampling fronts: an AIPO poll of Americans about Canada, and a second WIB-CIPO national survey of Canadians. In early March, Ketchum drafted questions for a survey of American attitudes towards Canada and its war effort, whose findings would help the board's Washington staff 'measure the effect of their work' in the United States. Grierson approved the plan and Porter handled the arrangements with the Princeton office, which charged the WIB $100 per question. In mid-May, Porter supplied Ketchum an advance copy of the AIPO 'Canadian' questionnaire, a practice that was 'strictly against our policies' and should remain confidential.[61] Ketchum too demanded discretion on a key point: 'the connection of WIB with this survey must not be hinted at in any way whatever. Princeton should merely say that the questions were asked on a regular Gallup Poll.' The survey figures were in Ketchum's hands by late June,[62] and he then lobbied Porter to have the AIPO publish select results, especially the finding that just 28 per cent of Americans were sure that Canada paid no taxes to Great Britain. The story could expose this popular misconception and educate Americans about Canada's constitutional status.[63] However, the Canadian material was not published until November 1943 when Wilfrid Sanders, on a two-week working visit in Princeton, wrote an AIPO column highlighting the survey's findings, albeit six months out of date. References to Canada as the Allies' fourth largest producer of war goods and the recent move by Ottawa and Washington to elevate their respective legations to embassy rank augmented the column's publicity value to Canadian officials.[64] The survey thus served the dual function of providing the board's Washington staff with statistical measures of their propaganda efforts, and, upon release, raising public awareness about Canada and its war effort in some one hundred American dailies. It also enhanced the cachet of the Gallup group, which alone could coordinate and carry out such bi-national surveys.

During this period, Ketchum organized the board's second national opinion survey of Canadians. By mid-March, he had compiled a series of questions, but the CIPO's crowded interviewing schedule delayed the poll's start date until late April. Interestingly, the survey's questionnaire carried a Canadian Opinion Company header, suggesting a firmer separation between the organization's commercial and newspaper polling, but nearly all the accompanying correspondence appeared on CIPO letterhead. The general themes, similar to the December survey, included Ottawa's management of the war; general views of the war effort; news reception by media type; and foreign affairs. There were also inquiries on rationing.[65] As with the earlier WIB poll, open-ended questions were common, securing 'hundreds of spontaneous comments ... as to the reasons for pride in Canada or lack of it, the factors affecting seriousness about the war, the grounds for feeling that particular areas or groups are discriminated against,' among others.[66] Again, Ketchum solicited demographic breakdowns for questions involving war information and media interaction. For example, for the question, 'When information is given out about something Canada is doing, which of these ways will get it across best as far as you are concerned?' the most common responses were newspaper articles and radio programs and announcements. But the two media appealed to different audiences; radio resonated more with labourers and farmers, while newspapers had 'a much stronger hold on the Big Business and White Collar groups.'[67] The survey revealed that government information was unevenly absorbed: young people, the low-educated, women, and the poor knew less about war measures and national goals than older, educated, and financially secure respondents. The link between information-deficient citizens and optimal media was not always obvious. For example, overall, posters and films rated low as preferred conduits for war information, but among younger, less-educated respondents they scored higher.[68] Well-informed persons, Ketchum later noted, typically displayed higher levels of morale, and were 'more willing to make sacrifices, more ready to support necessary regulations, more tolerant of Canadian minorities, [and] more internationally-minded.' Beginning in mid-1943, Young documents, the WIB retooled its operations to reach out to 'apathetic Canadians,' and increasingly designed information appeals along functional lines based on substantive issues rather than generic patriotism. Consequently, information programs specific to industrial workers, youths, and consumers, among others, were implemented, as were campaigns around issues like rehabilitation, citizenship, food, and economic stability.[69] In such a schema, polling mirrored the function of market research surveys used by advertisers and marketers to dissect consumer demand and formulate effective selling strategies. This time, however, many of the targeted 'consumers' of government information were those least valued by market researchers: the disaffected, the poor, the uneducated.

For Ketchum, survey research was a rational, technical-instrumental means to assess the state's information needs and to design and disseminate corresponding propaganda with maximum efficiency. Its closest cousin was the market research survey, but its authoritative claims derived as much from social science discourse as from the rhetoric of business know-how. The political-bureaucratic maelstrom of wartime Ottawa, however, was a far cry from the imperturbable ivory tower; and some critics during the war, notably Harold Innis, charged that this social-science-for-hire milieu, stressing short-term solutions for government problems, would ultimately impede or taint scientific advances.[70] Similarly, the war presented government officials the opportunity to employ social scientific knowledge less as a means to enhance the expertise of democratic governance than as a tool to legitimate the exercise of political power or the promotion of policy positions.[71]

Both these concerns were vindicated by a remarkable WIB survey on wage and price controls commissioned in September 1943. The Advisory Committee of the National Liberal Federation (NLF) was scheduled to convene in late September, immediately following a special Liberal caucus meeting. Ketchum, Grierson, and WPTB officials anticipated that some Liberal back-benchers would push to ease economic controls, believing they were the cause of the decline in support for the government. The WIB was preparing educational programs on economic stabilization and food conservation and did not want them jeopardized or inflation renewed by cabinet's 'yielding to the clamour of Liberal politicians who probably don't know what they are talking about.' A CIPO poll showing public support for price and wage controls, Ketchum and Grierson thought, would strengthen their hand with the government. The poll's blatant political motive, the lack of any pretence of 'objectivity' from its professorial promoter, can be seen in Ketchum's appeal to Porter on 13 September:

Grierson shied away from our undertaking the thing ourselves as it is so politically dangerous and told me to put it to you as an urgent personal request from an old friend! ... I am convinced that WIB would be ready to 'buy' the question from you in spite of Grierson's remarks. It might have to be hidden in a future survey of our own or something, but I fancy we could work it, though I have no authorization to say so. It will partly depend on the replies of course, from our point of view we want a big majority for maintenance of the system of controls.[72]

The institute duly obliged. A hastily arranged 'telegraph poll,' in which field workers telegraphed results to the CIPO shortly after interviewing, enabled the release of a column on 25 September, two days before the NLF meeting. The poll's sponsor was not revealed. Sixty-nine per cent supported wage-price ceilings, 20 per cent were opposed, and 11 per cent were undecided. The survey was not a national cross-section; farm dwellers, who formed 27 per cent of the population in 1941,[73] were left out, owing to 'interviewing difficulties involved in a quick poll.' The survey compared the September findings with the non-farm totals from an identical CIPO question from February 1943, for which 80 per cent supported controls, 14 per cent did not, and 6 per cent were unsure. The exclusion of farm residents the second time around would not skew the overall totals, the institute claimed, because agrarian opinion in the earlier poll was 'only a point or two away from the national figure.' No rural-urban breakdowns were provided for the earlier poll, but the column's only reference to the topic ('approval in the farming areas ... is less than that in the towns') suggests that farm and non-farm opinion were not closely aligned.[74] It would be unusual if they were, for farmers, unlike town and city dwellers, benefited directly from higher commodity prices. To wit, during the First World War when economic controls were few and mostly ineffective, agricultural wholesale prices rose 133 per cent from 1913 to 1919, compared to a 63 per cent increase in the cost of living.[75] High inflation hurt consumers, but not primary producers whose goods, like foodstuffs during war, were in high demand. While the farm population's omission was attributed to time constraints, it may have worked as well to secure results favouring Ketchum's predisposition.

Poll numbers on economic controls soon circulated among government officials. Grierson supplied King's assistant J.W. Pickersgill, a staunch advocate of wartime controls,[76] with data showing support for wage-price regulation, which was later forwarded to the prime minister. The survey, Ketchum wrote Porter, would unquestionably 'raise the status of the Gallup Poll in Government quarters,' as many cabinet members had received 'several sets of figures and interpretations' based on its findings.[77] The Liberal government stayed the course with price-wage ceilings; indeed, the Advisory Council endorsed a wide array of interventionist and welfarist policies.[78] And one month later the WIB received a strong cabinet vote of confidence when Grierson lobbied for and got a $370,000 supplement – a 64 per cent increase – to the board's 1943–4 budget.[79]

Again with the board's third national opinion poll, commissioned in October 1943, there were questions on price–wage controls and news-information dissemination, but the survey was most notable for its emphasis on postwar concerns, a total of eight of seventeen polled topics. This was understandable, since by mid-1943 postwar planning had become a cottage industry of sorts within bureaucratic Ottawa. In December 1939, King authorized the Cabinet Committee on Demobilization and Reconstruction, and four years later seventeen additional committees and subcommittees laboured to facilitate a smooth transition to peacetime.[80] These activities were as much a response to popular anxiety about the prospect of a return to Depression-era conditions as they were the technocratic impulse of state planners to avoid the kind of economic and social disruption that had followed the Great War. That reconstruction and social welfare were uppermost in people's minds is witnessed by responses to the open-ended question: 'If you could sit down and talk with the member of parliament for your riding before he returns to Ottawa, what question would you like to ask him about problems here in Canada?' Of decided Canadians, 50 per cent cited postwar and social security concerns. When asked to choose from a list of topics for which they wanted additional information, 57 per cent cited 'plans for after the war,' compared to 34 per cent for the second-place finisher, 'labour unions and working conditions.' Similarly, respondents were asked to select specific postwar plans deemed most important. In ascending order, these were recreational opportunities, housing, farm improvements, education, health care, old age security, and employment. Though by late 1943 the federal government was awash with reconstruction blueprints, Canadians were not placated; 59 per cent of decided respondents thought Ottawa was not planning sufficiently for the postwar era. As with other WIB-COC surveys, all figures were cross-tabulated by sex, region, class, and occupational group.[81] And favourable results, like the finding that 78 per cent of people (including 56 per cent in Quebec) backed the use of Canadian servicemen in postwar peace-keeping, could be given to the CIPO for release to publicize such a popular consensus. (Conversely, findings that twice as many Canadians believed French–English relations had worsened than had improved since 1939 did not make it into print.) The political implications for such polling were obvious, even to a 'disinterested' functionary like Ketchum: 'It seems to me that you could make a good case for arguing that the Government is losing elections because of [its] failure to meet these post-war demands and not because of [its] economic controls.'[82]

Among Liberal politicians, Claxton was the most enamoured of polling's charms. His constituency polling is discussed in the next chapter. But as the prime minister's parliamentary assistant from May 1943 to October 1944, when he served as King's representative on the WIB board, and thereafter as minister of national health and welfare, Claxton often consulted the polls while planning policy. Here he acted both as public official and partisan politician. In June 1943, Dunton provided him with a memo, which included polling data, on the public's mounting preoccupation with postwar problems. When King announced plans in early 1944 for a federal–provincial conference, Claxton was appointed chairman of a committee to compile information for Ottawa's case.[83] Claxton wanted the CIPO to determine public support for the postwar transfer of provincial powers to the federal government, and even drafted a highly biased question.[84] Ketchum and institute officials discussed the matter, and a more balanced question was inserted on the 10 March questionnaire. Three weeks later, the results, including provincial and sex breakdowns, were forwarded to Ketchum and Claxton.[85] In the end, the polling venture proved all for naught, as King cancelled the conference following acrimonious outbursts by Ontario premier George Drew. Also in March 1944, Claxton made a 'private' request to Gallup officials via Ketchum for age breakdowns on recent voting preference questions. The following month he received cross-tabulated CIPO tallies on three foreign policy questions and another on adopting a new national flag. Around the same time, Claxton, miffed about a March CIPO poll that asked people to choose between a foreign policy of outright independence or membership in the Commonwealth but did not provide a third choice of 'independence plus consultation,' wanted the institute to conduct another poll with the latter option. Ketchum passed on the request to Porter, who, in order to meet the deadline of an upcoming CIPO survey, quickly drafted two questions, neither of which, however, dealt adequately with Claxton's concern.[86] In any event, the results were published three weeks later.[87] In July and August 1945, in advance of the Dominion–Provincial Conference, Claxton solicited the WIB for recent poll findings on federal–provincial affairs.[88]

The importance of Gallup polling to the WIB and officials like Claxton hit home in 1943 and again in 1944 when they faced the prospect of losing Porter and Morris to the wartime draft. In September 1943, Porter received a call-up notice from the National Selective Service (NSS), the agency responsible for efficiently allocating civilian manpower for war production needs.[89] Alarmed by this prospect, Grierson wrote the NSS, requesting that Porter be granted a deferment, citing the CIPO's important work for the board. He followed this up with an appeal to deputy minister of labour Arthur MacNamara: the Gallup Poll was of 'increasing value to many government departments' and Porter's presence was essential in maintaining this flow of vital information. The lobbying effort paid off, and Porter received a six-month postponement. When this neared expiration, Dunton, now WIB general manager, appealed to MacNamara for another extension for Porter. A six-month search, Dunton claimed disingenuously, had turned up no one with Porter's 'knowledge of the science of opinion measurement.'[90] Again, the appeal was won.

Even more worrisome for Canadian officials was the prospect of losing Morris to an American draft board. As a skilled statistician in population sampling, he was even more prized than Porter. Upon word of his call-up in February 1944, Dunton wrote Morris's New Jersey draft board in support of a deferment, emphasizing his unique value to the Canadian government as a survey specialist. The following month, Sanders visited Ottawa to plead Morris's case in the Department of External Affairs, but his reluctance to disclose to low-level employees the close links between the CIPO and the federal government caused WIB officials to worry that the appeal would proceed as a mere request from a private company. Accordingly, Ketchum asked Dunton to have undersecretary of state for external affairs Norman Robertson advise Lester Pearson in the Washington embassy of the situation, in order to ensure a more senior-level appeal to American authorities. External Affairs obliged, MacNamara also wrote on Morris's behalf, and these efforts secured his exemption from military service. One year later, Morris, again with the help of WIB officials, obtained another exemption.[91] The irony here is palpable. The same government which in 1941 temporarily denied immigration visas to Gallup employees and two years later briefly banned the WIB from using CIPO polls was now acting to keep institute officials in Canada and the polling pipeline open.

And during the latter war years, the WIB continued to work closely with Gallup officials. Four additional COC surveys were sponsored, for a total of seven, which encompassed data from over one hundred questions. Total billings for this work reached over $16,000.[92] The WIB also continued to influence the selection of topics for regular CIPO polls, absorbing as well a steady flow of figures from this source. In September 1944 Ketchum lobbied successfully for a CIPO question on whether Canadians preferred that their servicemen later fought alongside American or British forces in the Pacific theatre. In November, against the backdrop of the second conscription crisis, Ketchum pushed for and got a CIPO question on overseas conscription, which later appeared in the institute's 30 December release. A March 1945 request from the Department of National Health and Welfare for a poll on family allowances – likely Claxton's handiwork – culminated in the CIPO column 'Majority of Public Feels Bonus Will Not Be Misused by Parents,' appearing twelve days before the election. After the vote, the WIB secured additional breakdowns for the CIPO's 16 June column asking: 'What do you think will be the greatest task the federal government elected in June will have to face in the next few years?' On an earlier occasion Gallup officials won board approval to use data from a COC survey for a CIPO column. Conversely, in February 1945, Ketchum's request to circulate unpublished CIPO polling on the United Nations Relief and Rehabilitation Administration (UNRRA) was granted by Porter, provided it was 'done in a thoroughly confidential way and ... not termed a "Gallup Poll."' Such poll swapping carried its share of risk, as seen in September 1944 when two CIPO columns on full employment and international peace were published shortly after the figures had appeared in a WIB report. As Ketchum explained to Morris, 'when that happens it seems to me that those who get our survey might be justified in assuming a very close tie-up between WIB and the Gallup Poll. This would, of course, be undesirable in the light of the questions asked in the House by Tommy Church and others.'[93]

As the war progressed, increasing numbers of federal officials dined on a burgeoning diet of polling prepared by the WIB. Along with survey results printed in *Information Briefs*, 'WIB Survey,' and weekly cabinet memoranda,[94] innumerable other poll findings made the bureaucratic rounds. An October 1943 WIB report described the Report Branch's mounting preoccupation with published and private surveys: 'this material is filed topically so that we may be in a position to answer rapidly any questions on current public opinion that may come to us. Such inquiries are becoming more frequent.' Next month, the WIB noted that topical poll results were being 'made available in advance of the regular reports to certain interested government officials.' In March 1944, Reports Branch officials provided survey data or discussed the use of polls with representatives from the Department of Munitions and Supply, the National War Finance Committee, the Economic Stabilization Information Committee, and the Chief of Information, Armed Services. Ketchum also gave technical advice to the Canadian Youth Commission about a youth survey.[95] Three months later, the board again reported the increasing number of governmental requests for polling figures, including public reactions to CBC policies and programs. COC work for the Department of Labour in late 1944, Ketchum reported to Sanders in November 1944, 'had won you some converts there,' including Arthur MacNamara. In December 1944, poll summaries on health issues were sent to the deputy minister of national health and welfare, and the following month additional survey findings were given to the Demobilization and Rehabilitation Information Committee. Soon after, External Affairs officer H.F. Angus requested poll numbers on sending Canadian food to postwar Europe. In March 1945, polls on American attitudes towards manpower controls were forwarded to the Department of Labour. Before arriving at the San Francisco Conference, the Canadian delegation received survey results on public 'attitudes towards the issues under discussion.'[96] It should not, of course, be assumed that polling affected policy making in every instance;[97] unquestionably, Ottawa's decision making, occurring in a milieu of competing interests and contradictory information, could not function with a mind only to the polls. Politics negated this. But these developments do suggest that by 1945 the instrumental technique of polling had made considerable inroads in the policy-making process, a phenomenon which only three years earlier was unknown.

Alongside the WIB, another branch of government made extensive use of survey research. Established on 3 September 1939, the Wartime Prices and Trade Board functioned to contain inflationary pressures and manage the supply and distribution of scarce commodities. The board's initial scope was limited, dealing mostly with rent controls and price regulation for staple goods like wheat and coal. The inability of this circumscribed system to control inflation, which rose 18 per cent from August 1939 to October 1941, prompted the King government to overhaul the board. In August 1941 it was transferred from the auspices of the Ministry of Labour to those of Finance, and three months later Donald Gordon, the energetic deputy governor of the Bank of Canada, took control of the organization. Most important, the government decided in October 1941 to impose a comprehensive freeze on wages and prices. The implementation and enforcement of these inflation-capping measures – coupled with the 1942 introduction of coupon rationing for sugar, butter, tea, and gasoline – expanded greatly the board's purview and public awareness. Indeed, with its myriad orders and regulations affecting pay stubs in the workplace and consumer spending in the marketplace, the WPTB arguably affected Canadians' daily lives more than any other wartime agency. The end result, as measured by inflation, was an unparalleled success; the cost-of-living index rose just 2.8 per cent from October 1941 to April 1945. Occasional griping about rationing and recurrent black market selling in restricted goods, however, served as occasional reminders that public compliance with board measures was not always willing or universal.[98]

Because the WPTB relied on exhortation and moral suasion alongside state fiat to curb consumption and dampen inflation, it benefited greatly from a knowledge of public opinion on consumption habits and current or prospective board measures. Accordingly, it solicited the services of the CIPO. The institute's inaugural survey of November 1941 gauged support for the recent wage–price freeze, and one month later it asked a series of questions on its personal impact.[99] The next survey in late December inquired if people expected certain goods to be rationed, which items they wanted rationed first, and whether they had noticed any shortages in local stores.[100] Subsequent institute surveys in 1942 carried questions on such 'public' issues as sugar usage, driving patterns and expected wearing-out dates of tires, the number of dresses and suits people had and the minimum they required per year, and whether men usually bought one or two pairs of trousers with suits. In November, the CIPO surveyed 'what the average Canadian eats in the course of a day,' recording the breakfast, lunch, and dinner foods for respondents and their children. By 1943, CIPO polls on rationing, conservation, and wage-price controls, of which there were dozens, were being handled by the WIB, which then passed on findings to the WPTB.[101] Did Canadians favour the sale of oleomargarine in stores? How many were planning gardens to stretch the country's food resources? How did people react to the curtailment of beer sales? What major purchases were Canadians planning for after the war?[102] There are obvious parallels between these queries and the consumer surveys examined in chapter 1 but for one important difference: WPTB officials turned to sample surveys to help contain consumer spending; market researchers used them, in large part, to augment consumption. The findings, equipped with the now requisite social and geographic breakdowns, helped WPTB officials plan programs and devise information appeals, particularly from 1943 on, when support for some board measures began to wane.[103]

In 1944, the Statistics Branch of the WPTB's Research Division became more closely involved with survey research exemplified by two endeavours: the development of a cross-country network of 'consumer panels,' and the commissioning of a series of Gallup surveys in 1944 and 1945. Market researchers in the United States, notably Paul Lazarsfeld, had developed such panels during the interwar years. The panels consisted of selected consumers (usually women, numbering from a few dozen to many hundreds) who tested products, tried out new recipes, listened to radio shows, and answered questionnaires, in addition to other 'assignments' levied by company marketers. While not a scientific sampling of consumer opinion, such panels carried a twofold appeal: they were a relatively inexpensive way to acquire broad-based consumer feedback, and they could track responses over time, measuring behavioural and attitudinal changes during the course of product use. In Canada in the 1930s, Lever Brothers Inc. maintained its 'Lever Research Corps,' a nationwide panel of hundreds of women who regularly answered mailed questionnaires about soap use and related topics. As well, *Chatelaine* magazine counted over a thousand women in its 'Chatelaine Consulting Board,' who periodically answered surveys about 'housekeeping' matters. Lazarsfeld later applied the consumer panel concept to politics when he set up the Erie voter panel during the 1940 election.[104]

The first consumer panels were created in 1943 to inform the WPTB about women's preserves-related spending on rationed goods like sugar and other sweeteners. With the help of home economists, dietitians, and the Women's Institute, additional panels were established soon after.[105] When home economists curtailed their involvement with the panels in mid-1944, the WPTB's Consumer Branch stepped in to fill the void. Headed by Byrne Hope Sanders, the dynamic editor of *Chatelaine* and sister of Wilfrid Sanders (and in the 1950s a director at the CIPO), the Consumer Branch in 1942 established the Women's Regional Advisory Committees (WRAC), to oversee the actions of sixteen thousand women volunteers who monitored retail prices nationwide and were, in the words of one historian, 'the real spine of price control' during the war.[106] This extensive network of price watchdogs, WPTB officials maintained, could also double as a sample base for consumer panels. The board's ini-

tial survey efforts, however, proved somewhat disappointing; the paucity of rural panel members, especially in Quebec, coupled with high
turnover rates, meant, according to one board official, that these early
'panels were not (statistically) all that could be desired.' These problems
were compounded by low response rates; for example, a Consumer
Branch questionnaire on metal household appliances sent to over 2,500
panellists in 1944 produced only 533 responses.[107]

In early 1945, officials from the Consumer and Statistics branches
joined forces to ameliorate the situation. Prominent among the latter
group was Henry King, the former director of research at Cockfield,
Brown and Canada's pioneer consumer researcher.[108] King and statistician Clyde McDonald proposed a novel survey design. Consumer
Branch would send questionnaires to the thousands of women on
WRAC and Women's Institute panels, and Statistics Branch would use
quota sampling to select five hundred to a thousand responses repre-
senting a national cross-section of consumers. Because 'housewives'
were thought to control 85 per cent of consumer purchasing, the sample
contained few unmarried women. The first of these 'rejuvenated consumer panel' surveys were mailed out in May 1945, but slow response
times and difficulties with 'the process of building up a representative
sample of responding volunteers' delayed the final report until September. A low return rate from Quebec excluded it from the survey's findings. The study recorded average prices paid for dresses and reported
that 85 per cent of panellists had an approximate idea that 'sanforizing'
referred to pre-shrunken fabrics. An incredible 97 per cent of homemakers claimed to have done some preserving or canning the past fall, an
average household tally of ninety-three pints of fruit in syrup, eighteen
pounds of jams, jellies, and marmalades, and sixty-one pints of vegeta-
bles. A second questionnaire went out in late July, and this time the
selected sample of about a thousand cases included Quebec. The survey
gauged demand for aluminum kitchen utensils and rates of sugar consumption, but its accuracy was weakened by uneven representation: the
sample was 'admittedly biased somewhat in the direction of persons in
the upper income groups.' The third and final panel survey occurring in
October and November 1945 contained a similar class bias. It recorded
the incidence of canning and preserving (down somewhat from 1944),
along with corresponding sugar use. In the behaviourist style reminiscent of J. Walter Thompson soap surveys of the 1930s, the poll documented soap consumption patterns, highlighting among other items
that prairie women were the largest per capita users of castile and car-

bolic toilet soaps and British Columbians were the most frequent buyers of fine laundry soaps.[109]

→ These three panel studies were a watershed in Canadian survey research history: they were the first extensive representative sample surveys done entirely in-house by the federal government. Polling and market research firms played no part in this unconventional sampling exercise. That these milestone polls targeted homemakers and were limited to consumer queries was highly fitting, given the purchasing and female-directed origins of sample surveys. They were also decidedly behaviourist, McDonald underscored, designed to secure 'facts' about consumer behaviour and not 'opinions' on consumer issues.[110] Their principal function as an instrumental tool to facilitate board planning – and not as a democratic means to illuminate popular desire – is revealed by the Lippmannesque standpoint of key WPTB officials:

... the idea of a Consumer Panel survey as suggested by Henry King and others designed to bring out some idea of what the public needs in the way of metal articles has been ruled out of court by the Chairman [Donald Gordon] and [Deputy Chairman] Max Mackenzie. They object to the idea on the following grounds: (a) that it would carry the presumption that we are obliged to produce the goods which the survey shows to be necessary; (b) that the public would tell us what they want as well as what they believe to be their minimum needs and the public is incapable of distinguishing between the two concepts (by inference the Board is assumed to be able to judge better than the public itself).[111]

The fact that this 'public' was a female preserve may have promoted such forms of top-down planning and citizen consultation.

While retooling its consumer panels, the WPTB also moved to measure the dual-sex public pulse on wartime controls. In June 1944, it commissioned a complete questionnaire survey from the COC. The 2,008-person sample, made up of near-equal numbers of men and women and stratified by social and geographic variables, gauged knowledge of and support for current and postwar rationing, the distribution of products, the black market in gasoline, and wage-price ceilings. Distinguishing this survey from the consumer panels was its emphasis on securing actual 'opinions,' and not just consumer-related 'facts.' Respondents relayed which, if any, controlled goods should cease to be rationed. While a plurality were content with the choice of rationed items, dissenters most often cited butter and sugar as needlessly regulated. Those who had had dealings with local WPTB officials registered their degree of satisfaction. People were asked if both buyers and sellers or only sellers of black market items should be punished. (A majority opted for both; in Quebec, however, 25 per cent said 'neither.') Women favoured this year's sugar-rationing provisions for canning over those from 1943.[112]

The next WPTB-COC collaborative effort took place in March 1945, the first of three semi-monthly surveys on economic controls done for the board's Information Branch. The three surveys shared the common purpose of providing Information Branch officials with data to enable them to 'market' more effectively wartime controls to the Canadian public during the waning war months and the postwar period. For example, WPTB officials maintained that two of the advance, *raison d'être* questions were answered in whole or in part by the survey: 'What are the main problems from a public relations point of view?' and 'What are the lines – as indicated by the poll – along which publicity is most needed?' Overall, results were generally encouraging. There was increased public support for the ideas that inflation continued to pose a danger, that price controls had successfully contained inflation, and that rationing was fairly conducted. The second survey, completed soon after V-E Day, polled on similar topics and again emphasized its 'public relations' function. The report differentiated three categories of data drawn from the survey, the most important one being 'the "putting across" of certain wisely chosen ideas and slogans, [the] assimilation of which will promote the successful operation of controls.' This so-called field of *'opinion proper'* afforded greater opportunities for 'suggestion and publicity' because it dealt with topics outside the 'scrutiny of personal experiences' such as housing. Once again, support for economic controls remained steady.[113] The July survey report contained additional cryptic references to 'opinion proper' survey data, while also noting that support for rationing and wage–price ceilings was tapering off. To shore up support for rationing, a supplementary report drew on survey findings to devise an information campaign:

From a public relations point of view acceptance of rationing would be satisfactory if the public could be 'sold' on 4 points: (i) rationing is the best method of distributing goods required by all that are in short supply; (ii) rationing is justified in terms of the actual commodities being so distributed; (iii) if justified on humanitarian grounds, rationing should be extended to cover other commodities; (iv) all violations of ration regulation, even those occurring 'just once in a while' are wrong and should be punished.[114]

As the above examples illustrate, Christopher Waddell's claim that polling provided the WPTB with 'a more precise method of gauging public beliefs and of shaping programmes to calm public concerns'[115] was empirically valid. Moreover, when these data were combined with those from consumer panels, they afforded board planners an even stronger quantitative grasp of consumer behaviour and thoughts.

'The essence of statesmanship,' Walter Lippmann wrote in 1929, 'consists in giving the people not what they want but what they will learn to want.' During the Second World War, when mass 'learning' and state propaganda became coterminous, Lippmann's dictum resounded loudly as liberal individualism and democratic practices became subsumed by 'the beneficent rationality of the state.'[116] In the bid to mobilize the nation's human and material resources for total war, decision making gravitated to the executive and bureaucratic branches of government. The dilemma this presented to Gallup-sanctioned opinion polling was palpable, if quickly papered over by those involved. An ostensibly independent and 'objective' technique promoting the general good by articulating the views of ordinary citizens, the CIPO confronted a political climate in which Ottawa had harnessed 'value-neutral' social science for its own purposes, and where state goals had firmly superseded those of any lingering 'public interest.'[117] As Max Weber had theorized, the logic of instrumental rationality – expert-managed administration – had prevailed over that of democracy, in which 'the unpredictability of the electorate undermines the values of consistency and efficiency central to large-scale corporations and large-scale government.'[118] The CIPO's intense and secretive involvement with federal officials violated its expressed public role – its purported democratic mission – as an independent vehicle for popular expression. But when viewed historically, such close collaboration becomes understandable – in fact 'logical' from the standpoint of instrumental rationality. Market research surveys were born of a business impulse to improve the efficiency of marketing, the demand-side corollary to rationalized production during the Second Industrial Revolution. When Canada's first 'large-scale government' mushroomed during the war, it was not surprising that technocratic officials turned to rationalized methods not only for the mass production of war goods but for the mobilization of mass consent behind state-prescribed goals.

5

Pols and Polls

In this day and age until we've learned how the technique of selling soap works, we'll go on making a mighty poor fist of selling socialism to the lower middle and working classes, the younger voters, and the women.

Philip Spencer, 1941

It will be possible for us again to survey nationally to determine which approach should be used in selling to the public the [Liberal] Party's stand on any particular issue ... In this way we will know not only what the public feel strongest about but also the best way in which to sell to them the Liberal party's stand on that issue.

F.W. Gross, 1944

The services of the [Gallup] Poll are not available to any political party or group, and it is completely objective and non-political in its outlook.

CIPO column, 1945[1]

'The twentieth century and Canadian politics come to terms this year,' Richard Gwyn wrote in the *Financial Post* in April 1962, for the country was on the brink of its 'first scientific election.' Two 'completely new weapons' were reconfiguring the electoral landscape – 'privately hired, public opinion surveys,' and their adjunct, 'sophisticated, probing, statistical analysis.' When combined with state-of-the-art advertising and communication techniques, the election promised a turning-point in Canadian politics, a critical juncture in which 'the skills of sociologists, statisticians, advertising experts, pollsters, and mass-communications experts' would match or surpass the 'age-old talents of politicians.'[2] Modernity, both its scientific and commercial forms, it seemed, had finally caught up with the archaic 'profession' of politics, which, for better or worse, would now be reconstituted as had other Victorian-rooted institutions and practices. Gwyn's pronouncement, buttressed by a detailed sketch of Liberal and Tory polling activities in 1962, set the standard for other accounts situating the arrival of electoral polling in the early 1960s. Joseph Wearing, while briefly remarking that Liberals and Conservatives 'attempted some polling in the 1950s,' credits the Liberal party's hiring of Democratic party pollster Louis Harris in the early 1960s as the effective launch date of Canadian electoral polling.[3] Pollster and political scientist David C. Walker and Khayyam Zev Paltiel similarly situate partisan polling's substantive beginnings with Harris's arrival.[4] These accounts, among others, have given rise to one of the more enduring myths of Canadian politics.[5]

Political party polling originated in the 1940s, not the 1960s. Indeed, many features of 1960s party polling were strikingly in evidence a generation earlier. Both times the Liberal party was the primary player, and both times it relied on the survey expertise of Americans – in 1944, the Princeton psychologist Hadley Cantril. Both periods witnessed a close working relationship between Liberal officials and advertising professionals. Walter Gordon, the policy specialist and party technocrat who eagerly embraced polling in 1961, had his counterpart in the similarly talented and equally polling-obsessed Brooke Claxton of the 1940s. Keith Davey, the radio station sales manager turned party-organizer who brought Harris to Ottawa,[6] was a latter-day, if less self-effacing, version of Bob Kidd, the Cockfield, Brown ad executive and Liberal polling point man during the war.

The two polling periods, however, differed in at least two ways. In the 1940s, polling was largely a one-party show, with Tory and CCF efforts proving marginal to none. Wartime Liberal party polling also did not match the scale and sophistication of the surveys performed in the 1960s. But these 1940s polls constituted the Canadian genesis of what came to be known as 'political marketing,'[7] the adaptation of market research techniques to party policy formation and electoral politics. In this respect, the 'twentieth century' arrived two decades before Gwyn's pronouncement.

Readers of *Canadian Forum*'s October and December 1940 issues might have wondered if the socialist monthly had been commandeered by Madison Avenue emissaries. The titles alone of the pseudonymous[8]

Philip Spencer's articles ('Does It Sell the Stuff?' and 'Pardon Me, Madam, How Often Do You Take a Bath?') were a far cry from staple erudite offerings from leftist literati like Frank Scott, Barker Fairley, or Frank Underhill. Spencer's argument went further beyond the pale of most progressive intellectuals: socialists, and especially the CCF, should wholeheartedly embrace market surveys and advertising to fashion party policy and wage elections. Commercial advertising based on research methods and psychological insight, Spencer championed with characteristic hyperbole, was 'one thousand per cent more effective than the appeals [now] turned out by political advertisers.'[9] Two months later he introduced *Forum* readers to three types of market research: 'parasitic' research, the culling of available data from sources like the Dominion Bureau of Statistics, would abet economic and social policy planning; 'strategy' research, analysing electoral returns and past campaign dynamics, would pinpoint winnable CCF ridings; and the third and most important research genre, discussed under the heading 'The New Fuller Brush Man,' was the market research survey as pioneered by George Gallup and Elmo Roper. In a passage extraordinary for its melding of commercial and political marketing, Spencer mapped out a research program for a hypothetical launch of a cigarette brand. Sample surveys and other research tools would determine the total number of smokers and their socio-economic distribution; what smokers liked about their current brands; what previous brands they had smoked and why they switched; which cigarettes were preferred for 'mildness,' 'flavour,' or 'economy.' Ad copy testing would be done, and by cross-tabulating these results with other demographic and response variables the advertiser could 'evaluate the effectiveness of one selling story against another ... the degree of penetration of a selling appeal ... [and] whether advertising for a product [was] reaching the market intended.' After outlining the four-paragraph research plan, Spencer directed the reader to revisit it with a political cast of mind:

For the word 'market' substitute the word 'population' or 'voters.' For 'cigarette' and 'smoke' substitute either 'appeal and 'believe in,' or 'function' and 'perform.' Change 'mildness' and 'flavor' to any political or social descriptive noun you wish. Leave 'advertising' as it is. Re-read the description of this typical survey and it will become evident how it could be applied to a thousand socialist problems.

The CCF would never achieve political strength, Spencer contended, so long as it relied on 'old-fashioned methods of "intellectual persuasion,"' rooted more in eighteenth-century 'rationalism' than in twentieth-century mass democracy. The party should shed the '"education-method" of our grandfathers' and adopt policies and campaign strategies with a mind to voters' emotional and impressionable natures. 'Until we know what people do and think and read, until we have developed a strategy that is really relevant to the readers of Popeye and the listeners [to] Charlie McCarthy, we can't hope to make socialism the loud, imperative and compelling shout that it should be.'[10]

What should one make of Spencer's brash unorthodoxy? The CCF in 1940, in the minds of most supporters, constituted an educative socialist movement as well as a political party.[11] To 'sell' socialism like chewing gum or cigarettes was at best trivializing a virtuous political crusade, at worst denigrating it. *Forum* editors, drawn from the ranks of the CCF 'brain trust,' the League for Social Reconstruction,[12] evidently thought otherwise; in each of the next four issues, articles from Spencer appeared, poring over the findings of a 'political consumer survey' he conducted among Torontonians. The size of the sample was not disclosed and 'amateur investigators' served as field workers, who filled interview schedules stratified by age, sex, and class quotas. Once again, newspaper and magazine reading habits were avidly elicited. For lower-income earners – the 'C' and 'D' groups making less than $50 weekly and totalling 75 per cent of the sample – the comics and sports pages together outstripped the news pages as the most popular newspaper sections. Women read fewer papers but more magazines than men, half of which were female-specific. Blending condescension with marketing savvy, Spencer propounded that women were 'living in their own world of cosy chats about baby's diet and how I stopped middle-aged spread.' The only effective way to 'bring new ideas to this majority of women' was via the women's magazines themselves. Similarly, radio listening revealed tabloid tastes and diversionary impulses. Drama and variety shows, especially American ones, were more popular than news and public affairs broadcasts, notably among hoped-for CCF voters. As Spencer quipped sarcastically, 'it's pretty nasty, isn't it?, that the lower classes whom socialists want to reach, the youngsters, and leftists *themselves*, vote more heavily for escapism.'[13]

Having established the parameters of people's newspaper, magazine, and radio interaction, the survey scrutinized opinion on conventional left-wing issues. Did Torontonians think they paid an 'unfair price' for everyday staples? Why was this? Did monopolies keep prices unnecessarily high for consumers? If so, for what products? A strong correlation between those blaming monopolies for inflating prices and those believing they overpaid for staples meant, Spencer concluded, that 'it should be the job of a progressive movement to see to it that *every* individual who blames monopolies has it knocked into his head that this condition also affects the everyday things he buys.' Other issues queried included the treatment of soldiers, cooperatives, suggestions for neighbourhood and city-wide improvements, local relief, the quality of public schools, and the merits of municipally managed milk distribution. The popularity of the last item suggested the CCF 'would be backing a hopeful horse if it plugged this.'[14]

Alongside customary demographic variables like age, sex, and class, Spencer devised another denoting 'left' and 'right' political affinity. Respondents were asked to choose a preferred *ideal* government type, ranging from one which 'kept stricter control of labor unions and radical groups' to one which 'believed in parliamentary socialism.' Those expressing no political ideal were lumped in with the rightist camp, which overall constituted 63 per cent of the sample, compared to 37 per cent on the left. Among 'D' voters, though, left supporters totalled 48 per cent, and for thirty- to forty–year-olds they reached 53 per cent. Slightly more men than women were left-leaning. A target market for the CCF was coming into focus. Working-class males under forty, generally, were more predisposed to socialist tenets and thus more likely to endorse CCF ideas and policies. Party appeals, Spencer emphasized, should be designed with these specific groups in mind, employing messages and communicative strategies which registered on a personal level, not an abstract, ideological one.[15]

Within the non-political camp, there were also vote-garnering opportunities. For example, this group supported municipally run milk distribution by a two-to-one margin, making it an obvious issue upon which to broaden CCF appeal. But disinterested voters required fundamentally different tactics and appeals. A key problem was the group's high level of political ignorance. When asked to name the federal Liberals' 'parliamentary leader' (admittedly harder than naming the prime minister), only 53 per cent of apolitical respondents could do so. For the entire sample, just 68 per cent answered correctly, an outcome instilling contempt in Spencer: 'One wonders what percentage would be able to identify the celestial head of the Christian church.' That more people could identify the sponsor of the Jack Benny show than had named King underscored the effectiveness of linking political messages to popular culture and commercial advertising: 'What chance has a small party ... of selling its product until it has made the effort of planning innumerable dramatic activities capable of making impressions on an un-political people, innumerable activities pre-judged and executed on the basis of modern business technology and social psychology?' Indeed, the CCF was in dire need of its own selling job. Nearly six in ten voters drew a blank when asked what the CCF 'stood for.' Among identified 'reformist' respondents, the figure was 76 per cent, nearly the same level for non-politicals. Salvation here would not come from the 'usual dry-as-dust socialist speech-making pap,' but from harnessing the promotional will to 'act realistically and thoroughly on the basis of modern psychology and science.'[16]

Spencer's clarion call, juxtaposing an advertiser's bravado with socialist platitudes, provided a peculiar spectacle, to say the least. Appearing in the country's preeminent leftist magazine, it was the first known politically inspired opinion poll in Canada, albeit one done by 'amateur' canvassers and with only partial methodological disclosure. Spencer's series was also the first published apologia for the application of market research techniques to politics. Political marketing in Canada had been conceived and trumpeted, but by an apostle seeking to curtail the very domain which spawned it, free-enterprise capitalism. And how did *Forum* readers react to learning that the road to the New Jerusalem was necessarily lined with billboards plugging succulent grapes and golden honey? If the readers' responses printed were any indication, they didn't; no letters about the articles appeared, nor did any subsequent writings by Spencer. For the remaining war years, the *Forum* steered largely clear of advertising, market research, and opinion polling, focusing instead on characteristic topics like state planning, civil liberties, and monopoly capitalism, along with the usual complement of poetry and fiction.[17]

Did Spencer's message resonate with the CCF? Judging from the paucity of polling material in party records it would seem unlikely. In January 1941, an Ontario CCF committee inquired into means of improving party publicity, which included 'polls of public opinion,' but seemingly nothing came of this.[18] For the federal CCF, the concern with opinion polling also proved marginal. Party files contain only a few Gallup column clippings and some CIPO promotional material.[19] As well, there is an unsigned 1942 federal government memo sent to Saul Rae (and somehow forwarded to the CCF) questioning the logic of CIPO poll reporting of party standings. The Gallup Poll pegged the CCF's popular support at the time of the 1940 election at 8 per cent, even though the party fielded candidates in fewer than half the country's 245 ridings. The author asked Rae to contact Gallup officials to see if a more accurate indicator of CCF national support in 1940 could be determined. Only once did party officials draft a strategy paper based on polling figures. A 27 March 1943 Gallup release showed support for the provincial CCF in Ontario at 26 per cent, compared to 35 and 36 per cent respectively for the Liberals and Tories. The memo estimated, based on the poll and internal intelligence, that in some forty ridings CCF support averaged 40 per cent, in twenty ridings it hovered around 26 per cent, and in thirty constituencies it registered only about 8 per cent. The party was in strong command of twenty-five to thirty-five ridings, with another twenty or so within reach. The Liberals presented the main challenge, as Tory support was thought too thinly spread over rural and urban areas to capture many seats – an obviously flawed analysis, as five months later the Tories won a plurality of seats with 36 per cent of the vote. The memo also touched on a theme raised earlier by Spencer and couched in similar paternalistic reasoning. Gallup polls consistently counted far more men than women among CCF voters, which was 'a clear indication that we must make better efforts to interest the women in our program. They may think they are not interested in politics, but they are certainly interested in what will happen to their families after the war. Candidates particularly should not permit themselves to forget that at least half the voters are women.'[20] Though the CCF party press and its advertising occasionally formulated specific appeals for women voters,[21] the party never followed through with opinion surveys or other marketing techniques to determine the effectiveness of these entreaties, either for women or for other underrepresented groups beneath the CCF canopy.[22]

On polling and the CCF, perhaps a more useful question would be: *Could* CCF leaders have adopted and acted upon the marketing ethos if they so wanted? A number of factors thwarted such a possibility. The CCF's hybrid character, the mingling of social movement and political party, functioned as a barrier to political action driven by opinion polling and advertising. A key axiom for Spencer was the generally irrational, malleable nature of most people, both as consumers and citizens. Commercial advertisers knew this; hence their frequent preference for emotion-centred ad copy over appeals to reason or intellect. But this premise was anathema to the CCF world view, especially among those most enamoured of socialist proselytizing. People might read Popeye and listen to Charlie McCarthy for recreation, but their fundamental human nature remained rational and educable. Strongly opposed to nineteenth-century economic liberalism, the CCF incorporated one important liberal precept from that era: a belief in the perfectibility of people through reason and knowledge. In populist idiom akin to Gallup's own evangelizing of opinion polling (but not market research), the CCF viewed the common people as uncommonly endowed with good judgment and homespun wisdom. They could be trusted to act prudently on public matters, reconciling their own interests with those of the general good, provided they received accurate facts and straightforward arguments. This deep-seated faith in public rationality served as the party's guiding principle for ideological dissemination and political promotion. 'The CCF believed,' Walter Young observed, 'that it could win by rational conversion and organization. The basis of organization was the sending of the converted into the streets to proselytize on the doorstep, to set up clubs, to chair discussion groups, to publish pamphlets, to educate.'[23] From this standpoint, techniques for selling soap were inimical to the building of a Cooperative Commonwealth.

The CCF's party structure posed another impediment to the adoption of market research methods. In his seminal typology of political parties, Maurice Duverger formulated two broad categories. 'Cadre' parties were characterized by an emphasis on electoral operations, relatively few dues-paying members, and the dominant role of government leaders, financiers, bureaucrats, and professional experts in shaping party protocol and policies. 'Mass' parties functioned during and *between* elections, were more democratically organized, and counted many active members, most of whom shared an ideological affinity with party doctrines. Frequently, member groups were organized in non-electoral units, i.e. workplaces or neighbourhood associations. The Liberals and Tories, according to Engelmann and Schwartz, conformed to the cadre model, while the CCF adhered to the mass party type.[24] For example, the CCF founded its first constituency association only in 1938, an organizational model which only gradually replaced the bevy of clubs and study groups (sometimes two or more per riding) constituting the party. Party fundraising, largely unsuccessful until the late 1940s, was premised on soliciting donations from grassroots members. This diffuse, decentralized party structure was often beset by sectarian rivalry and a 'lack of coordinated effort at elections,' especially before the mid-1940s.[25]

The CCF also distinguished itself from the established parties by its degree of internal democracy. While, for example, the federal Liberals had last held a party convention in 1919, the CCF convened eight national conventions between 1932 and 1944. Party members elected local, provincial, and national officials and leaders, as well as most delegates to provincial and national conventions. Delegates presented resolutions to the convention floor and voted on party policies. The epitome of this democratic style was in Saskatchewan, where widespread grassroots activism infused CCF riding and provincial affairs, especially in rural areas. This does not refute entirely Young's argument that an 'oligarchic' clique of CCF officials and leaders exercised considerable influence in policy formation and party decision making. Officials such as David Lewis, the national secretary from 1937 to 1950, no doubt set the tone and tempo for a good deal of the party's affairs. But Young's critique of the CCF's democratic structure is set against an *ideal* type of grassroots party democracy and not the actual state of Canadian political parties. Had his analysis incorporated the Grit and Tory parties' meagre measures of internal democracy, it is likely his assessment of CCF democratic practices, properly contextualized, would have been more conciliatory.[26] One begins to see why a mass party like the early CCF – defined by grassroots activism, a relatively diffuse power base, and a shared animating ideology – was an unlikely candidate for opinion polling before 1945. According to the CCF credo, policy making and political intelligence gathering were as much the preserve and responsibility of the rank and file as of 'elite' decision makers. To go further and have 'outsiders' like opinion pollsters perform these functions would no doubt have alienated grassroots supporters, the organizational bedrock of a movement-cum-party. David Walker, underscoring polling's centripetal impact on electioneering and party decision making, writes: Their [pollsters'] success is based on limiting access to information and maintaining a mystique regarding the collection and analysis of data. Their world is dominated by hierarchical organizations in which it is taken for granted that they negotiate and confide with only a few at the top. The democratization of this world is still a long way off.'[27] Paradoxically, polling, heralded by Gallup and CIPO officials as a democratizing agent, was least amendable to parties most beholden to their rank and file.[28]

Another factor militating against the CCF's use of polls was the party's relative lack of contact with established advertisers and market researchers. As will be seen below with the Liberal party, direct and enduring ties with market researchers, both commercial and academic, were vital for launching and sustaining a polling program. The standard histories of the CCF provide little information about the party's use of advertising or its relations with ad firms prior to 1945.[29] What fragments are available suggest that CCF advertising was often primitive and lacklustre. A 1944 committee chaired by Ontario provincial secretary Morden Lazarus concluded that CCF ads and literature were 'dull, badly laid-out, repetitious, and lacking in personal appeal.' The committee recommended they become more 'colourful, catchy, and entertaining,' and that they 'DON'T PREACH.'[30] During the war, CCF advertising was often 'depression-oriented,' a sort of political scare copy admonishing voters to back the CCF to prevent a return to economic calamity.[31] Some ads were also trite and crude, like those in 1944 attacking big business by depicting a grasping, malevolent octopus choking a soldier, housewife, and farmer. Another ad, Caplan describes, showed 'two fat cat capitalists, bedecked in top hats and tails, slinging mud at an advancing army of socialist realism–created workers, farmers, and soldiers.'[32] Of course, had CCF officials sought out an advertising or market research firm for a political poll they likely would have been rebuffed. As any perusal of the advertising and marketing trade press will attest,[33] ad men and marketers were unrestrained boosters of free enterprise and mass consumption. Socialism, when mentioned, was usually excoriated. As the customers of advertising and market research firms were mostly other companies, word of a CCF association could very well harm client relations and future business prospects.

Had CCF popularity remained mired at pre-war levels, the absence of voter research and opinion polling probably would have mattered little. The party garnered just under 9 per cent of votes in the 1935 and 1940 elections, and its support remained largely confined to parts of western Canada, Cape Breton, and a sprinkling of northern and urban ridings in Ontario. But this would change suddenly after 1942. In an oft-cited series of events, CCF fortunes catapulted skyward, ushering in a short-lived 'Golden Age' of Canadian socialism.[34] Joe Noseworthy's thrashing of Arthur Meighen in York South in February 1942, the Ontario CCF's capture of thirty-four seats in August 1943, and Tommy Douglas's resounding triumph in Saskatchewan a year later were the electoral milestones of a rising socialist tide that promised – or threatened, depending on one's standpoint – to engulf federal politics. The party registered 20 per cent or more in CIPO polling from late 1942 until April 1945, even once, in September 1943, posting a one-point edge over the Liberals and Tories, a 'lead,' however, which fell well within the poll's margin of error.[35] CCF membership jumped from under thirty thousand in 1942 to nearly one hundred thousand two years later. During the same period, party revenues tripled to more than $28,000. Issues long championed by the CCF – state planning, public ownership, social security, unionization – had migrated from the political periphery to the hub of public debate. But just as precipitously as the CCF's star rose, so would it crash. The much-anticipated Ontario and federal elections of June 1945 saw the provincial party reduced to eight seats and its federal counterpart shut out of all Ontario ridings. Nationally, the CCF took twenty-eight seats, eighteen in Saskatchewan, and its 15.6 per cent share of the popular vote, while a marked improvement from 1940, was well below expectations. Various explanations abound. The end of the European war one month earlier had sapped some of the general resolve for state planning. Concerns for social security remained, but these were also being met by the protean King Liberals, whose moderate welfarist platform promised a 'New Social Order,' made possible, in part, by co-opting CCF ideas and policies. John English, in a polling-informed analysis of changing voter sentiment in southwestern Ontario, attributes part of the CCF rise to rural–urban migration and the corresponding uncertainty whether war-engendered security would continue. When these CCF converts began to realize that the larger society, with the mainstream parties in tow, would incorporate many of the war-spawned social changes, they gradually relinquished their alternative visions and reverted to traditional voting patterns.[36]

CCF officials and historians commonly point to another reason for the party's 1945 defeat – the anti-CCF smear campaigns by Gladstone Murray and B.A. Trestrail.[37] Murray, a former CBC general manager, founded 'Responsible Enterprise Limited' in April 1943 as a clearing-house to publicize free enterprise and assail socialism and the CCF. Capitalizing on his broadcasting and public relations work with the CBC and BBC (during the 1926 General Strike he worked as a government propagandist), Murray enlisted business backers in a venture employing 'imaginative planning' and 'psychological initiative' to stem the spread of socialism. By September, he counted among his supporters Arthur Meighen, former finance minister C.A. Dunning, and the presidents of Imperial Oil, Noranda Mines, Massey-Harris Company, National Breweries, International Nickel, and Continental Life Insurance Co. Murray's operation, Caplan claims, eventually garnered the financial backing of fifty-two company presidents and seventeen vice-presidents. Murray's publicity work centred on writing propaganda tracts, reprinting his and others' speeches, and publishing *Outlook*, an anti-CCF newsletter. He also supplied anti-socialist material to radio stations, daily and weekly newspapers, and politicians. Stephen Leacock was even enlisted to write material.[38]

Trestrail lacked Murray's blue-chip backing, but he more than compensated with a keen writer's ear for homespun idiom and kitchen-table logic, combined with a Goebbels-like ability to render the Big Lie believable. No finer compliment could be had than when in 1944 a CCF report on publicity recommended that party literature mirror the colloquial, breezy style of one of Trestrail's anti-CCF booklets.[39] An American by birth, he settled in Canada in the 1910s while in his twenties. He claimed to have earned a sizeable fortune in the 1920s, only to lose it during the Depression. A self-described 'Industrial Relations Counsel' during the war, in 1944 he founded 'Public Informational Association,' which solicited business donations to finance anti-socialism/CCF publicity. His 1945 booklet *Social Suicide* (a condensed version of the 1944 book *Stand Up and Be Counted*) was, Trestrail claimed, mailed to every postal address in the country prior to the federal election, a total of three million copies at a cost of more than $300,000, according to one CCF estimate.[40]

Taken together, the tracts are superb examples, indeed seminal classics, of political attack literature, marrying commercial salesmanship with a polished knack for exploiting emotional and negative motifs. Half of *Social Suicide*'s title page was taken up with the message '$5000 Cash Awards: See Back Cover,' which referred to a contest awarding $500 prizes to the best titles submitted for a cartoon of a CCF 'acrobat' juggling and balancing a number of balls inscribed with CCF policies. Some twenty-seven thousand people reportedly wrote in.[41] The pamphlet also carried testimonials from satisfied 'customers' of *Stand Up and Be Counted*. 'I have lived seven years under state socialism in Russia,' one individual wrote, 'and don't want to go through the nightmare again here in Canada.' Mrs W.G. Robert, self-described as 'just one of the ordinary working class,' had bought several copies for friends and expressed the hope that 'thousands more will see and buy your booklet.' Trestrail's ostensible mode of persuasion was by honest appeal from one ordinary citizen to another. 'I will express myself in the language of the so-called "common people," of whom I am one, and with whom I have spent most of my life.' Such people generally exercised good common sense, *if you will just give them the facts.*' The 'facts' presented, however, were in most cases gross distortions and outright fabrications. A CCF government would regiment and bureaucratize civil society while nationalizing most businesses. Individual freedom would be crushed under the heel of totalitarianism. Ludicrous parallels between the 'National Socialism' of Nazi Germany and the CCF were drawn. An anti-Semitic, xenophobic raw nerve was exposed with references to Lewis as the son of a 'Russian Jew,' and suggestions that this 'Jewish immigrant boy' might soon 'write the ticket for the social and economic program of this nation.'[42] Added to this was strident anti-intellectualism; CCF officials were 'Professional Social Students,' and the cartoon drawings by the *Globe*'s Jack Boothe, in addition to accentuating Lewis's Semitic features, depicted an eggheaded Frank Scott in convocation cap and gown. CCF leaders were not Of The People like Trestrail and his initiated readers; they were alien malingerers, untouched by the meaning of ordinary work and everyday concerns.

Trestrail's propaganda pieces were not just the product of one man's intuitive reading of the voters' psyche. He claimed to have benefited from insights gleaned from opinion polls. At one point in *Social Suicide*, he refers to 'the figures of six recent surveys' which revealed that only half of Canadians could offer a definition for 'State Socialism.'[43] The polls' sources and sponsors were not revealed. In a May 1945 fundraising letter, Trestrail outlined plans for a national anti-CCF campaign, which would be 'based on the findings of surveys covering more than 2000 Canadians in all walks of life.' He noted that a 1944 'experimental campaign' in Toronto had been conducted to 'ascertain to what extent public interest could be aroused over the issue of State Socialism and the degree to which such thinking could be influenced.' The survey indicated that 25 to 40 per cent of people could 'be diverted from the possibility of voting for any candidate committed to State Socialism – if they are provided with proper information in the proper manner.'[44] Here again, the source and content of the purported polls are unknown; they could well have been slapdash, unscientific undertakings. But on at least one occasion Trestrail seemingly did benefit from direct contact with a professional pollster. *Stand Up and Be Counted* contains a May 1944 publication date. The book cites a Gallup Poll finding that only 23 per cent of people favoured state ownership of banks, and that among CCF voters fewer than half backed the measure. The question appeared on a 10 March 1944 CIPO survey and was released 3 May. It would seem highly likely, given the lead time needed to edit and print the book, that Trestrail acquired the Gallup result well before its May release. This contention is also supported by the book's acknowledgment thanking 'Sandy' and 'Wilf'; either could have applied to the CIPO's Wilfrid

Sanders, a former business press journalist, known as 'Sandy' to friends and colleagues.[45]

Trestrail's use of opinion polls paled in comparison to another business-sponsored venture carried out by the market research firm Elliott-Haynes Limited. The company began operations in 1937 as a credit-reporting service, but by the early 1940s had moved into survey research work, primarily with radio-listening audiences. In September 1944 it launched a semi-annual survey, 'The Study of Public Attitudes toward Business and Industry,' which would continue into the early 1950s. The survey was partially modelled on polling done by the Psychological Corporation for the Du Pont Corporation during the late 1930s and early 1940s. These surveys registered American attitudes towards the company, probed their etiology, and evaluated the effectiveness of Du Pont promotional activities in shaping public opinion. Americans holding a 'generally favourable' view of the chemical conglomerate increased from 56 per cent in 1936 to 69 per cent in 1940.[46] The six-thousand-person Elliott-Haynes national survey – one of the largest samples ever to that time – solicited general opinions about business and industry, as well as specific views on individual companies. To offset costs, sponsorship of the 'omnibus poll' was spread among a number of companies, each of whom received data specific to their firms, along with findings of a general nature.[47] These surveys represent the first systematic use of polling for public relations purposes in Canada.[48] Their impetus and operating rationale were closely tied to the socialist surge. As an early 1945 survey report made clear, the study's principal objectives were 'to provide overall measurements of the magnitude of threats against business in general,' to track these views over time, and to delineate 'the cultural areas of population sub-groups within which the major changes are occurring.' It was vitally important that big business acquaint itself with mass opinion on this score, for 'some of the forces swaying public attitudes are not in line with the continued good health of Canadian private enterprise.'[49]

The September 1944 survey found support for government ownership on the rise. Thirty-seven per cent of Canadians favoured 'government owner-management' for *all* of the following industries: hydro-electricity, railways, airlines, banks, insurance, telegraphs and telephones, radio, logging, mining, and steamships. Individually, hydro-electricity had the most public support for state control, logging the least. The survey also probed Canadians' views on the following companies: Bell Telephone Co. of Canada, Canadian General Electric, Canadian Industries, Cana-

dian Westinghouse, Chrysler Corporation, Dominion Rubber, Ford
Motor Company of Canada, General Motors of Canada, Goodyear Tire
and Rubber Co. of Canada, Imperial Oil, Imperial Tobacco Co. of Canada,
Northern Electric, and RCA-Victor. The report prepared for Canadian
General Electric contained 'favourable' and 'unfavourable' ratings for it
and some of its competitors, and provided advice, based on cross-tabular
analyses, on ways to reduce the 35 per cent total of 'indifferent' and 'don't
know' responses. One explanation for the relatively high levels of support for state enterprise, the report advanced, were the 'consistent efforts
of the C.C.F. and [other] socialistic-minded' politicians. The general
appeal of the survey was twofold: it provided Canadian corporations
with an overall view of the mass opinion landscape, particularly concerning issues of state regulation and nationalization. It also penetrated attitudes on specific companies and their competitors -not just views on
products or services. A wealth of geographic and demographic breakdowns, made more reliable by the exceptionally large base sample, facil-
itated fine-tuned analyses and planning – 'the use of the "rifle" technique
of promotion and education rather than the "shotgun" technique.'[50]

How many of these poll findings, if any, made their way to Murray or
Trestrail is unknown. Some of the aforementioned companies – Imperial
Oil, Imperial Tobacco, Bell Telephone – counted among Murray's business sponsors, and conceivably survey results could have been passed
on.[51] In any event, the above events highlight the disparity of polling
preparedness between the political Left and the business Right leading
up to the 1945 election. Caplan makes the point that the CCF was orga-
nizationally ill equipped for 'counter-propaganda' activities, and that it
had greatly overestimated the 'revered Common Man's' capacity to dis-
cern Trestrail's and Murray's 'self-evident' lies. Lewis, acknowledging
Trestrail's work as a 'masterpiece of propaganda,' attributed the CCF's
response to a 'lack of political sophistication,' one compounded by a
'failure to appreciate the strength of the acquisitive psychology
implanted in Canadians by the materialistic environment of North
America, and, more importantly, the electoral strength of cleavages
other than those of class.'[52] One can see how even a remedial polling
program would have better informed CCF officials on these counts, both
on the extent of Trestrail's and Murray's influence on voters, and on the
demographics and political outlook of non-class cleavages. But, as
recounted above, the CCF faced structural-ideological barriers to adopting the marketing dictum, even though the party's intelligentsia were
among the first to publish a 'political-consumer' survey. That Trestrail

and other business interests were early movers in adapting consumer research techniques to the political arena was foreseeable: market research surveys had been part of the commercial landscape since the late 1920s.⎣That their efforts were in turn used against the CCF reads as much like Greek tragedy as it does an early achievement of commercial politics.⎦

While the CCF wartime experience invokes a classical reference, that of the Conservatives conjures up the Keystone Kops. No other national party was so plagued by internecine feuding, lacklustre leadership, and general ineptitude as were the Tories during the Second World War.[53] The party leadership passed through five men between 1938 and 1942. In both the 1935 and 1940 general elections, the Conservatives won just thirty-nine seats, their worst ever performances – until 1993.[54] Following the 1940 vote, not one province counted a Conservative government – indeed only five provinces had Tory party leaders – and the federal organization was verging on a 'state of collapse.'[55] Financial donations began drying up. By 1943, only Ontario and parts of the Maritimes registered reassuring levels of popular support, but even in these areas on-the-ground organization was uneven. Quebec was virtually written off, and the CCF surge had seriously depleted Tory support in the western provinces.

The party's repeated response to its ongoing dolour was to change its leader and its stripes. Robert Manion, the Catholic anti-conscriptionist, was jettisoned after the 1940 election for the arch-conscriptionist, anglophile Arthur Meighen. His by-election defeat made way in December 1942 for Manitoba premier John Bracken, who engineered the 'Progressive' addition to the party name and led the Tories' half-hearted move to the political Left to compete with the CCF. But these about-turns left many on the sidelines grumbling. An 'Old Guard' of Toronto Tories, led by George Drew and *Globe and Mail* publisher George McCullagh, railed against the party's softening stance towards social welfare, while demanding a stronger push for overseas conscription. By mid-1943 it was apparent that Bracken could not deliver politically as he had done in Manitoba for over twenty years. Disparaging Bracken in August 1943 for failing to contest a Commons seat, Tory MP Rodney Adamson pegged him an 'absolutely useless leader'; a month later he confided to a colleague that the Tories were 'old and fossilized. And incapable of learning. In other words ... we stink.'[56] Bracken's biographer similarly noted of his subject: '[Bracken] gave no real lead in policy formation, he was ineffectual as a party broker, he was an atrocious public speaker, and he seemed politically naive on the larger stage of national politics.'[57] While a few bright organizational minds – J.M. Macdonnell, Richard Bell, and Ross Brown – laboured behind the scenes, the Tories' public image remained one of maladroit decision making and intra-party sniping. That McCullagh and not Bracken delivered the party's final radio address in the 1945 election attested as much to Bracken's dismal speaking style as it did to the enduring influence of the 'Old Guard.' The Tories' 27 per cent share of the popular vote in 1945 was four points lower than in 1940, but favourable centre-left vote splits resulting from a stronger CCF enabled the party to boost its seat count to sixty-seven.[58]

It was during this tumultuous period of the party's history that public opinion polling arrived in Canada. Given these tribulations (and other factors to be discussed below), it is understandable that a novel and sophisticated technique like sample surveying was not taken up directly by the Conservative party, even though it did conform to the cadre party model.[59] But party officials were not entirely blind to polling's instrumental value, and in 1943 they began systematically amassing Gallup Poll results and forming contacts with CIPO officials. In June, Ross Brown, the party's director of public relations, sent a memo to caucus members and senior Tory officials charting the federal parties' CIPO standings in Ontario and Quebec from January 1942 until June 1943. By November, party headquarters were receiving regular CIPO releases, and by early 1944 so too was the office of Gordon Graydon, the party's House leader.[60] The general climate created by polling's arrival may have affected the choice of name for the party's monthly newspaper, *Public Opinion*, founded in August 1943 'not ... to be partisan in any narrow sense,' but to 'express rational views.' John Bird of the *Winnipeg Tribune*, a CIPO subscriber, joked to Brown soon after the paper's launch that he would 'try to persuade the Gallup people, and others, not to sue you for too high damages in stealing their label – "Public Opinion."'[61]

Had Bird's offer been serious, it would have been unnecessary in light of the affable rapport which existed between Brown and Wilfrid Sanders. On the eve of the Ontario provincial election, Sanders sent Brown a whimsical (and cryptic) telegram with the institute's popular vote prediction: 'Read em and Weep Snuffles, 36 Roses [CCF] 33 Petunia [PC] 31 Sleep Tight [Lib.].' In April 1944, CIPO statistician O.J. Morris wrote Brown (addressed as 'Dear Ross') in response to the latter's request to Sanders for unpublished breakdowns on federal party standings in Ontario and the West. Morris passed on some findings, regretting that a busy schedule prevented him from providing 'a whole flock' of other breakdowns. Brown expressed his appreciation for the material, which alerted him to unexpected Liberal growth in Ontario.[62] Additional correspondence further questions the CIPO assertion that it had 'no connection with governments or political parties.'[63] In July 1944, Brown wrote 'Wilf' for copies of 'all of those [CIPO releases] concerning political trends,' and any other relevant material with which he could part. Sanders's response is not known, but a subsequent letter to Brown provided him with advance information on the Union Nationale's rapid rise during the ongoing Quebec election, along with a pledge to 'shoot you [more] figures when they materialize.' Sanders's waggish parting line, 'Best love, and a throbbing kiss,' more than hinted at the pair's ribald sense of close camaraderie.[64]

Though in regular receipt of Gallup Polls and on good terms with CIPO officials, Tory organizers did not commission political polls prior to the 1945 election. On one level, this is somewhat surprising, for the party made definite strides towards improving its organization and operations, especially after the arrival of Richard Bell as national director in April 1943. Bell promptly appointed a publicity director and formed a national advisory committee on public relations and publicity. *Public Opinion* was launched. The near-moribund Dominion Progressive Conservative Association (DPCA) was rejuvenated with the 'retirement' of its inept, long-standing president, John R. MacNicol. Serious attention was directed to strengthening the coordination of federal and provincial organizers. DPCA annual reports of 1944 and 1945, however, contain no polling references, nor are there any in the minutes of the Committee on Publicity and Public Relations.[65] Indeed, the earliest Tory-sponsored political poll found in the federal party's records was one commissioned by the *Ontario* party for the 1948 South Huron provincial by-election, which saw the return of the Drew government candidate. Canadian Facts conducted the survey and McKim Advertising, the principal Tory ad firm, acted as liaison between pollster and politician.[66]

Key aspects of this poll – that a party in power commissioned it, and the presence of McKim Advertising – suggest two other reasons for the federal Tories' belated use of political polling. Advertising firms, lured by the tantalizing prospect of government advertising revenues, were far more inclined to do political or electoral work – often at or below cost – for parties in power or those likely to assume power. For example, by war's end, Ottawa had spent over $30 million on advertising for war bonds and the like, making it the country's largest single advertiser. At least two-thirds of this work was handled by ad agencies. As Reginald Whitaker underscores, 'this meant that there was a very substantial "pork barrel" for advertising patronage in the making; it also meant that the attention of politicians would inevitably be drawn to the potential of ad agencies for political as well as governmental work. Everything was in the cards for a happy and lasting *ménage à trois* between the government, the party, and the ad agency.'[67] Such a symbiosis put the hapless Tories, out of office since 1935 and holders of the government purse strings for only six years since 1921, at an obvious disadvantage. They could not hope to attract advertisers of the same calibre as could the Liberals. This point is important with respect to polling, for few ad firms possessed the requisite market research know-how and resources to conduct or properly analyse representative sample surveys.

McKim Advertising evidently did not. Formed in 1889, it was Canada's oldest ad agency, but it had not kept pace with the research achievements of rivals like Cockfield, Brown. A book published on the occasion of the firm's fiftieth anniversary and co-written by a current and a former McKim executive, makes no mention of market research surveys.[68] Another employee, A.S. Coldridge, later recalled that the firm's early 1940s use of copy-testing, a remedial form of advertising research, was 'nervously minimal.'[69] Certainly, the decision by McKim and Tory officials in 1945 to focus their electoral advertising on the drab and ineffectual Bracken raises serious questions about the firm's ability to read the popular pulse. Ads promoting 'John Bracken – The Farmer,' 'John Bracken – The Man,' and 'Win with Bracken' not only spotlighted a lacklustre campaigner but exposed the Tories to Liberal barbs that they were flogging their leader like 'a new breakfast food, or a new brand of soap.' Despite total party spending in excess of $1,500,000 during the election (more than half of which went to advertising), the Bracken-centred ad campaign appeared largely ineffective. A post-election CIPO poll of Tory voters found just 23 per cent listing 'calibre of candidates' as the main reason for supporting the party, well back of the 33 per cent citing 'policies or platform.'[70]

For the Liberal party, the wartime years saw mercurial swings of fortune. The CIPO's first party standing poll in January 1942 pegged Liberal support at 55 per cent, three points higher than its share of the 1940 vote. But soon after, Grit support began to tumble. In the fall of 1942, its CIPO numbers were under 40 per cent, and by the following September support had bottomed out at 28 per cent. In Ontario in 1943 and Saskatchewan the year after, Liberal governments were pummelled by voters. Similarly, the Godbout Liberals in Quebec were replaced in 1944 by the Union Nationale. Badly haemorrhaging support to the CCF in English Canada, King's party confronted the unenviable prospect that had befallen Britain's Liberals: political marginalization in the wake of left-right polarization. After Liberal by-election losses in August 1943, King wrote in his diary of the CCF and Communist gains: 'In my heart, I am not sorry to see the mass of the people coming a little more into their own but I do regret that it is not a Liberal party that is winning that position for them.'[71] How King succeeded in 'winning that position for them,' eventually securing a slim majority government in 1945, has been well documented[72] and need not be recounted here in detail. Party notables, like Norman Lambert and Brooke Claxton, reactivated the dormant National Liberal Federation (NLF) in September 1943. The NLF Advisory Council subsequently endorsed a range of progressive policies touching on full employment, social security, old age pensions, and family allowances. The government's January throne speech reconfirmed the party's commitment to reconstruction and social welfare. The Liberals' cautious welfarist program contained just enough to woo back CCF defectors but not enough to trigger a serious exodus of right-wing and business supporters to the Tories. The cadre party Liberals, in Whitaker's apt assessment, had again positioned themselves in their customary (and paradoxical) role 'as the defender of the people against the big interests and the defender of the big interests against the people.'[73]

The role of party organization, finance, and advertising in contributing to the Liberal victory has been explored by Whitaker and Granatstein.[74] But neither author addresses in detail the party's use of polling. As discussed in the last chapter, Gallup polling done for the Wartime Information Board, and made available to Claxton and cabinet colleagues, formed a vast statistical body of knowledge on public attitudes and policy preferences. That this valuable resource, though publicly funded, would also inform the political considerations of members of the 'Government Party' is hardly surprising. The distinction between public interest and Liberal interests was increasingly muddied by the mid-1940s. By themselves alone, the WIB-CIPO polls provided the governing Liberals with a clear-cut advantage over their political opponents: key Liberal strategists were privy to public opinion data known to few others. But in addition to this survey data, three other polling projects, organized by the ad firm Cockfield, Brown, also benefited Liberal politicians. Two surveys of Claxton's riding were undertaken. A national poll gauged the popular appeal of campaign slogans. And an extraordinary series of surveys in forty-three Ontario ridings measured Liberal strengths and weaknesses in the province shaping up as the key electoral battleground.

As seen in chapter 1, Cockfield, Brown was Canada's first advertising agency to perform systematic market research, having established in 1929 a Commercial Research and Economic Investigation Department soon after its founding. Assisted by university-based consultants, the company conducted or coordinated consumer research in numerous locales across the country. Henry King's contributions have been detailed, but another Cockfield, Brown employee, H.E. Kidd, was also important to the firm's early research development. Born in Stockholm in 1902 to British parents and educated in Sweden, he moved to Vancouver in 1921. After a year's work in a sawmill, he landed a reporting job with the *Vancouver Daily World*. In 1926 he joined the Eastman Advertising Company as a research and account executive, and four years later he signed on as a field representative in Cockfield, Brown's research department, working out of the Vancouver office. Subsequently, Kidd travelled widely, conducting marketing investigations for British Columbia industries like cedar shingles, apples, and the Pacific fishery. He would later spend several months among Maritime, Ontario, and Quebec farmers, compiling a market survey of farm conditions for an agricultural weekly newspaper. In 1937, Kidd moved to the firm's Montreal head office to become an account executive, and shortly after he was handling the files of prestigious clients like the Dominion Textile Company, the Aluminum Company of Canada, and the Canadian Bankers' Association.[75]

Kidd professed long-standing ties to the Liberal party, claiming to have 'worked with and in the Liberal organization since 1925.'[76] However, his direct links to the party hierarchy (which culminated in his 1949 appointment as NLF secretary) began in earnest in 1940 when Claxton, seeking to unseat the long-time Tory incumbent in the Montreal riding of St Lawrence–St George, engaged the services of Cockfield, Brown. He was assigned Kidd, who effectively organized campaign publicity, emphasizing the use of radio advertising. Kidd's efforts did not go unappreciated by Claxton, who handily won the contest. While other senior campaign workers, like Davidson Dunton, received an engraved flask or cigarette case, Kidd alone was given a clock. Kidd's ties to Claxton remained close after the election, when he served as volunteer publicist for the newly minted MP, forwarding copies of Claxton's speeches and articles to dozens of magazines and newspapers, along with press releases on Claxton's public activities.[77] No other back-bencher benefited from such a coordinated public relations campaign. The bright, hard-working, and politically astute Claxton, though an awkward glad-hander, would no doubt have eventually achieved political prominence with or without Kidd's input. But the speed with which this novice MP ascended the governing ladder, becoming King's parliamentary assistant in 1943 and a year later minister of national health and welfare, suggests that Kidd's efforts to distinguish Claxton from a very crowded field of Liberal back-benchers were not inconsequential.

Judging from the confidence which Claxton placed in Kidd, the up-and-coming MP was well attuned to the political uses of the professional ad man. When King asked him to help organize the NLF Advisory Committee meeting of September 1943, Claxton turned to Kidd and other Cockfield, Brown executives for advice on policy options, the state of Liberal organization, and business reactions to Liberal defeats in the Ontario election and recent federal by-elections. Kidd rallied support within the agency for partisan involvement, overcoming one colleague's disdain for the unreliable paymaster 'hypocrites of Ottawa,' and by early 1944 Cockfield, Brown had cemented a deal making it the Liberal party's sole provider of national, English-language advertising.[78] Having skilfully outmanoeuvred MacLaren Advertising, its principal Liberal-affiliated rival, Cockfield, Brown transferred Kidd to Ottawa to liaise directly with the NLF and to begin work on restoring the Liberals' sagging fortunes.[79]

Soon after Claxton's invitation to Cockfield, Brown, in September 1943, Kidd suggested to him that a 'careful survey of [his] constituency should be made fairly soon.'[80] In early 1944 Claxton took up the offer. The first of its kind in Canada, the quota sample constituency poll, completed sometime in late February or March, was conducted by the Cockfield, Brown research department at cost – 15 cents for each of the approximately two hundred interviews. The survey report does not survive, but that of an April follow-up poll of St Lawrence–St George voters is available. The 190-person, in-home survey contained breakdowns by sex, age, language, income, and marital status. Significantly, women made up just 39 per cent of the sample, a fact meriting no accompanying explanation. The survey asked if it mattered much or little which party ran the country's affairs, and whether the voter's party loyalties were strengthening or diminishing. Half the sample were undecided voters, but of the remainder 61 per cent opted for the Liberals, with the Tories placing a distant second at 20 per cent. The news was not all reassuring for Claxton: only 22 per cent of voters could name their MP. The report also grouped the riding's polls by 'A-B-C-D' census class designations, information which could be later useful when devising door-to-door campaign strategies. Another information service was also provided to enhance Claxton's electoral prospects. Interviewers were disingenuously instructed to introduce themselves as researchers 'making a series of studies on political problems in Canada' and to tell respondents that 'we do not want your name – just your opinion.' Nonetheless, a list of addresses of people voting Liberal was included in the report. Kidd's matter-of-fact way of conveying this to Claxton ('you will also find attached the addresses of respondents saying they would vote Liberal') suggests that this breach of respondents' anonymity was a perfectly acceptable means of securing information about voters.[81] It might also account for the survey stipulation that all interviews take place in the home and not on the street.

Cockfield, Brown and the NLF formalized their contractual arrangement on 15 March 1944, and three days later Claxton and Kidd discussed the prospect of opinion surveys. Their deliberations would eventually result in two separate endeavours – a national survey to 'pretest' campaign slogans, and the riding polls in southern Ontario. However, the polling project was originally conceived, incredibly, as a series of surveys in most of Canada's 245 federal ridings. Claxton, insisting that the survey be scientifically rigorous, suggested that Kidd contact AIPO officials or Hadley Cantril at Princeton University. Kidd sought to have Harold Poole, Cockfield, Brown's director of research, visit Princeton right away, but a busy schedule prevented his immediate departure.[82] Instead, F.W. Gross, an account executive with a marketer's flair for 'political merchandising,'[83] contacted Cantril by phone. The Princeton professor proved highly accommodating, even agreeing to visit Montreal to offer survey advice, but he was adamant that his involvement remain strictly confidential. Cockfield, Brown officials thought the survey should be restricted to voting-related questions, but Cantril advocated a more expansive approach, as Gross later reported to Kidd:

Cantril ... is very strongly of the opinion that it is in the field of campaign issues and policy where we may be of greatest help to the Liberal party. His view was that, supposing we do determine how a particular constituency will vote, of what use is that information without some knowledge of why it will vote that way. He answered my objection regarding the complications by saying that campaign issues and policy matters should be surveyed only on a National basis ...

He recommends, therefore, that we conduct a number of sample surveys to determine what in the public view, are the main issues in the national sense involved in the coming election.

Gross also solicited advice on handling the Liberals' perceived Achilles' heel: the unpopularity of King, who, Gross callously claimed, was viewed by voters as a 'dictatorial automaton without humanness and colour.' Cantril offered some reassurance; his polling for President Roosevelt had shown that many voters resented his 'cocksureness.' Roosevelt subsequently gave a humility-laden speech, emphasizing that he had made past mistakes and would undoubtably make future ones. The result, according to Cantril, was that public sentiment 'changed almost over night.' Gross thought, quite rightly, that King would be far less amendable to similar attempts at an image make-over. Cantril also dissuaded Gross from polling in most ridings. The cost and logistical problems would be enormous, and ample political data could be attained from a selected sample of ridings.[84] By late March, Cantril's suggestion that 'campaign issues and policy matters' be surveyed nationally was given closer consideration.

On 30 March, Claxton wrote Cantril, soliciting survey research and social psychological insight on a proposed political message: 'If the government can organize the country for war, it can do it for peace. The members of the government have proved their skill.' Cantril, responding shortly after to 'Dear Brooke,' warned of the 'very real danger' of this political appeal. If the Canadian political situation were analogous to the American one, such an appeal 'would spell suicide for the Administration as an argument,' for voters saw wartime and peacetime governing as fundamentally different phenomena. Americans strongly supported Roosevelt's wartime administration, but if peace came soon the president would almost certainly lose the next election. (Churchill's later defeat lends some credibility to this analysis.) Cantril, however, did agree with Claxton's idea of 'moving ahead with the liberal [sic] party,' underlining that the key problem was 'how to present your theme, how to say it,' and to do so 'in a better way than the other chaps.'[85]

Soon after, Cockfield, Brown organized a national survey on political slogans to determine the most effective way 'to say it.' As Kidd later relayed to Cantril, the poll's purpose 'was to establish whether it is practical to pre-determine the value of a slogan by finding out which one people will go for.'[86] The 1,068–person survey cost the NLF $450, and, in characteristic fashion, responses were broken down by sex, age, urban-rural, income, occupation, and party affiliation designates. Respondents were asked to select from a list of six slogans the one which 'best tells the story of what the country could expect from the political party you favour.' These were: 1) Work-Progress-Unity, 2) Bring Victory Home, 3)Let's March Forward Together, 4)Keep Moving Forward, 5)Let's Stay Prosperous, and 6)The (X) Party Gets Things Done. The overall first choice, picked by 27 per cent of respondents, was 'Work-Progress-Unity.' But among Liberals, the slogan scored only 23 per cent, compared to 39 per cent for CCF supporters. Such a slogan might lure CCF supporters to the Liberals, but it also carried the risk of reinforcing a political message associated with socialist principles. A seemingly better choice for the Grits was 'Bring Victory Home,' which scored first among Liberal supporters (29 per cent) and also among undecided voters (38 per cent), while faring poorly with CCFers (14 per cent). But this slogan's utility obviously hinged on the prospects and timing of Allied victory. Before D-Day, public support for such sentiment was naturally quite high, but once Allied victory became a foregone conclusion, say by early 1945, its appeal would be significantly lessened as people's sights became more fixed on postwar concerns.

The least preferred option was 'The (X) Party Gets Things Done,' which scored only 7 per cent overall, but 13 per cent among Liberals. And yet, surprisingly, this slogan was chosen by Cockfield, Brown to anchor a proposed ad campaign for the summer of 1944. A short run of 'The Liberal Party Gets Things Done' actually appeared in the Saskatchewan election, which saw the governing Liberals reduced to a five-seat rump.[87] Cockfield, Brown executives' rationale for this choice, advanced on 23 May, was that this 'background' advertising campaign would reinforce in voters' minds that the Liberal party 'does accomplish what it sets out to do.' Later when Liberal election promises were made they would be 'more readily believed if the people [were] convinced before hand' that the party had 'the ability to accomplish anything they promise.' The slogan's low survey ranking, however, presented a problem for the ad planners, and a consensus arose that 'not a great deal of usefulness would be served in presenting the results of this survey.'[88] When Kidd later sent Cantril a copy of the poll along with reasons for the selected slogan, Cantril responded with a polite refutation: 'If one thinks of those slogans in terms of an investment, it certainly shows how much more return one gets for the money by using the first appeal [Work-Progress-Unity] than the last one [The Liberal Party Gets Things Done].' The proposed $150,000 ad campaign, approved by Jimmy Gardiner, the minister in charge of electoral organization, and the Publicity Committee of the cabinet, however, never got off the ground. In a problem that would plague NLF–Cockfield, Brown relations, and which will be examined below, the necessary 'financial arrangements' for the national campaign 'were not completed.'[89]

Concurrent with the work of the slogan survey, Claxton and Cockfield, Brown officials discussed plans for a series of constituency polls.[90] Claxton's initial idea of surveying each of the Liberals' 176 seats was soon jettisoned on the altar of cost and logistical capability. Cantril had earlier suggested to Gross that ridings be grouped into categories of 'fairly certain,' 'doubtful,' and 'extremely doubtful,' with polling mainly targeting the latter two. One week later, on 31 March, plans were set in motion for a survey of some fifty ridings in Toronto and southwestern Ontario. The rationale for this geographic choice was not explicitly stated, but it likely derived from two key considerations. Politically, the Liberals in early 1944 were reasonably strong in French Quebec and the Maritimes. In the West, however, party prospects were generally bleak (the Grits would take only nineteen of seventy-one seats in 1945). Consequently, Ontario, with its eighty-two seats, loomed large as an important make-or-break Liberal battleground. The party commanded strong support in the province's northern and eastern ridings, owing in part to higher Catholic and French Canadian representation, but its support in Toronto and southwestern Ontario was far less secure. Of the eventual forty-three seats surveyed,[91] twenty-six were Liberal, but roughly three-quarters of these had voted Tory until 1935.[92] Retaining as many of these 'swing' seats as possible was vital to the party's chances for reelection. A second and more pragmatic consideration was these ridings' proximity to Toronto, where Cockfield, Brown had a branch office and from which the survey could be managed.

Toronto was also home to Canadian Facts and the CIPO, two organizations which would also expedite the poll. Harold Poole was given charge of the survey assignment, and in late March he went to Toronto to meet with John Graydon, president of Canadian Facts, and Arthur Porter and O.J. Morris of the CIPO, seeking to secure their services. Graydon initially thought the job too big for Canadian Facts to handle alone, but he offered to assist with the training of field workers. Porter and Morris advised Poole that the CIPO could have no formal association with the poll, for its newspaper subscribers, which included Tory-leaning papers, would surely object to such a partisan undertaking. But this did not rule out Porter and Morris from 'privately' offering their services on an 'extra curricular' basis, for which they would expect an 'honorarium.' Morris's sampling expertise, Poole believed, would be especially valuable. Porter and Morris advised that a travelling crew of interviewers would work best for such a riding-by-riding polling assignment. The pair also offered their own services for questionnaire writing, sampling design, and data analysis. They even supplied Poole with a budget estimate for three weeks of polling and subsequent tabulation; the $5,790 total included a $600 item for 'estimated honorarium.'[93]

After receiving Gardiner's approval and a $5,000 advance from the NLF, Cockfield, Brown began work on the project on 11 April. Under Poole's direction, questionnaire pre-testing commenced in Toronto, with the help of three Canadian Facts interviewers hand picked by Graydon. The initial short questionnaire, limited to voting questions, was replaced by a longer one touching on a broad range of issues. These included the success of Canada's war effort; King's performance as prime minister; the nature of Bracken's 'progressivism'; whether labour should be more strongly represented in government; whether the CCF's rise was responsible for Liberal and Tory social welfare proposals; and voting preferences. Morris, however, when consulted on the matter, judged this questionnaire 'too leading.' As well, with its more than ten questions, it would likely result in interviewing costs that would exceed the $150 budgeted for each riding's one-hundred–person survey. As a result, a 'compromise,' mid-length questionnaire was tested and ultimately adopted, whose questions were similar to those from the Claxton constituency poll. These dealt with whether it mattered which party ran the country, and if so whether it most mattered between Liberal and Tories or between the CCF and the 'older parties'; the state of voter party loyalty; whether people could identify their MP; how and in which riding they had voted in 1940 and in the Ontario election; and how they would vote today. Thus, the survey was mainly limited to voting and party matters, and did not attempt to identify the most salient issues among riding constituents. As such, it fell somewhat short of Cantril's (and Spencer's) dictum that political polling should integrate voting and issues questions. By late April, polls in three Toronto ridings – York East, Danforth, and Eglinton – had been done by Canadian Facts interviewers, with the raw data statistically weighted by Morris, 'confidentially, of course,' Poole reported to Kidd.[94]

By early May, work on the remaining ten Toronto-area polls was winding down, and Poole began arranging for out-of-town surveying, which meant acquiring cars and rationed gasoline. After some delay, three cars were rented from an auto dealer at $3 each per day, a supply of petrol was secured, and by mid-May Canadian Facts field workers were interviewing outside of Toronto. It soon became evident, however, that rural polling was more expensive than its urban counterpart. Though Gardiner was adamant that the survey not exceed its $5,000 allotment, Poole informed Kidd on 22 May that Graydon's quote for the twenty-seven completed or in-progress polls was $3,730, and the estimate for all ridings would be $6,013. Moreover, this figure did not include Cockfield, Brown's 'out-of-pocket,' or overhead, expenses, which would be an additional 100 per cent. The total bill to the NLF would be in the area of $12,000 and thus it was necessary, Poole informed Kidd, to contact NLF officials and 'get some more money in the bank.' (The 100 per cent mark-up was subsequently lowered when it was determined that Canadian Facts would do most of the survey tabulation.)[95] It is not known how much, if any, additional money was secured, but the surveys continued apace, and by mid-June forty-three ridings had been canvassed, from Toronto to Windsor and from the Niagara Peninsula to Lake Huron.

And what did the results reveal? As a Claxton memo to King summarizing the findings made clear, Liberal prospects in southern Ontario were fairly gloomy. The Grits held twenty-six of the forty-three polled ridings, but only twelve seats were likely to return Liberal members. The CCF stood to gain seventeen seats, the Tories to lose three. Of Ontario's eighty-two seats, Claxton estimated the Liberals would capture twenty, the CCF twenty-six, the Tories thirty-five, and the Communists one. In some Liberal ridings, Grit seepage to the CCF was astounding. In Hamilton East, the CCF stood at 50 per cent, the Liberals 26 per cent. In Hamilton West and Trinity, the comparative numbers were 47 and 24 per cent, and 44 and 23 per cent. Such bad tidings, Claxton suggested, should not be widely circulated, lest some MPs' nascent 'defeatism' become more ingrained. Rather, the results should be limited to cabinet ministers and key party officials.[96] Claxton's unsettling news was the likely catalyst for King's tirade the same day to cabinet colleagues lamenting the shoddy state of party organization.[97]

With the Ontario poll assignment complete by mid-June, Kidd turned his attention to other survey possibilities. He proposed to NLF officials that Nova Scotia might be considered for similar polling, and he also pushed for a post-election survey in Saskatchewan to uncover 'just what the people expect from the new [CCF] Government.' He even thought the Great West Life Insurance Company might help finance the poll if it meant learning whether Saskatchewan voters expected 'nationalization of banks and other financial institutions as soon as the prairie fire reaches Ottawa.' Neither proposal came to fruition. Most significantly, plans were launched to extend polling to Ontario's remaining ridings, with the exception of the less accessible northern ones. A $6,000 budget for thirty additional riding surveys was drawn up and presented to Liberal party chairman Gordon Fogo on 18 July. The 'factual material' from these surveys, Kidd argued, would prove useful in the likely event that 'the Ontario campaign would ... be waged in special ridings, and, therefore, not be regarded as an overall provincial campaign.' But Fogo viewed the proposed survey as an unwarranted – and probably unaffordable – expense, and turned it down. He did, however, authorize an additional $375 to complete a statistical breakdown of survey results from nineteen southwestern Ontario ridings, currently being done by Canadian Facts.[98]

The impetus for this statistical analysis had come from Graydon himself. Writing to Poole in early June, Graydon provided a textbook enunciation of the consumer researcher's marketing vision, only this time pertaining to a 'political' marketplace:

I think we are agreed that the results of the interviewing in the Ontario ridings can only be of the greatest value if they are analyzed to bring out differences in the thinking of different groups so that promotion plans can be aimed at specific groups. For example, you and your client should know how much difference, if any, there is in the political thinking of men and women, between members of labour unions and non-members, between various age groups, between income classes and between city sizes or urban and rural residents.

Graydon originally proposed that the statistical analysis cover the roughly 4,400 cases comprising most of the surveyed ridings. In the end, however, for reasons which are not entirely clear, the analysis was limited to a 2,200-person sample drawn from the nineteen southwestern ridings.[99]

By August, polling work for the Liberals was largely complete, and no subsequent surveys were commissioned.[100] Two reasons likely account for this cessation. Many in the Liberal camp in the spring and summer of 1944, including King as late as 13 July, believed a fall election was likely. But by late summer it was apparent the federal writ would not drop soon. Concerns in September about the readiness of the Liberal organization in Quebec were followed by the events of the second conscription crisis, and King resolved to postpone voting until fighting in the European theatre had neared completion, likely the following spring.[101] The organizational imperative tied to an impending election was removed, thus lessening the immediate need of voter surveys. Secondly, and more important, Liberal party organizers at this time were increasingly hard pressed to raise the necessary funds for research and promotional activities. Liberal payments to Cockfield, Brown were held up, and relations became tense enough for Kidd to feel compelled to write Claxton that 'the money deadlock must be broken.'[102] The exact amount of money passing from Liberal to Cockfield, Brown hands during this period is not known. Whitaker points to an NLF report stating that $14,537 was paid to the firm from March 1944 to January 1945. However, agency invoices for about $23,000 were also sent to the NLF over the same period.[103] Presumably, the actual figure fell somewhere in the middle. It would seem, therefore, that polling costs formed a considerable part of overall Cockfield, Brown billings. Records show that the NLF gave the agency $5,375 for the Ontario surveys and accompanying analysis, plus $450 for the national slogan poll. But additional revenue would also have been needed to cover the $6,013 cost of interviewing by Canadian Facts and whatever overhead charges Cockfield, Brown would have tacked on top.

Similarly, it is not possible to determine the precise extent to which poll findings influenced campaign strategies and advertising in the June 1945 election.[104] Of the forty-three surveyed ridings in Ontario, only thirteen voted Liberal in 1945, which suggests a limited instrumental value for the surveys at the constituency level, if indeed local Liberals even knew of their existence. A fall 1944 Cockfield, Brown memo drew on data from the Ontario survey to report that many voters had moved ridings since 1940 and that most could not name their MPs. Undecided voters predominated among 'young people, women, and middle-agers with depression memories,' and these groups should be especially appealed to by Liberals. Kidd, in a post-election report, again referred to the Ontario and slogan surveys, emphasizing that the 'results of these polls of public opinion were carefully studied.'[105] The forward-looking, demographic-specific nature of Liberal election advertising also suggests a measure of marketing insight. As Whitaker describes – in language which recalls the WIB's polling-informed propaganda designed along functional lines and directed at specific social groups – Liberal advertising 'appeals went out to specific sectors of the population, to farmers, to union workers, to returned soldiers, to small businessmen, and to housewives – with a dual emphasis in each case on the actual achievements of the government with regard to the special interests of the recipient.'[106] This certainly points to a more efficient and effective advertising approach than that suggested by such generic appeals as 'Win With Bracken' or 'They [financiers] Can't Hold Back the CCF March.' Evidently, as Cantril had earlier counselled, the Liberals had indeed learned to 'present [their] themes' in a 'better way than the other chaps.'

⌊The origins of party polling were nothing if not ironic⌋ A socialist magazine published Canada's first 'political-consumer survey,' but polling would make the fewest inroads with the CCF. Indeed, the party would bear the brunt of business attacks shaped in part by polling itself. While Progressive Conservatives were derided for 'selling' Bracken like 'a new brand of soap,' the Tories in fact possessed little in the way of marketing or advertising research in their campaign arsenal. The Liberals were the first movers in party polling, and in so doing they were best able to develop an issue-centred electoral agenda, one which enabled them to tailor appeals to different social groups. In our own, somewhat cynical, political age, it has become common to equate electoral polling with 'image' and personality-driven politics. But the point should not be lost that opinion surveys in the 1940s for the first time enabled parties, or at least the Liberals, to assess systematically the salience of a variety of issues across a wide spectrum of the electorate. The party could then develop corresponding policy positions. The Liberal party won the 1945 election because it promoted social and economic policies which proved generally popular. The victory had little to do with King's (lack of) popularity, and neither did xenophobic and emotional appeals to race or religion move many voters.

That the Liberal party became the main protagonist and primary beneficiary of political surveying is not surprising. The cadre party Liberals were little beholden to the rank and file, with party decision making effectively centralized in a coterie of key organizers and cabinet ministers. The party's lengthy tenure in office had fostered close ties with advertising agencies like Cockfield, Brown, which possessed a strong market research capacity. Such research personnel were also ideally placed to link up with firms like Canadian Facts and the CIPO for more specialized survey work. Of course, the incoming stream of WIB polling data also benefited Liberal political planning. And advice emanating from Hadley Cantril, who became known to Liberals through his involvement with the federal government, similarly served the party well. But the most important factor was surely the presence of two talented men: Bob Kidd, the research-wise advertiser; and Brooke Claxton, the 'organizational genius'[107] of the Liberal party. These two pols, more than anyone else in Canada, would usher in the arrival of 'twentieth-century' political marketing.

Conclusion

Today our only shared culture is a commercial one, a substitute for a political culture, and what exists of politics is formed as a metaphor of commerce and an imperative of markets. While that culture, with its commitment to markets, can do many things, it cannot produce a politics, or it can produce nothing more than a politics of interests.

James Carey, 1995[1]

During the early hours of 28 March 1938, Mackenzie King, the former industrial relations counsellor to the Rockefeller empire, dreamt about public relations. 'I was planning a course and noting the different subjects that should be a part of it – economics, international law, constitutional history, etc.'[2] Nine years later, however, when the University of Toronto's Department of University Extension offered Canada's first public relations course, its content would bear little resemblance to King's nocturnal musings. Co-sponsored by the Association of Canadian Advertisers and the Advertising and Sales Club of Toronto, the twelve-week evening course, targeted to a business audience, featured a number of American and Canadian public relations specialists as guest lecturers, along with a small contingent of academics. Among the lecture titles were 'The Psychology of Public Opinion,' 'How Important Is Public Opinion?' and 'Basic Tools of Public Relations,' none of which bore directly on economics, law, or history – nor for that matter did any of the other topics. The third session, entitled 'Research – A Public Relations Tool,' featured presentations by J.D. Ketchum and Wilfrid Sanders. The latter's address, 'Determining Opinions of a Specific "Public,"' covered the rudiments of survey planning, questionnaire design, interview methods, and opinion data interpretation. Ketchum's speech, 'Analyzing Public Opinion,' built on his wartime research involving public morale and the mobilizing effects of propaganda, only this time directed to postwar economic and social uncertainty:

People are not clear where they stand, they are disorganized and adrift ... Man cannot act satisfactorily until the situation is defined, and there is today, in your field as in others, a tremendous demand for a definition to be given, a word to be spoken, that will bring more clarity into the situation. Anything that suggests a new approach to the confused problems of the industrial world will be eagerly seized upon, and I know of no one better fitted to make that definition, to speak that word, than some of the talented young men in this audience.[3]

While during the war the task of 'defining' and 'clarifying' issues for the general public had been performed by state propagandists like Ketchum and John Grierson, in the postwar era this function would increasingly fall to business leaders. Representative sample surveys, spawned in the 1920s by a business impulse to gauge consumer preferences and behaviour concerning products, could now track opinions about individual companies, industrial sectors, or free enterprise itself. And if the public relations polling carried out by Elliott-Haynes, and discussed in chapter 5, was any indication, Canadians were warming up to the private sector. While in 1945 just 39 per cent of respondents supported complete private ownership of the automotive, brewing, broadcasting, banking, distilling, hydro-electric, life insurance, and petroleum sectors, by 1949 fully 62 per cent backed the idea.[4] It was perhaps telling that Canada's first attempt at a national opinion poll in 1939 – the aborted Bren Gun survey by Canadian Facts – was conceived by Maclean Publishing as a public relations tool to discredit the federal government.

The business lecture appearances by Ketchum, an academic social scientist, and Sanders, an official from the CIPO whose ostensible mission was to promote the views of ordinary citizens over those of vested interests (i.e., public relations officers), would at first glance seem highly incongruous. But, as this study has demonstrated, the boundaries between academe and business, and between the public interest and commercial interests, had largely eroded by the mid-1940s. In the United States, Harvard's Bureau of Business Research, Henry Link's Psychological Corporation, Paul Lazarsfeld's consumer surveys at

Columbia University, and Hadley Cantril's two-pronged research at Princeton University and the AIPO all pointed to the cross-fertilization of academic and commercial research. Likewise, in Canada, the work of the University of Western Ontario's Department of Business Administration and Cockfield, Brown's extensive use of university academics highlighted the co-penetration of scholarship and commerce with respect to market research.

Similarly, polling's role as a democratizing agent, as exalted by Gallup and CIPO officials, was conditioned (and ultimately negated) by a specific business context. Not only were AIPO and CIPO polls designed for and sold to a select market of newspapers, but in both countries Gallup polling operated in close step with market research surveying. In Canada, the CIPO performed clandestine market research during its first year, and thereafter it formalized these activities with the creation of the Canadian Opinion Company; however, the separation between it and the CIPO proved more nominal than actual. Importantly, it became a commercial imperative to demonstrate polling's accuracy by predicting election results, a fact which spawned a sampling design underrepresenting perceived apathetic voters: blacks, women, and the poor in the United States; and women and low socio-economic groups in Canada. Indeed, the fledgling CIPO regarded election predictions as so crucial to its operational success that it did not balk at inflating its forecasting record.

While polling's egalitarian promise was severely compromised by commercial imperatives, its purported promotion of an independent 'public interest' was similarly sacrificed on the altar of the wartime state. This was hardly surprising, for the War Measures Act, the Defence of Canada Regulations, and many other government measures imposed severe restraints on individual freedom, while granting widespread powers to the federal state. The centralization of decision making around a coterie of cabinet officials and key bureaucrats, coupled with the rationalized, economies-of-scale approach to the production of war materials, suggests a rough parallel with the *modus operandi* of large-scale manufacturers during the Second Industrial Revolution. When technocrats, like Brooke Claxton and Walter Turnbull, experienced problems with the promulgation or 'marketing' of state-prescribed goals to the general public (namely, Quebec after the plebiscite), they turned for help, as industrialists had done before them in a different context, to opinion-sampling authorities. While initially abetting Ottawa on an *ad hoc* basis, the CIPO by late 1942 had become an integral and indispensable component of planning and promotion by the Wartime Information Board and the Wartime Prices and Trade Board. Such polling unabashedly served Ottawa's propaganda needs, as determined by officials like Claxton, Grierson, and Ketchum. And the prime function of this propaganda, as Claxton had earlier enunciated, was to 'influence opinion and conduct,' serving not 'the good of the person subjected to it' but only the 'ends of the propagandists.'[5] There was no 'public interest' to serve, only state interests. Opinion polling, emulating consumer research surveys, provided quantitative measures of aggregate opinion, while simultaneously securing data which could be broken down and analysed by any number of demographic or geographic variables. Such delineated popular feedback helped officials devise more effective information appeals aimed at specific 'publics.' In turn, cross-tabulated responses on media use could identify optimal radio and print venues for corresponding 'advertising' campaigns. It was as a technique of instrumental rationality, a centralized and calculable means of gauging public opinion and mobilizing popular consent, that CIPO polling proved its worth to Ottawa officials. Democratic rationales were rare.[6]

By 1945, CIPO poll results were a burgeoning presence in the federal bureaucracy, but polling by political parties proved far less prevalent. Though Canada's first 'political consumer survey' appeared in the *Canadian Forum*, challenging leftists to apply market research techniques to political organizing, the CCF avoided party polling. A fusion of educative socialist movement and political party, the CCF faced unique structural and ideological barriers to the adoption of the marketing ethos. The party counted many active grassroots members and possessed a democratic structure, both of which were inimical to polling's centripetal effect on policy making and electioneering. Wedded to a belief in individual rationality, the CCF world-view rejected advertisers' and marketers' assumptions about consumers' fundamental emotional, irrational, and malleable natures. Furthermore, the CCF had no contacts with advertising or market research firms versed in opinion sampling. The Progressive Conservatives, while in touch with CIPO officials and keeping a watchful eye on published Gallup Poll results, similarly did not commission any party polls. The party's main advertising agency, McKim Advertising, knew little about market research techniques, but, more important, the Tories' incessant internal feuding worked against the adoption of a novel technique like polling. The Liberal party commanded the entire field of political polling prior to 1945. Senior Liberals like Claxton were privy to reams of secret CIPO data funnelled through the WIB, much of which served partisan alongside state interests. When in 1944 Liberal strategists moved to conduct internal party polling, they had at their disposal an advertising affiliate well steeped in market research expertise, Cockfield, Brown, which in turn had close contacts with Canadian Facts, Canada's leading market research firm. Though financial constraints forced a premature end to the polling program, it nonetheless proved a watershed in Canadian politics, constituting the birth of 'political marketing.' Its impact was symbolically display-ed soon after when Canadian Facts revamped its letterhead motto to read: 'Canada's Oldest Dominion-Wide Marketing and *Public Opinion Research Organization.*'[7] Consumer and citizen polling were now two sides of the same marketing coin.

In one of his many jeremiads against the enlistment of the social sci-ences for state and commercial purposes, Harold Innis lamented the use of economists by politicians 'to foster the interests of the party and the state. The economist becomes a political economist. He has enlisted with pressure groups in the struggle against other pressure groups or he has enlisted with the state as centralized power.' CIPO pollsters, along with Ketchum, were similarly 'politicized,' both in service to state and, to a lesser extent, to party. Indeed, the sample survey's role in scientifically affirming 'centralized power' undermined polling's democratizing claims. Efficiency, instrumental rationality, and scientific management – the mantras of economies-of-scale production and Ottawa's wartime social and economic engineering – were hardly compatible with the non-linear workings of democratic decision making. As John M. Jordan has argued with respect to American social engineering and liberalism, 'the logic of the machine process' was not amendable to that of 'demo-cratic politics unless politics no longer turns on the principles of free debate.' Political pluralism generated 'multiple phrasings of the relevant questions, not to mention competing answers to all questions.'[8] Notably, it was during the war, as C.B. Macpherson documents, that a new inter-pretive model of liberal democracy, emphasizing 'an entrepreneurial market analogy,' arose among political theorists. Originally presented in Joseph Schumpeter's 1942 work *Capitalism, Socialism, and Democracy,* the model expunged moral questions from political governance, positing instead that the goal of democracy was to 'register the desires of people as they are, not to contribute to what they might be or might wish to be.' In this schema, according to Macpherson, 'democracy is simply a mar-ket mechanism: the voters are consumers; the politicians are the entre-preneurs.'[9] While consumer research and opinion polling played no direct role in this paradigmatic shift, the use of market metaphors and the conflation of consumer and political choice fitted well with Canada's emerging marketing polity engendered in good measure by opinion surveying. The quantitative technique devised to dissect consumers' thoughts and actions now performed this task with citizens.\Less in evidence by 1945, however, were promises linking polling with democratic rejuvenation\In its place stood a phalanx of political and business interests – politicians, civil servants, marketers, and public relations specialists, among others – whose nascent uses of opinion polling served more private advantage than public good.

Notes

Introduction

1 Seeley G. Mudd Manuscript Library, Princeton University Archives (PUA), Woodrow Wilson School of Public and International Affairs collection (WWSPIA), box 90, file 'Gallup, G.,' Gallup to Poole, 20 May 1939; Poole to Gallup, 7 June 1939; Gallup to Poole, 12 June 1939; Gallup to Poole, 14 June 1939. Interviews with the Honourable Bob Rae, 3 June 1993, 8 Nov. 1995. Saul Forbes Rae, 'The Concept of Public Opinion and Its Measurement' (PhD dissertation, London School of Economics, 1938). See also Saul Forbes Rae, 'The Oxford Bye-Election: A Study in the Straw-Vote,' *Political Quarterly*, 10, 2 (1939), 268–79.

2 Albert H. Cantril, foreword to Irving Crespi, *Public Opinion, Polls, and Democracy* (Boulder: Westview Press, 1989), xi.

3 George Gallup and Saul Forbes Rae, *The Pulse of Democracy: The Public-Opinion Poll and How It Works* (New York: Simon and Schuster, 1940), 6, 14, 44–5.

4 Cited in Hugh Whalen, 'The Perils of Polling,' in Paul W. Fox, ed., *Politics: Canada*, 4th edition (Toronto: McGraw-Hill Ryerson, 1977), 203.

5. Michael Adams, 'Pro Polling,' *Policy Options*, July 1987, 30; Adams, *Sex in the Snow: Canadian Social Values at the End of the Millennium* (Toronto: Viking, 1997), 2.

6 Martin Goldfarb and Thomas Axworthy, *Marching to a Different Drummer: An Essay on the Liberals and Conservatives in Convention* (Toronto: Stoddart, 1988), xii, xxii. For recent American examples of survey researchers offering similar views, see Sidney Verba, 'The Citizen as Respondent: Sample Surveys and American Democracy (Presidential Address, American Political Science Association, 1995),' *American Political Science Review*, 90, 1 (March 1996), 1–7;

Andrew Kohut, 'Opinion Polls and the Democratic Process: 1945/1995,'
Public Opinion Quarterly, 59 (Fall 1995), 463–71.

7 Goldfarb and Axworthy, xii. There is, however, a mounting body of academic
and journalistic critiques of polling, notably its impact on the democratic pro-
cess. The early classics are Herbert Blumer, 'Public Opinion and Public Opin-
ion Polling,' *American Sociological Review,* 13, 5 (Oct. 1948), 542–9, and Lindsay
Rogers, *The Pollsters: Public Opinion, Politics and Democratic Leadership* (New
York: Alfred A. Knopf, 1949). For more recent examples, see Jeffrey Simpson,
'Pollstruck,' *Policy Options,* 8, 2 (March 1987), 3–7; Christopher Hitchens,
'Voting in the Passive Voice,' *Harper's,* April 1992, 45–52; Benjamin Ginsberg,
The Captive Public: How Mass Opinion Promotes State Power (New York: Basic
Books, 1986); John S. Dryzek, 'The Mismeasure of Political Man,' *Journal of Pol-
itics,* 50, 3 (Aug. 1988), 705–25; Michael Wheeler, *Lies, Damn Lies, and Statistics:
The Manipulation of Public Opinion in America* (New York: Liveright, 1977);
Pierre Bourdieu, 'Public Opinion Does Not Exist,' in Armand Mattelart and
Seth Siegelaub, eds., *Communication and Class Struggle,* vol. 1: *Capitalism, Impe-
rialism* (New York: International General, 1979), 124–30; and Charles T.
Salmon and Theodore L. Glasser, 'The Politics of Polling and the Limits of
Consent,' in Glasser and Salmon, eds., *Public Opinion and the Communication of
Consent* (New York: Guilford Press, 1995), 437–58.

8 Jean M. Converse, *Survey Research in the United States: Roots and Emergence
1890–1960* (Berkeley: University of California Press, 1987); Susan Herbst,
Numbered Voices: How Opinion Polling Has Shaped American Politics (Chicago:
University of Chicago Press, 1993).

9 Claire Hoy, *Margin of Error: Pollsters and the Manipulation of Canadian Politics*
(Toronto: Key Porter, 1989), 10–17.

10 Guy Lachapelle, *Polls and the Media in Canadian Elections: Taking the Pulse*
(Toronto: Dundurn Press, 1991). For example: the last *Literary Digest* straw
poll was in 1936, not 1940. George Gallup's first national opinion poll was in
1935, not 1936. The Canadian Institute of Public Opinion conducted its first
election poll in 1943, not 1945. The market research firm Canadian Facts was
founded in 1932, not 'between 1965 and 1980' (ibid., 6, 7, 10, 11).

11 A.B. Blankenship, Chuck Chakrapani, and W. Harold Poole, *A History of
Marketing Research in Canada* (Toronto: Professional Marketing Research
Society, 1985).

12 This observation is drawn from Richard Ohmann, *Selling Culture: Magazines,
Markets, and Class at the Turn of the Century* (London: Verso, 1996), 361.

13 See especially Ginsberg, *The Captive Public.*

14 'Deliberative polling,' studied and promoted by James Fishkin, provides one
recent example of the use of a variant of survey research to reinvigorate

American democracy. See his *Democracy and Deliberation: New Directions for Democratic Reform* (New Haven: Yale University Press, 1991).

1: Polling Consumers

1 Stuart Peabody, 'Research Big Development in Advertising,' *Canadian Advertising*, Dec. 1935, 15–16; Walter A. Thompson, 'Tendencies toward a More Rational Approach to Marketing,' *Quarterly Review of Commerce*, 3, 1 (Autumn 1936), 26.

2 Daniel J. Boorstin, *The Americans: The Democratic Experience* (New York: Vintage, 1973), 148.

3 Richard S. Tedlow, *New and Improved: The Story of Mass Marketing in America* (New York: Basic Books, 1990), 16.

4 M.C. Urquhart and K.A.H. Buckley, eds., *Historical Statistics of Canada* (Toronto: Macmillan, 1965), 141.

5 Robert Bothwell, Ian Drummond, and John English, *Canada 1900–1945* (Toronto: University of Toronto Press, 1987), 74; Graham D. Taylor and Peter A. Baskerville, *A Concise History of Business in Canada* (Toronto: Oxford University Press, 1994), 309–12, 336–8; Graham S. Lowe, *Women in the Administrative Revolution: The Feminization of Clerical Work* (Oxford: Polity Press, 1987), 37–46; For examples of scientific management methods used by Canadian firms, see Craig Heron and Bryan D. Palmer, 'Through the Prism of the Strike: Industrial Conflict in Southern Ontario, 1901–14,' *Canadian Historical Review*, 58, 4 (Dec. 1977), 430–4. Michael Bliss, however, downplays the importance of scientific management in early 1900s business organization. *Northern Enterprise: Five Centuries of Canadian Business* (Toronto: McClelland and Stewart, 1987), 606; and *A Living Profit: Studies in the Social History of Canadian Business, 1883–1911* (Toronto: McClelland and Stewart, 1974), 11. On the counterproductive impact of scientific management at the Hudson's Bay Company in the 1920s, see David Monod, 'Bay Days: The Managerial Revolution and Hudson's Bay Company Department Stores, 1912–1939,' *Historical Papers* (1986), 173–96. On the founding of Canada's first management consulting firm, see Edward Bruce Mellett, *From Stopwatch to Strategy: A History of the First Twenty-Five Years of the Canadian Association of Management Consultants* (Toronto: Canadian Association of Management Consultants, 1988), 2–4. For the American context, see the exemplary works of Alfred D. Chandler, Jr, *The Visible Hand: The Managerial Revolution in American Business* (Cambridge: Harvard University Press, 1977) and *Scale and Scope: The Dynamics of Industrial Enterprise* (Cambridge: Harvard University Press, 1990).

6 Robert Craig Brown and Ramsay Cook, *Canada, 1896–1921: A Nation Trans-*

formed (Toronto: McClelland and Stewart, 1974), 91–2; Tom Traves, *The State and Enterprise: Canadian Manufacturers and the Federal Government* (Toronto: University of Toronto Press, 1979), 5; Paul Craven, *'An Impartial Umpire': Industrial Relations and the Canadian State, 1900–1911* (Toronto: University of Toronto Press, 1980), 380 (original emphasis). Craven examined managerial growth in 161 industries from 1901 to 1911. In 102 industries the ratio of administrative to production employees (A/P ratio) stayed constant or actually fell ten years later. However, because administrative overhead increased significantly in the remaining, mostly large-scale, industries, there was a 14 per cent mean increase in the A/P ratio for all industries, a figure consistent with that of other western economies.

7 M.C. Urquhart, 'Three Builders of Canada's Statistical System,' *Canadian Historical Review*, 68, 3 (Sept. 1987), 423; Canada, *Dominion Bureau of Statistics: History, Function, Organization* (Ottawa: King's Printer, 1952), 9.

8 Canada, *Dominion Bureau of Statistics*, 10; Urquhart and Buckley, *Historical Statistics of Canada*, 454; Urquhart, 'Three Builders of Canada's Statistical System,' 428; R.H. Coats, 'Beginnings in Canadian Statistics,' *Canadian Historical Review*, 27, 2 (June 1946), 127–9.

9 R.H. Coats, 'Vital Statistics for National Advertisers,' *Canadian Advertising Data*, Dec. 1928, 74; Canada, *Dominion Bureau of Statistics: Its Origins, Constitution and Organization* (Ottawa: King's Printer, 1935), 19.

10 Lowe, *Women in the Administrative Revolution*, 24. See also Barry Ferguson, *Remaking Liberalism: The Intellectual Legacy of Adam Shortt, O.D. Skelton, W.C. Clark, and W.A. Mackintosh, 1890-1925* (Montreal and Kingston: McGill-Queen's University Press, 1993), 214–15.

11 Ian H. Macdonald, 'U.S.A. Makes Census of Distribution,' *Canadian Advertising Data*, Feb. 1930, 78. Few historical works examine marketing in Canada. On retailing see Joy L. Santink, *Timothy Eaton and the Rise of His Department Store* (Toronto: University of Toronto Press, 1990). See also David Monod, 'Bay Days,' and especially his *Store Wars: Shopkeepers and the Culture of Mass Marketing, 1890–1939* (Toronto: University of Toronto Press, 1996), 102–48.

12 Walter A. Thompson, 'Tendencies toward a More Rational Approach to Marketing,' *Quarterly Review of Commerce*, 3, 1 (Autumn 1936), 22–7; *Dominion Bureau of Statistics: Origins* (Ottawa: King's Printer, 1935), 19.

13 'Distribution Statistics in Canada,' *Canadian Advertising Data*, July 1930, 13; See also H.E. Mihell, 'Basing Advertising on Facts,' *Canadian Advertising Data*, July 1928, 83–4; Charles F. Abbott, 'Market Analysis a First Requisite,' *Industrial Canada*, Oct. 1931, 42–4; Canada, Dominion Bureau of Statistics, *Canada Year Book 1932* (Ottawa, King's Printer, 1932), 527.

14 Herbert Marshall, 'The Statistical Basis of Marketing Policy,' in H.R. Kemp,

ed., *Canadian Marketing Problems* (Toronto: University of Toronto Press, 1939), 13; anon., 'The Reasons for Taking Census of Merchandising in Canada,' *Canadian Advertising Data*, July 1931, 8.

15 Canada, *Dominion Bureau of Statistics: Origins* (1935), 20, 47; Canada, *Census of Canada, 1931*, vol. 10, *Merchandising and Services, Part 1* (Ottawa: King's Printer, 1934), and vol. 11, *Merchandising and Services, Part 2* (Ottawa: King's Printer, 1934); Marshall, 'The Statistical Basis of Marketing Policy,' 13–20; Urquhart and Buckley, eds., *Historical Statistics of Canada*, 562–3.

16 Canada, *Canada Year Book, 1933.* (Ottawa: King's Printer), 627–41; For other DBS merchandising publications, see *Historical Catalogue of Dominion Bureau of Statistics Publications, 1918-1960* (Ottawa: Dominion Bureau of Statistics, 1966), 115–37. See also *Consumer Market Data, 1931* (Ottawa: DBS, 1940), and *Consumer Market Data, 1941* (Ottawa: DBS, 1945). Wholesale and retail annual surveys were halted during World War Two, except for the complete annual survey of retail chain stores. Urquhart and Buckley, *Historical Statistics of Canada*, 563.

17 Marshall, 'Statistical Basis of Marketing Policy,' 19–20; and Thompson, 'Tendencies toward a More Rational Approach to Marketing,' 25. On the vagaries of Depression-era retailing, see Monod, *Store Wars*, 290–301.

18 Stuart Peabody, 'Research Big Development in Advertising,' *Canadian Advertising*, Dec. 1935, 15–16.

19 James R. Beniger, *The Control Revolution: Technological and Economic Origins of the Information Society* (Cambridge: Harvard University Press, 1986), 20.

20 Henry King, 'The Beginning of Marketing Research in Canada,' in W.H. Mahatoo, ed., *Marketing Research in Canada* (Toronto: Thomas Nelson and Sons, 1968), 20–2; see also A.B. Blankenship, Chuck Chakrapani, and W. Harold Poole, *A History of Marketing Research in Canada* (Toronto: Professional Marketing Research Society, 1985), 28.

21 Charles Parlin, *The Merchandising of Automobiles, An Address to Retailers* (Philadelphia: Curtis Publishing, 1915); Douglas B. Ward, 'Tracking the Culture of Consumption: Curtis Publishing, Charles Coolidge Parlin, and the Origins of Market Research, 1911–1930' (PhD dissertation, University of Maryland, 1996); Beniger, *The Control Revolution*; Jean M. Converse, *Survey Research in the United States: Roots and Emergence, 1890–1960* (Berkeley: University of California Press, 1987), 89; Robert Bartels, *The Development of Marketing Thought* (Homewood, Ill: R.D. Irwin, 1962), 109.

22 Lawrence C. Lockley, 'Notes on the History of Market Research, *Journal of Marketing*, 14, 5 (April 1950), 735; Converse, *Survey Research in the United States*, 90; Daniel Pope, *The Making of Modern Advertising* (New York: Basic Books, 1983), 26.

23 Harwell Wells, 'Charting Consumer America: J. Walter Thompson and the Rise of Market Research,' paper presented at Business History Conference, Fort Lauderdale, 19 March 1995, p. 6; Pope, *The Making of Modern Advertising*, 142–3; Susan Strasser, *Satisfaction Guaranteed: The Making of the American Mass Market* (New York: Pantheon, 1989), 153; Peggy Jean Kreshel, 'Toward a Cultural History of Advertising Research: A Case Study of J. Walter Thompson, 1908–1925' (PhD dissertation, University of Illinois at Urbana-Champaign, 1989), 212–385; and Kreshel, 'The "Culture" of J. Walter Thompson, 1915–1925,' *Public Relations Review*, 16, 3 (Fall 1990), 80–93.

24 Converse, *Survey Research in the United States*, 113–14.

25 On radio listening research in the 1930s, see E.P.H. James, 'The Development of Research in Broadcast Advertising,' *Journal of Marketing*, 2 (1937), 141–5; Boorstin, *The Americans: The Democratic Experience*, 154–5; Hugh Malcolm Beville, Jr, *Audience Ratings: Radio, Television, and Cable*, revised edition (Hillsdale, NJ: Lawrence Earlbaum Associates 1988), 4–11.

26 Archibald M. Crossley, 'Early Days of Public Opinion Research,' *Public Opinion Quarterly*, 21, 1 (Spring 1957), 159–61; Converse, *Survey Research*, 111–13, 90.

27 George Gallup and Saul Forbes Rae, *The Pulse of Democracy: The Public-Opinion Poll and How It Works* (New York: Simon and Schuster, 1940), 69–70; William Leach, *Land of Desire: Merchants, Power, and the Rise of a New American Culture* (New York: Pantheon, 1993), 162–3, 285–92; Converse, *Survey Research*, 94. For a general history of the Harvard Business School, see Jeffrey L. Cruikshank, *A Delicate Experiment: The Harvard Business School, 1908–1945* (Boston: Harvard Business School Press, 1987).

28 Robert Bartels, *The Development of Marketing Thought*, 106. Examples of the more noteworthy works include Carson S. Duncan, *Commercial Research* (New York: Macmillan, 1919); Percival White, *Market Analysis: Its Principles and Methods* (New York: McGraw-Hill, 1921), and *Marketing Research Technique* (New York: Harper and Bros., 1931); Frank R. Coutant and J. Russell Doubman, *Simplified Market Research* (Philadelphia: Walther Printing House, 1935); William J. Reilly, *Marketing Investigations* (New York: Ronald Press, 1929); Ferdinand C. Wheeler, ed., *The Technique of Marketing Research* (New York: McGraw-Hill, 1937); Lyndon O. Brown, *Market Research and Analysis* (New York: Ronald Press, 1937); and Advertising Research Foundation, *Copy Testing* (New York: Ronald Press, 1939).

29 N.H. Engle, 'Gaps in Marketing Research,' *Journal of Marketing*, 4, 1 (April 1940), 346.

30 Henry Link, *The New Psychology of Selling and Advertising* (New York: Macmillan, 1932); Link, 'A New Method of Testing Advertising Effectiveness,'

Harvard Business Review, 11, 2 (Jan. 1933), 165–77; Michael M. Sokal, 'The Origins of the Psychological Corporation,' *Journal of the History of the Behavioral Sciences*, 17 (1981), 54–67; Converse, *Survey Research*, 108.

31 Otis Pease, *The Responsibilities of American Advertising: Private Control and Public Influence, 1920–1940* (New Haven: Yale University Press, 1958), 170–1; T.J. Jackson Lears, 'From Salvation to Self-Realization: Advertising and the Therapeutic Roots of the Consumer Culture, 1880–1920,' in Richard Wightman Fox and T.J. Jackson Lears, eds., *The Culture of Consumption: Critical Essays in American History, 1880–1980* (New York: Pantheon, 1983), 18–19. In Canada, Douglas J. Wilson wrote in 1936 that 'psycho-technologists' aiming to improve advertising's efficiency should emulate the approach of engineers and scientists developing techniques of mass production. 'Psychological Aspects of Market Research,' *Quarterly Review of Commerce*, 3, 2 (Winter 1936), 67–70.

32 Beniger, *The Control Revolution*, 18–20, 346–56, 378–89.

33 John R.W. Gwynne-Timothy, *Western's First Century* (London: University of Western Ontario, 1978), 462–4.

34 Some of the pertinent theses include O.C. Simmers, 'Consumer Opinion of Retail Store Clerks' (1933); D.E. Lofft, 'Store Preference' (1933); F.D. Carney, 'Brand Preference' (1933); W.R.A. Thomson, 'Brand Preference in the Drug Field as Shown in London, Ontario' (1933); G.D. Beaumont, 'Testing Advertising' (1934); K.S. Murray, 'Radio Listening Habits' (1937). See 'Research Problems,' *Quarterly Review of Commerce*, 5, 2 (Winter 1938), 47–53; and Blankenship et al., *A History of Marketing Research*, 25–6.

35 Walter A. Thompson, 'Brand Policy,' *Quarterly Review of Commerce*, 1, 1 (Autumn 1933), 31–4.

36 Walter D. Tamblyn, 'Consumer Opinion of Retail Store Clerks,' *Quarterly Review of Commerce*, 1, 3 (Spring 1934), 118–23.

37 Gilbert C. Clarke, 'A Survey of Gasoline Consumer Buying Habits,' *Quarterly Review of Commerce* (QRC), 1, 2 (Winter 1934), 94–102.

38 Walter A. Thompson, 'Consumer Purchasing outside the City of London,' QRC, 2, 2 (Winter 1935), 15–22. For a copy of Theodore Brown's table displaying the relationship between sample size and probable error, see Gallup and Rae, *The Pulse of Democracy*, 70.

39 Kenneth Murray, 'Radio Listening Habits,' QRC, 5, 2 (Winter 1938), 41–6; and Blankenship et al., *A History of Marketing Research*, 26.

40 For other market research articles in QRC, see Beverley E. Smith and Randal K. Bythell, 'The Buying Habits of Used Car Purchases,' QRC, 3, 2 (Winter 1936), 51–8; Frank R. Coutant, 'Profitable Marketing through Scientifically Planned Advertising,' QRC, 6, 1 (Autumn 1938), 15–19; J.L. Dampier, 'Adver-

tising Research,' *QRC*, 6, 3 (Spring 1939), 109–17; Donald R.G. Cowan, 'Consumer Testing of Products,' *QRC* 7, 3 (Spring 1940); Tom Faust, Jr, 'Merchandise Returns – Customer's Viewpoint,' *QRC*, 8, 2 (Winter 1940–1), 152–66.

41 Walter Thompson, 'Retailing from the Consumer's Point of View,' in H.R. Kemp, ed., *Canadian Marketing Problems* (Toronto: University of Toronto Press, 1939), 50. See also Henry King, 'The Need for More Market Knowledge in Canada,' *QRC* 7, 3 (Spring 1940), 124.

42 Blankenship et al., *A History of Marketing Research in Canada*, 18–19.

43 W.H. Poole, 'Marketing Research in Canada,' *Commerce Journal*, Feb. 1957, 21; King, 'The Beginning of Marketing Research in Canada,' 21.

44 National Archives of Canada (NAC), H.E. Kidd Papers, MG 32 G9, vol. 26, Goforth to Kidd, 17 June 1930.

45 Ibid.

46 Kidd Papers, vol. 25, file 14, 'Partial List of Market Surveys.' In spite of his firm's prolific outpouring of market research studies, Henry King still lamented in 1940 that Canada lagged far behind the United States in this regard. 'The Need for More Market Knowledge in Canada,' 124–9.

47 'Orange Crush Base Campaign on Nation-Wide Survey,' *Canadian Advertising Data*, May 1932, 3; H.R. Cockfield, 'Trend in Advertising Agency Practice (Part II),' *Canadian Advertising Data*, Jan. 1931, 19; Henry King, 'New Problems in Advertising and Steps towards Their Solution,' in H.R. Kemp, ed., *Canadian Marketing Problems* (Toronto: University of Toronto Press, 1939), 73.

48 Blankenship et al., 18; David Hayes, 'Who Killed Cockfield Brown?' *Saturday Night*, Feb. 1984, 44–52.

49 For Cockfield, Brown and other firms discussed below, little is known about the sums charged clients for such services. While many marketing reports survive, related correspondence and financial records unfortunately do not. As well, many consumer surveys were not conducted for specific clients; instead, they were used by ad agencies and publishers to promote advertising's merits to a wide range of actual and potential advertisers.

50 Kidd Papers, vol. 25, file 14, 'Extracts from the "Psychological Brand Barometers,"' circa 1935.

51 Kidd Papers, vol. 25, file 14, 'Partial List of Clients, Cockfield, Brown & Company Limited,' 'Partial List of Market Surveys prepared by Cockfield, Brown & Company Limited,' both circa 1936; G.A. Barrat to Cockfield, Brown, 17 June 1936.

52 Duke University, Special Collections Library, J. Walter Thompson (JWT) Papers, box 2, minutes of representatives meetings, 14 May 1930; 'Montreal Office Growing Rapidly,' *J.W.T. News*, June 1930, 3. On JWT consumer sur-

veys in the United States, see Kreshel, 'Toward a Cultural History of Advertising Research,' 226–47.

53 In addition to the Canadian surveys discussed below, the following are available in Duke University's J. Walter Thompson collection. Reel 224, 'Survey among Gillex Users in Montreal and Toronto,' Nov. 1933; reel 223, 'Consumer Survey on Cameras and Films,' Nov. 1933; reel 224, 'Survey on Use of Yeast Cakes among Housewives in Rural Canada' Aug. 1934; reel 233, 'Garment Tag Survey,' Sept. 1936.

54 JWT Papers, reel 223, survey report, 'Facts on Canadian Media,' Dec. 1930.

55 Ibid., 'Survey of the Canadian Market for Household Ammonia,' Jan. 1931.

56 Roland Marchand, *Advertising the American Dream: Making Way for Modernity* (Berkeley: University of California Press, 1985), 66. On gender and consumption, see Victoria de Grazia and Ellen Furlough, eds., *The Sex of Things: Gender and Consumption in Historical Perspective* (Berkeley: University of California Press, 1996).

57 JWT Papers, reel 224, 'Survey of the Baking Powder Market in 4 Canadian Cities,' June 1933.

58 JWT Papers, reel 232, 'A Consumer Survey of the Canadian Market for Ready-to-Eat Cereals,' Aug. 1938.

59 Urquhart and Buckley, *Historical Statistics of Canada*, 96.

60 JWT Papers, reel 224, 'Survey of Newspaper Reading Habits of Adolescents,' July 1938. On comic strips and advertising, see 'Boom in Comics,' *Canadian Advertising*, March 1935, 27–8; Spalding Black, 'Adapting Colored Comics to Advertising,' *Canadian Advertising*, April 1937, 11–12; and 'Even the Politicians Go for the Strip,' *Canadian Advertising*, Oct. 1937, 22.

61 JWT Papers, reels 232 and 233, 'Face Washing Survey: Ontario and Quebec,' April 1938.

62 JWT Papers, reel 338, 'General Soap and Market Survey – 1939,' May 1940.

63 Blankenship et al., *History of Marketing Research*, 28; Coutant, 'Profitable Marketing through Scientifically Planned Advertising,' 15–19; Dampier, 'Advertising Research,' 109–17; H.A. Innis, 'The Necessity of Research in Marketing,' *Commerce Journal*, March 1940, 12–14.

64 For a copy of Watson's speech on behaviourism and advertising delivered in 1935 to the Toronto Advertising and Sales Club, see 'That Strange Animal – The Consumer,' *Canadian Advertising*, Nov. 1935, 18–19, 29.

65 JWT Papers, reel 338, 'General Soap and Market Survey – 1939,' May 1940. On early 1900s soap advertising in America, see Vincent Vinikas, *Soft Soap, Hard Sell: American Hygiene in an Age of Advertisement* (Ames: Iowa State University Press, 1992), 79–94. See also Richard L. Bushman and Claudia L. Bushman, 'The Early History of Cleanliness in America,' *Journal of American*

History, 74, 4 (March 1988), 1234–9. For Canadian references to soap as a social purity metaphor in the pre-1918 period, see Mariana Valverde, *The Age of Light, Soap, and Water: Moral Reform in English Canada, 1885–1925* (Toronto: McClelland and Stewart, 1991), 40–1.

66 On this note, see Innis, 'The Necessity of Research in Marketing,' 12–14.

67 On this subject, see Ross A. Eaman, *Channels of Influence: CBC Audience Research and the Canadian Public* (Toronto: University of Toronto Press, 1994).

68 Canadian Facts (Toronto), company records, 'Canadian Facts at Fifty,' circa 1982. Blankenship et al., *History of Marketing Research,* 22; Eaman, *Channels of Influence,* 50. On the early days of radio advertising, see Russell Johnston, 'The Emergence of Broadcast Advertising in Canada, 1919–1932,' *Historical Journal of Film, Radio and Television,* 17, 1 (1997), 29–47.

69 'Mr. Manufacturer: Meet Your Market' (ad), *Marketing,* 24 Dec. 1938, 8; 'FACTS Are Your Stepping Stones to PROFITS' (ad), *Canadian Advertising,* Jan. 1939, 21.

70 Archives of Ontario (AO), Maclean-Hunter Papers, vol. 403, file 'Surveys, Opinion-General,' Colwell to Irwin, 21 June 1939.

71 Canadian Facts, survey report, 'An Analysis of Listening Habits and Opinions of Children's Radio Programs Conducted in Selected Markets,' Jan. 1939; N.P. Colwell, 'Avoiding Pitfalls in Marketing Research,' *Canadian Advertising* (Fourth Quarter, 1940), 10.

72 AO, Maclean-Hunter Papers, vol. 403, file 'Surveys,' Canadian Facts survey, 'Report of a Readership Study on Maclean's Magazine in Twenty-three Canadian Cities,' Dec. 1940; Irwin memo, 'Notes on Survey of Reader Reaction to Maclean's Magazine, December 1940,' n.d. Since the early 1930s, *Maclean's* had conducted or sponsored small-scale, *ad hoc* surveys of its readers. Blankenship et al., *History of Marketing Research,* 23. For a humorous account of Mavor Moore's experiences as a survey interviewer for *Maclean's* in 1934, read his *Reinventing Myself: Memoirs* (Toronto: Stoddart, 1994), 38–9. For other satirical and sardonic depictions of market research polling in Canadian fiction, see Margaret Atwood, *The Edible Woman* (Toronto: Seal Books, 1969), 38–50; and Mordecai Richler, *Joshua Then and Now* (Toronto: McClelland and Stewart, 1980), 117–18.

73 Maclean-Hunter Papers, vol. 403, file 'Surveys'; Irwin memo, 'Notes on Survey of Reader Reaction to Maclean's Magazine, December 1940,' n.d. On journalists' complaints in the early 1980s about the use of marketing surveys to determine editorial content – derided as 'Pablum Canada' by one reporter – see Canada, *Report of the Royal Commission on Newspapers* (Ottawa: Queen's Printer, 1981), 172.

74 Maclean-Hunter Papers, vol. 402, file 'W.A. Irwin – correspondence, 1941,' Irwin to T. McLaughlin (Curtis Publishing), 5 April 1941; Irwin to R. Robin-

son (Crowell Publishing), 5 April 1941; McLaughlin to Irwin, 8 April 1941; Robinson to Irwin, 8 April 1941. For examples of market research articles, see 'General Motors Ask the Buyer for Opinions,' *Canadian Advertising Data*, Nov. 1932, 14, 25; Henry G. Weaver, 'Educating the Consumer,' *Canadian Business*, 10 (Feb. 1937), 30–3; 'These Seven Steps in Market Research Simplify Task and Ensure Accuracy,' *Marketing*, 29 July 1939, 3; Henry King, 'The Need for More Market Knowledge in Canada,' *Quarterly Review of Commerce*, 7, 3 (Spring 1940), 124–9; and G. Walter Brown, 'Information, Please!' *Canadian Business*, 13 (Nov. 1940), 20–4.

75 Maclean-Hunter Papers, vol. 402, file 'W.A. Irwin – notes, drafts,' 'Reader Survey of *Chatelaine* and *Maclean's*,' 15 April 1941.

76 When a 1931 tariff on U.S. magazines was lifted in 1936, the value of American magazines shot up from $2,625,000 in 1936 to $5,900,000 in 1937. Isaiah Litvak and Christopher Maule, *Cultural Sovereignty: The Time and Reader's Digest Case in Canada* (New York: Praeger, 1974), 28. See also Mary Vipond, *The Mass Media in Canada*, 2nd edition (Toronto: Lorimer, 1992), 29; Paul Rutherford, *The Making of the Canadian Media* (Toronto: McGraw-Hill Ryerson, 1978), 45–8; Phillis Axford, 'Marketing Canadian Magazines,' *Commerce Journal*, March 1939, 24–30; and Noel Robert Barbour, *Those Amazing People! The Story of the Canadian Magazine Industry, 1778–1967* (Toronto: Crucible Press, 1982), 104. For a popular history of magazine publishing, see Fraser Sutherland, *The Monthly Epic: A History of Canadian Magazines 1789–1989* (Markham: Fitzhenry and Whiteside, 1989).

77 Maclean-Hunter Papers, vol. 402, file 'Surveys – Chatelaine,' 'Second Readership Study of Editorial Items in Chatelaine, Dec. 1941; 'Report of Item-by-Item Study of Readership of Two Consecutive Issues of Chatelaine,' 17 Jan. 1944; vol. 404, file 'Maclean's Readership Survey 1941–42,' 'Study of Readership on an Item-by-item Basis of Two Consecutive Issues of Maclean's Magazine,' 24 Dec. 1942; 'Survey M.M. [Maclean's] Readership, 1944,' n.d.; file 'Survey Audience 1944,' 'Report of Results of Study of Canadian Publication Audiences,' 6 June 1945; Floyd S. Chalmers, 'Canada a New Market,' *Commerce Journal*, April 1944, 54. Since 1925, Maclean Publishing had produced the annual *Financial Post Business Year Book, Canada and Newfoundland*, which compiled manufacturing and marketing statistics for business audiences.

78 William G. Rook, *Their Purchasing Power* (Toronto: Canadian Woman's Magazine Publishing, 1912), 3, 5. In Progressive-era America, Mary Ellen Waller-Zuckerman argues, women's magazine publishers 'were among the leaders in performing [market] research, pioneering studies of reader demographics, consumer preferences, comparative advertising data, and market surveys for

products of major advertisers.' See her '"Old Homes, in a City of Perpetual Change": Women's Magazines, 1890–1916,' *Business History Review* 63, 4 (Winter 1989), 752. On turn-of-the-century American magazines' depictions of upscale readers, see Richard Ohmann, *Selling Culture: Magazines, Markets, and Class at the Turn of the Century* (London: Verso, 1996), 113–14.

79 'Canadian Farm Market,' *Canadian Advertising*, Jan. 1938, 13; 'A.C.A. Analyzes Magazine Contents,' *Marketing*, 11 June 1938, 8.

80 H.R. Kesterton, *A History of Journalism in Canada* (Toronto: McClelland and Stewart, 1967), 71; Carlton McNaught, *Canada Gets the News* (Toronto: Ryerson Press, 1940), 9–10, 24; Rutherford, *Making of the Canadian Media*, 48–9; Canada, *Report of the Royal Commission on Publications* (Ottawa: Queen's Printer, 1961), 245; *Report of the Royal Commission on Newspapers*, 65.

81 Vipond, *The Mass Media in Canada*, 17.

82 McNaught, *Canada Gets the News*, 19; See also Harold Innis, *The Press: A Neglected Factor in the Economic History of the Twentieth Century* (London: Oxford University Press, 1949), 12; Rutherford, *The Making of the Canadian Media*, 50–2; and Minko Sotiron, *From Politics to Profit: The Commercialization of Canadian Daily Newspapers, 1890–1920* (Montreal and Kingston: McGill-Queen's University Press, 1997), 4–9.

83 'Star Strength in Toronto' (ad), *Canadian Advertising Data* 3, 2 (March 1930), 47; 'Still Bigger Value for Your Advertising Dollar' (ad), *Marketing*, 4 Aug. 1934, 5. For similar promotional ads for the *Montreal Daily Star* propounding reader purchasing power, see 'Logic!' *Marketing*, 10 Feb. 1934, 3, and 'Are You Keeping Step with This Market?' *Marketing*, 29 May 1937, 3.

84 'Survey of Buying Power,' *Marketing*, 10 Dec. 1938, 9.

85 Canadian Daily Newspapers Association (CDNA), Toronto, 'Report of Nineteenth Annual Meeting of the Canadian Daily Newspaper Association,' 22 April 1938, 37–9; W.A. Craick, *A History of Canadian Journalism*, vol. 2 (Toronto: Ontario Publishing Company, 1959), 210–12; 'Canadian Markets Shown in Volume of Vivid Charts, *Canadian Advertising*, Oct. 1937, 23. See also CDNA, *The Canadian Market: 1938 Supplement; A Graphic Summary of Canadian Statistics, and an Analysis of Retail Trade* (Toronto: CDNA, 1938).

86 CDNA, 'Report of the Twenty-First Annual Meeting of the Canadian Daily Newspapers Association,' 30–31 May 1940, 40; 'C.D.N.A. Market Study Ready in September,' *Marketing*, 22 July 1939, 8. Canadian data on newspaper markets were available in the American trade publications, *Editor and Publisher: Market Guide* and *Editor and Publisher: The Fourth Estate*. Also of note was the annual, *Lydiatt's Book of Canadian Market and Advertising Data*.

87 CDNA, 'Report of Nineteenth Annual Meeting of the Canadian Daily

Newspaper Association,' 22 April 1938, 42; Craick, *History of Canadian Journalism*, 213.

88 Duncan MacInnes, 'What of Newspaper Advertising?' *Quarterly Review of Commerce* 8, 3 (Spring 1941), 230–9; Thomas C. Leonard, *News for All: America's Coming-of-Age with the Press* (New York: Oxford University Press, 1995), 133–4.

89 CDNA, 'Report of the Twenty-First Annual Meeting of the Canadian Daily Newspapers Association,' 30–31 May 1940, 52–3. Wilder Breckenridge was the speaker.

90 CDNA, 'Report of the Twenty-First Annual Meeting of the Canadian Daily Newspapers Association,' 30–31 May 1940, 46–7; 'Report of the Twenty-Second Annual Meeting,' 7 March 1941, 8–9; MacInnes, 'What of Newspaper Advertising?' 230–1.

91 Elmer P. Resseguie, 'Newspapers and Market Research,' in Jane McKee, ed., *Marketing Organization and Technique* (Toronto: University of Toronto Press, 1940), 68.

92 Henry Link, 'Some Milestones in Public Opinion Research,' *International Journal of Opinion and Attitude Research*, 1 (1947), 36; cited in Converse, *Survey Research in the United States*, 88.

93 See David MacKenzie, 'The Bren Gun Scandal and the Maclean Publishing Company's Investigation of Canadian Defence Contracts, 1938–1940,' *Journal of Canadian Studies*, 26, 3 (Fall 1991), 140–62; and his *Arthur Irwin: A Biography* (Toronto: University of Toronto Press, 1993), 116–47.

94 Cited in MacKenzie, 'The Bren Gun Scandal,' 150. Mackenzie's work does not examine this polling project.

95 Maclean-Hunter Papers, vol. 403, file 'Surveys-opinion-general,' Colwell to Irwin, 30 May 1939; Colwell to Irwin, 21 June 1939; Irwin to Tyrrell, 22 June 1939; Colwell to Maclean Publishing, 27 July 1939 and 31 July 1939.

96 Ibid., Hunter to Irwin, 29 Aug. 1939; Hunter to Irwin, 10 April 1941.

97 Wilson, 'Psychological Aspects of Market Research,' 67.

98 On this point, see Peggy J. Kreshel, 'Advertising Research in the Pre-Depression Years: A Cultural History,' *Journal of Current Issues and Research in Advertising*, 15, 1 (Spring 1993), 59–74.

99 James R. Beniger, 'The Popular Symbolic Repertoire and Mass Communication,' *Public Opinion Quarterly*, 47, 4 (Winter 1983), 482; Strasser, *Satisfaction Guaranteed*, 288; Converse, *Survey Research*, 92, 445n35.

100 Cited in Boorstin, *The Americans*, 152. On this point, see also William R. Leach, 'Transformation in a Culture of Consumption: Women and Department Stores, 1890–1925,' *Journal of American History*, 71, 2 (Sept. 1984), 319–42; and Marchand, *Advertising the American Dream*, 66–9.

2: 'Selling Toothpaste and Plumbing the Public Mind'

1 Claude E. Robinson, *Straw Votes: A Study of Political Prediction* (New York: Columbia University Press, 1932), 55–6.

2 Journalism straw polls employed different survey techniques with varying degrees of accuracy. The least reliable method, the 'ballot-in-the-paper,' entailed clipping, marking, and returning ballots by mail. Only slightly more accurate was the practice of sending postcard ballots to people on selected mailing lists. The most reliable survey method, but least used, was the personal canvass in which people's opinions were solicited in various locales. Robinson, *Straw Votes*, 52–5. On nineteenth-century straw polls see Tom Smith, 'The First Straw,' *Public Opinion Quarterly*, 54, 1 (Spring 1990), 21–36; Thomas A. Bowers, '"Precision Journalism" in North Carolina in the 1800s,' *Journalism Quarterly*, 54, 4 (Winter 1976), 738–40; and Steven J. Rosenstone, *Forecasting Presidential Elections* (New Haven: Yale University Press, 1983), 24–6.

3 Jean M. Converse, *Survey Research in the United States: Roots and Emergence, 1890–1960* (Berkeley: University of California Press, 1987), 118. Roughly 10 million ballots were mailed and some 2.3 million were returned. For the magazine's extensive reporting on incoming vote tallies, see *Literary Digest*, 12 Sept. 1936, 5–6; 19 Sept. 1936, 9–10; 26 Sept. 1936, 7–8; 3 Oct. 1936, 7–8; 10 Oct. 1936, 7–8; 17 Oct. 1936, 7–8; 24 Oct. 1936, 9–10; 31 Oct. 1936, 5–6.

4 Gallup surveyed a small sample of telephone and automobile owners, who made up the majority of the *Digest*'s voter pool, and predicted the *Digest*'s final tally for Landon would be 56 per cent. In fact it was 57 per cent. Gallup, 'Closest Election since 1916 Indicated by Poll's Results,' *New York Herald-Tribune*, 12 July 1936, sec. II, 1, 7.

5 *Digest*, 31 Oct. 1936, 6.

6 Peverill Square, 'Why the 1936 Literary Digest Poll Failed,' *Public Opinion Quarterly*, 52, 1 (1988), 125–33; Daniel Katz and Hadley Cantril, 'Public Opinion Polls,' *Sociometry*, 1, 1 (July–Oct. 1937), 164.

7 Mervin D. Field, 'Political Opinion Polling in the United States of America,' in Robert M. Worcester, ed., *Political Opinion Polling: An International Review* (London: Macmillan Press, 1983), 200.

8 George Gallup, *Public Opinion in a Democracy* (Princeton: Herbert L. Baker Foundation, 1939), 14; Gallup and Saul Rae, *The Pulse of Democracy: The Public Opinion Poll and How It Works* (New York: Simon and Schuster, 1940), 289; Gallup, *A Guide to Public Opinion Polls* (Princeton: Princeton University Press, 1944), v.

9 There are no archived 'Gallup papers' and most of the Gallup Corporation's

records from the 1930s and early 1940s, according to company officials, were lost in a warehouse fire. Consequently, this chapter draws on other primary and secondary sources, particularly Gallup's published writings.

10 Thomas Morain, *Prairie Grass Roots: An Iowa Small Town in the Early Twentieth Century* (Ames: Iowa State University Press, 1988), 26, 35, 43, 57–8; Becky Wilson Hawbaker, 'Taking "the Pulse of Democracy": George Gallup, Iowa, and the Origin of the Gallup Poll,' *Palimpsest*, 74, 3 (Fall 1993), 98–113.

11 Columbia University Oral History Project (CUOHP), George Gallup Interview, 15 March 1962, 2.

12 Morain, *Prairie Grass Roots*, 45.

13 CUOHP, Gallup interview, 13; Hawbaker, 'Taking "the Pulse of Democracy,"' 101.

14 Gallup, 'An Objective Method for Determining Reader Interest in the Content of a Newspaper' (PhD dissertation, University of Iowa, 1928); Hawbaker, 'Taking "the Pulse of Democracy,"' 105; Converse, *Survey Research*, 114–15; Raymond Moscowitz, *Stuffy: The Life of Newspaper Pioneer Basil 'Stuffy' Walters* (Ames: Iowa State University Press, 1982), 40–3; Alfred McClung Lee, *The Daily Newspaper in America: The Evolution of a Social Instrument* (New York: Macmillan, 1937), 357–8; Thomas C. Leonard, *News for All: America's Coming-of-Age with the Press* (New York: Oxford University Press, 1995), 133–4; Gallup testimony before Congress, *Hearings before the Committee to Investigate Campaign Expenditures*, House of Representatives 78th Congress, 2nd session, H. Res 551, vol. 1031, pt. 12 (28 Dec. 1944), 1259.

15 CUOHP, Gallup interview, 120, 103, 109–10, 36–51, 105–28; Gallup testimony before Congress, 1259; Converse, *Survey Research*, 114–16.

16 George Gallup, ed., *The Gallup Poll: Public Opinion, 1935–1971*, vol. 1: 1935–1948 (New York: Random House, 1972), 1. This was not the first published scientific opinion poll. That honour went to Elmo Roper, whose 'Roper Poll' first appeared in the July 1935 issue of *Fortune* magazine.

17 Frank Luther Mott, *American Journalism: A History of Newspapers in the United States through 250 Years, 1690–1940* (New York: Macmillan, 1941), 691–4; Alfred McClung Lee, *The Daily Newspaper in America: The Evolution of a Social Instrument* (New York: Macmillan, 1937), 576–602; Michael Schudson, *Discovering the News: A Social History of American Newspapers* (New York: Basic Books, 1978), 7; Thomas C. Leonard, *News for All: America's Coming-of-Age with the Press* (New York: Oxford University Press, 1995), 221.

18 John M. Fenton, *In Your Opinion* (Boston: Little, Brown, 1960), 11; Harwood L. Childs, 'Rule by Public Opinion,' *Atlantic Monthly*, June 1936, 759–61.

19 Interviews with John F. Maloney, Chappaqua, NY, 23 April 1994, and Paul Perry, Princeton, NJ, 7 Feb. 1994; Gallup and Rae, *The Pulse of Democracy*,

56–76; George Gallup and Claude Robinson, 'American Institute of Public Opinion – Surveys, 1935–38,' *Public Opinion Quarterly,* 2, 3 (July 1938), 373–4; Jerome H. Spingarn, 'These Public-Opinion Polls,' *Harper's Magazine,* Dec. 1938, 99; J.J. O'Malley, 'Black Beans and White Beans,' *New Yorker,* 2 March 1940, 20–4; Gallup, *Gallup Poll,* 1–85; F.S. Wickware, 'What the American People Want,' *Harper's Magazine,* Oct. 1938, 547–52; Hadley Cantril, *Gauging Public Opinion* (Princeton: Princeton University Press, 1944), 82.

20 Princeton University Archives (PUA), Woodrow Wilson School of Public and International Affairs (WWSPIA), box 90, file 'Gallup, George,' Gallup to Dewitt C. Poole, 30 Nov. 1937.

21 PUA, WWSPIA, box 90, file 'Gallup, G.,' Poole to Gallup, 7 June 1939; Gallup to Poole, 12 June 1939; box 91, file 'Public Opinion Quarterly 1938–39,' Free to Munro, 20 Dec. 1939; O'Malley, 'Black Beans and White Beans,' 20;. Gallup Congressional testimony, *Hearings,* 1260.

22 Franklin D. Roosevelt Library (FDRL), Hyde Park, NY, Official File (OF) 73, 'Motion Pictures, 1941,' Howard Cullman to Roosevelt, 22 Aug. 1941; Edmund Dorman to Roosevelt, 4 Nov. 1941.

23 Gallup, ed., *The Gallup Poll,* passim; Roper Center for Public Opinion Research (RCPOR), University of Connecticut, Elmo Roper Papers, file '1941: Ideas for and Concerning Surveys,' Wallace Thorsen to Roper, 23 June 1942.

24 For examples see, 'Portrait,' *Time,* 2 March 1936, 18; Don Wharton, 'Man of Straws,' *Today,* 12 Sept. 1936, 8–9; 'Dr. Gallup Closes a Gap between People and Government,' *Newsweek,* 14 Nov. 1936, 14–16; Jerome H. Spingarn, 'These Public-Opinion Polls,' *Harper's Magazine,* Dec. 1938, 97–104; 'Gallup's Growth,' *Newsweek,* 30 Oct. 1939, 30–1; Lindsay Rogers, 'Dr. Gallup's Statistics,' *New Republic,* 1 Nov. 1939, 358–9; Robert R. Updegraff, 'Democracy's New Mirror,' *Forum and Century,* Jan. 1940, 11–14; O'Malley, 'Black Beans and White Beans'; 'Gallup Polls,' *New Republic,* 22 July 1940, 122; R.G. Hubler, 'George Horace Gallup: Oracle in Tweed,' *Forum,* 103 (Fall 1940), 92–5; P. London, 'Ringing Doorbells with a Gallup Reporter,' *New York Times Magazine,* 1 Sept. 1940, 9; 'Dr. Gallup Cites Survey's Success,' *New York Times,* 7 Nov. 1940, L-15; M.M. Clark, 'Government by Gallup,' *Scribner's Commentator* (Sept. 1941), 31–6.

25 Cantril, *Gauging Public Opinion,* xi.

26 For examples, see 'Measuring Public Opinion,' *Vital Speeches,* 9 March 1936, 370–2; 'Putting Public Opinion to Work,' *Scribner's,* Nov. 1936, 36–9; 'Public Opinion in Our Cities,' *National Municipal Review,* 27, 2 (Feb. 1938), 69–71, 103; 'Way the People Are Thinking,' *Reader's Digest,* 32 (June 1938), 1–4; *Public Opinion in a Democracy;* 'Making Democracy Work Every Day: Public Opinion Polls,' *Scholastic,* 2 Oct. 1939, 29–30; 'Can We Trust the Common

People?' *Good Housekeeping*, Oct. 1940, 21; 'Polls and Prophets,' *Current History and Forum*, 7 Nov. 1940, 12–13; 'Public Opinion, 1941,' *Current History and Forum*, 23 Jan. 1941, 12–13; 'We, the People, Are Like This,' *New York Times Magazine*, 8 June 1941, 3, 24; *A Guide to Public Opinion Polls* (Princeton, 1944).

27 Gallup and Rae, *The Pulse of Democracy*, 125, 30; James Bryce, *The American Commonwealth*, 2 vols. (New York: Macmillan, 1888). For similar pronouncements on polling's democratizing function by Archibald Crossley and Elmo Roper, see Crossley, 'Straw Polls in 1936,' *Public Opinion Quarterly*, 1, 1 (Jan. 1937), 35; and Roper, 'Sampling Public Opinion,' *Journal of the American Statistical Association*, 35 (1940), 332, 334.

28 Gallup, *Public Opinion in a Democracy*, 14. See also Converse, *Survey Research*, 121–4.

29 Gallup, 'We, the People, Are Like This,' 24. For similar commentary, see Gallup, 'Testing Public Opinion,' *Public Opinion in a Democracy*, special supplement to *Public Opinion Quarterly* (Jan. 1938), 14; 'Public Opinion in Our Cities,' *National Municipal Review*, 27, 2 (Feb. 1938), 71; *Public Opinion in a Democracy*, 14; *A Guide to Public Opinion Polls*, 74–5.

30 Walter Lippmann, *Public Opinion* (New York: Macmillan, 1922) and *The Phantom Public* (New York: Harcourt, Brace, 1925); Thurman Arnold, *The Symbols of Government* (New Haven: Yale University Press, 1935); John Dickinson, 'Democratic Realities and Democratic Dogma,' *American Political Science Review*, 24, 2 (May 1930), 283–309; Harold D. Lasswell, *Politics: Who Gets What, When, How* (New York: Peter Smith, 1936). See also Edward A. Purcell, Jr, *The Crisis of Democratic Theory: Scientific Naturalism and the Problem of Value* (Lexington: University Press of Kentucky, 1973), 95–114; Daniel T. Rodgers, *Contested Truths: Keywords in American Politics since the Independence* (New York: Basic Books, 1987), 178–211; and William Graebner, *The Engineering of Consent: Democracy and Authority in Twentieth-Century America* (Madison: University of Wisconsin Press, 1987), 47–8, 63–5, 99–102.

31 On Dewey, see Robert B. Westbrook, *John Dewey and American Democracy* (Ithaca: Cornell University Press, 1991), 275–318.

32 Theodore M. Porter, *Trust in Numbers: The Pursuit of Objectivity in Science and Public Life* (Princeton: Princeton University Press, 1995), 73–6.

33 Gallup, 'Polling Public Opinion,' in Asher Christensen and Evron Kirkpatrick, eds., *The People, Politics and the Politicians: Readings in American Government* (New York: Holt, 1941), 258; *Pulse of Democracy*, 56.

34 For examples of the voluminous literature on the history of the social sciences, see Dorothy Ross, *The Origins of American Social Science* (New York: Cambridge University Press, 1991); Converse, *Survey Research*; Robert C. Bannister, *Sociology and Scientism: The American Quest for Objectivity, 1880–*

1940 (Chapel Hill: University of North Carolina Press, 1987); and Mark
Smith, *Social Science in the Crucible: The American Debate over Objectivity and
Purpose, 1918–1941* (Durham: Duke University Press, 1994).

35 Daniel Pope, *The Making of Modern Advertising* (New York: Basic Books,
1983), 26; Richard S. Tedlow, *New and Improved: The Story of Mass Marketing in
America* (New York: Basic Books, 1990); Susan Strasser, *Satisfaction Guaranteed: The Making of the American Mass Market* (New York: Pantheon, 1989),
146–61; Crossley, 'Early Days of Public Opinion Research,' *Public Opinion
Quarterly* 21, 1 (Spring 1957), 159–64; Childs, 'Rule by Public Opinion,' 757;
Robert Bartels, *The Development of Marketing Thought* (Homewood, Ill: R.D.
Irwin, 1962), 106–20; James R. Beniger, *The Control Revolution: Technological
and Economic Origins of the Information Society* (Cambridge: Harvard University Press, 1986), 387–9; Leonard, *News for All*, 166–7; Sally Clarke, 'Consumers, Information, and Marketing Efficiency at GM, 1921–1940,' *Business and
Economic History*, 25 (1996), 186–95; and Edwin Perkins, 'Market Research at
Merrill Lynch & Co., 1940–1945,' *Business and Economic History*, 25 (1996),
232–41.

36 Converse, *Survey Research*, 88, 91; Crossley, 'Early Days of Public Opinion
Research,' 159, 162; William Albig, *Modern Public Opinion* (New York:
McGraw-Hill, 1956), 184; Spingarn, 'These Public-Opinion Polls,' 98; Childs,
'Rule by Public Opinion,' 757.

37 Elmo Roper conducted the poll. 'A New Technique in Journalism,' *Fortune*,
July 1935, 65.

38 Harry S. Bunker, George H. Gallup, W. Harry Harper, and Charles H. Stout,
The Business Department of School Publications (Iowa City: Lombard Press,
1927).

39 Converse, *Survey Research*, 115. See also Gallup, *Factors of Reader Interest in
261 Advertisements* (New York, 1932).

40 Duke University, Special Collections Library, J. Walter Thompson Collection,
box 4, file 'Minutes of Representatives Meeting,' 17 Nov. 1931.

41 L.E. Firth, *Testing Advertisements: A Study of Copy Testing Methods in Theory
and Practice* (New York: McGraw-Hill, 1934), 227, 229; Donald A. Laird, *How
to Use Psychology in Business* (New York: McGraw-Hill, 1936), 112; H.K.
Nixon, *Principles of Advertising* (New York: McGraw-Hill, 1937), 356; Frank R.
Coutant, 'Testing Advertising Copy,' in E.B. Weiss, F.C. Kendall, and Carroll
B. Larrabee, eds., *The Handbook of Advertising* (New York: McGraw-Hill,
1938), 505; Harold Ernest Burtt, *Psychology of Advertising* (Boston: Houghton
Mifflin, 1938), 23–4; *Printers' Ink*, fiftieth anniversary edition, 28 July 1938,
414, 420; F. Allen Burt, *American Advertising Agencies: An Inquiry into Their
Origin, Growth, Functions and Future* (New York: Harper and Brothers, 1940),

123–4; George Burton Hotchkiss, *An Outline of Advertising: Its Philosophy, Science, Art and Strategy* (New York: Macmillan, 1940), 170, 214, 545; Mark Wiseman, *The Anatomy of Advertising*, vol. 1: *Campaign Planning* (New York: Harper, 1942), xiii, 172; and Herbert C. Ludeke and Ruth A. Inglis, 'A Technique for Validating Interviewing Methods in Reader Research,' *Sociometry*, 5, 2 (1942), 109.

42 Paul Hutchison, 'Who Makes Public Opinion?' *Survey Graphic*, June 1939, 374.

43 'Boy Meets Facts,' *Time*, 21 July 1941, 73; Leo A. Handel, *Hollywood Looks at Its Audience: A Report of Film Audience Research* (Urbana: University of Illinois Press, 1950), 4; David Ogilvy, *Confessions of an Advertising Man* (New York: Atheneum, 1963), 119; Marjorie Fiske and Leo Handel, 'Motion Picture Research: Content and Audience Analysis,' *Journal of Marketing*, 11, 2 (Oct. 1946), 129.

44 Interview with John F. Maloney, Chappaqua, NY, 23 April 1994.

45 O'Malley, 'Black Beans and White Beans,' 21. For example, Americans' cinema-going preferences and habits appeared four times as 'public opinion' in AIPO polls between 1939 and 1942. See Gallup, ed., *The Gallup Poll*, 141, 235–6, 266, 347.

46 CUOHP, Gallup interview, p. 123; FDRL, President's Personal File (PPF) 4721, file 'American Institute of Public Opinion 1936–1940,' William Maulsby to Marguerite LeHand, 31 Dec. 1935. Archibald Crossley similarly conflated commercial market research with public opinion polling: 'The task of locating the beginning of commercial public opinion research ... is made difficult by the fact that it has never been clearly distinguished from marketing research. The two grew together, and the point at which the one merges into the other is often impossible to locate.' 'Early Days of Public Opinion Research,' 158.

47 Converse, *Survey Research*, 109; Henry Link, *The New Psychology of Selling and Advertising* (New York: Macmillan, 1932); Michael M. Sokal, 'The Origins of the Psychological Corporation,' *Journal of the History of the Behavioral Sciences*, 17 (Jan. 1981), 54–67; Link, in a book review of *The Pulse of Democracy*, expressed uncategorical praise for polling: 'No single development in the history of social psychology – probably no development anywhere in the history of psychology – has produced such a wealth of scientifically important material in so short a time as have these polls.' *Psychological Bulletin*, 38 (1941), 117–18.

48 Kerry Buckley, *Mechanical Man: John Broadus Watson and the Beginnings of Behaviorism* (New York: Guilford Press, 1989), 134–47.

49 Pope, *The Making of Modern Advertising*, 6.

50 Merle Curti, 'The Changing Concept of "Human Nature" in the Literature of American Advertising,' *Business History Review*, 41, 4 (Winter 1967), 335–57. See also David P. Kuna, 'The Concept of Suggestion in the Early History of Advertising Psychology,' *Journal of the History of the Behavioral Sciences*, 12 (Oct. 1976), 347–53.

51 Burtt, *Psychology of Advertising*, 4–5. See also Otis Pease, *The Responsibilities of American Advertising: Private Control and Public Influence* (New Haven: Yale University Press, 1958), 203.

52 Hawbaker, 'Taking "the Pulse of Democracy,"' 15–16.

53 J.D. Tarcher, 'The Serious Side of the Comic-Strip,' *Printers' Ink*, 28 April 1932, 4. See also Stephen Fox, *The Mirror Makers: A History of American Advertising and Its Creators* (New York: Morrow, 1984), 138–9; and Pease, *The Responsibilities of American Advertising*, 185–6.

54 Wiseman, *The Anatomy of Advertising*, 172; Raoul Blumberg and Carroll Rheinstrom, 'How Advertising Techniques Are Rated by Gallup Survey,' *Printers' Ink*, 24 March 1932, 17–20.

55 Gallup, 'Newspaper Memorandum,' 26 Feb. 1936, 4, Raymond Rubicam Copy Research Data, Young and Rubicam Archives, New York, cited in Roland Marchand, *Advertising the American Dream: Making Way for Modernity, 1920–1940* (Berkeley: University of California Press, 1985), 70, 68.

56 Marchand, 66–7, 69. On advertising and women, see Susan Smulyan, 'Radio Advertising to Women in Twenties America: 'A latchkey to every home,' *Historical Journal of Film, Radio and Television*, 13, 3 (1993), 299–314; Marilyn Lavin, 'Creating Consumers in the 1930s: Irna Phillips and the Radio Soap Opera,' *Journal of Consumer Research*, 22 (June 1995), 75–89; Stewart Ewen, *Captains of Consciousness: Advertising and the Social Roots of the Consumer Culture* (New York: McGraw-Hill, 1976), 159–76; Michael Schudson, *Advertising, the Uneasy Persuasion: Its Dubious Impact on American Society* (New York: Basic Books, 1984), 178–208; and Andreas Huyssen, 'Mass Culture as Women: Modernism's Other,' in his *After the Great Divide* (Bloomington: Indiana University Press, 1987), 44–62. On gender and consumerism generally, see Victoria de Grazia and Ellen Furlough, eds., *The Sex of Things: Gender and Consumption in Historical Perspective* (Berkeley: University of California Press, 1996).

57 Gallup and Rae, *Pulse of Democracy*, 82; interview with Paul Perry, Princeton, 7 Feb. 1994. On the 1936 election's positive impact on the market research industry, see 'Advertising News and Notes,' *New York Times*, 5 Nov. 1936, 50; and 'Straw Polls Help Market Research,' *New York Times*, 8 Nov. 1936, sec. III, 9.

58 Gallup and Rae, *Pulse of Democracy*, 56–76, 73, 68, 233–4. The woman-as-parasite theme was not new to the twentieth century, as T. J. Jackson Lears

has argued: 'Nineteenth-century political thought politicized the discourse of authenticity, locating public virtue in plain speech and plain living, disdaining the "parasitical" vices of commerce, celebrating the leather-aproned "producer" as the ultimate embodiment of republican reality. The producers were invariably male, the parasites effeminate.' 'Sherwood Anderson: Looking for the White Spot,' in Richard Wightman Fox and Lears, eds., *The Power of Culture: Critical Essays in American History* (Chicago: University of Chicago Press, 1993), 15.

59 RCPOR, 'The 1936–1937 Composite Gallup Poll' data set.

60 For example, 43 per cent of women and 26 per cent of men favoured prohibition in December 1936. Women made up 28 per cent of this sample and the properly weighted results would be 35 dry and 65 wet, slightly different from the 33/67 results reported by the AIPO. A tendency to underreport female opinion by 1 to 3 per cent was also found with questions on capital punishment, voting for a woman as president, and sterilizing habitual criminals and the insane. To determine the full extent of the underreporting of female opinion would require analysing much additional AIPO data from the 1930s and 1940s, an extensive undertaking which exceeds this chapter's scope.

61 RCPOR, 1936–7 Gallup Composite Poll data set.

62 Charles Edward Merriam and Harold Foote Gosnell, *Non-Voting: Causes and Methods of Control* (Chicago: University of Chicago Press, 1924), 7, 25–6; See also Barry D. Karl, *Charles E. Merriam and the Study of Politics* (Chicago: University of Chicago Press, 1974), 148–51.

63 Sara Alpern and Dale Baum, 'Female Ballots: The Impact of the Nineteenth Amendment,' *Journal of Interdisciplinary History*, 16, 1 (Summer 1985), 52.

64 Nancy Cott, *The Grounding of Modern Feminism* (New Haven: Yale University Press, 1987), 104–5.

65 Russell, 'Is Woman Suffrage a Failure?' *Century*, March 1924, 724–30. See also Estelle B. Freedman, 'The New Woman: Changing Views of Women in the 1920s,' *Journal of American History*, 61, 2 (Sept. 1974), 372–5. For later works citing the Merriam-Gosnell study and Illinois turnout figures as proof of female voter apathy, see Gerald M. Pomper, *Voters' Choice: Varieties of American Electoral Behavior* (New York: Dodd, Mead, 1975), 69; and Robert E. Lane, *Political Life: Why People Get Involved in Politics* (Glencoe, Ill: Free Press, 1959), 210. Lane's comments are particularly relevant: 'It appears that a large percentage of the women in the 1920s, and a somewhat smaller per cent now, do not include "voting" in their concept of the things women do, that is, in their image of the female role.'

66 Indeed, this interpretation is found in the 'Gender Gap' entry in the *Handbook*

of American Women's History (New York: Garland, 1990), 227: 'The first generations of women voters after enfranchisement in 1920 seemed generally to
vote along similar lines with their husbands, fathers, and other males. It was
hard to see that women as a group cast their votes differently from men.'

67 Seba Eldridge, 'Public Intelligence: A Study of the Attitudes and Opinions of
Voters,' *Bulletin of the University of Kansas, Humanistic Studies*, 5, 1 (1936),
1–101, esp. 89; Sophinisba Breckinridge, *Women in the Twentieth Century:
A Study of Their Political, Social, and Economic Activities* (New York: McGraw,
1933), 249–56; Charles Hickman Titus, *Voting Behavior in the United States:
A Statistical Study* (Berkeley: University of California Press, 1935), 55.

68 U.S. Bureau of the Census, *Historical Statistics of the United States: Colonial
Times to 1970, pt. 2* (Washington: Bureau of the Census, 1975), 1071–2. In 1912
only the sparsely populated states of Wyoming, Colorado, Utah, Idaho, California, and Washington had full suffrage in place for presidential elections.
Stucker, 'Women as Voters,' 101.

69 Cantril, *Gauging Public Opinion*, 193.

70 AIPO, *The Gallup Political Almanac for 1946* (Manchester, NH, 1946), 230–1.

71 For later works refuting stereotypes of female political apathy and/or high-
lighting increasing rates of women voting in the late 1920s and 1930s, see
Paul Kleppner, 'Were Women to Blame? Female Suffrage and Voter Turnout,'
Journal of Interdisciplinary History, 12, 4 (Spring 1982), 621–43; Sara Alpern and
Dale Baum, 'Female Ballots: The Impact of the Nineteenth Amendment,'
Journal of Interdisciplinary History, 16, 1 (Summer 1985), 43–67; Kristi Ander-
sen, *After Suffrage: Women in Partisan and Electoral Politics before the New Deal*
(Chicago: University of Chicago Press, 1996); David Burner, *The Politics of
Provincialism: The Democratic Party in Transition, 1918–1932* (New York:
Knopf, 1968), 229; Norman H. Nie, Sidney Verba, and John R. Petrocik, *The
Changing American Voter* (Cambridge: Harvard University Press, 1976), 89;
John J. Stucker, 'Women as Voters: Their Maturation as Political Persons in
American Society,' in Laurily Keir Epstein, ed., *Women in the Professions* (Lex-
ington, Mass: Lexington Books, 1975), 106; Joel H. Goldstein, *The Effects of the
Adoption of Woman Suffrage: Sex Differences in Voting Behavior – Illinois, 1914–
21* (New York: Praeger, 1984), 214; and Walter Dean Burnham, 'Theory and
Voting Research: Some Reflections on Converse's "Change in the American
Electorate,"' *American Political Science Review*, 68, 3 (Sept. 1974), 1015.

72 Norval D. Glenn, 'Opportunities and Pitfalls,' in Philip K. Hastings, ed., *Survey Data for Trend Analysis* (Storrs, Conn.: Roper Center for Public Opinion
Research, 1975), I-10, I-13, I-36, I-40.

73 Gallup, 'Unattractive Women,' *Daily Iowan*, 21 July 1921, cited in Hawbaker,
'Taking "the Pulse of Democracy,"' 103.

74 PUA, Bruce and Beatrice Blackmar Gould Papers, box 7, file 41, Gallup to Bruce Gould, 27 May 1942.

75 Hadley Cantril, ed., *Public Opinion, 1935–1946* (Princeton: Princeton University Press, 1951), 556–7.

76 Genevieve Lloyd, *The Man of Reason: 'Male' and 'Female' in Western Philosophy* (London: Methuen, 1984).

77 For a three-thousand-person survey, then, on average fewer than sixty respondents were black, far too few to weight reliably these responses to reflect the black proportion of the American population.

78 *Historical Statistics of the United States*, 14. These figures should also be viewed sceptically, for as Margo J. Anderson has argued, the decennial census consistently underenumerated African Americans. For example, draft registration figures for 1940 indicated a 13 per cent undercount of black males in the 1940 census. *The American Census: A Social History* (New Haven: Yale University Press, 1988), 195, 210–11, 221–2.

79 Glenn, 'Opportunities and Pitfalls,' I-36.

80 Gallup and Rae, *Pulse of Democracy*, 65, 73; Spingarn, 'These Public-Opinion Polls,' 101. That this was also the case in 1944 is evidenced by Hadley Cantril's comments to White House staffer David Niles, who had enquired about black voting: 'Enclosed is the best information I have on it. I have taken this from various Gallup ballots run since September. Not many Negroes are included in any one sample and these figures are based on about 550 cases. So I can't say precisely how reliable they are ... P.S. These figures are from the "political sample" – hence don't include Negroes in the South.' FDRL, PSF 157, file 'Public Opinion Polls 1942–44,' Cantril to Niles, 20 Jan. 1944. I could find only one AIPO poll (Oct. 1936) reporting solely on African American opinion. It was limited to voting intentions – 69 per cent favoured FDR – and, consequently, was done outside of the South. Gallup, ed., *The Gallup Poll*, 36; 'Canvass Shows Negro Voters Favor Roosevelt,' *Cleveland Plain Dealer*, 11 Oct. 1936, 27.

81 Gunnar Myrdal, *An American Dilemma: The Negro Problem and Modern Democracy* (New York: Harper, 1944), 1329, ff. 74. See also Donald Young, *American Minority Peoples: A Study in Racial and Cultural Conflicts in the United States* (New York: Harper, 1932), 208; and Willis D. Weatherford and Charles S. Johnson, *Race Relations: Adjustment of Whites and Negroes in the United States* (New York: Negro Universities Press, 1934 [1969]), 419–20.

82 Harold Gosnell, *Negro Politicians: The Rise of Negro Politics in Chicago* (Chicago: University of Chicago Press, 1935 [1967]), 17; Myrdal, *An American Dilemma*, 493.

83 The following southern papers subscribed to the Gallup Poll in November

1936: *Atlanta Constitution, Birmingham News-Age-Herald, Charlotte News, Chattanooga Times, Durham Herald, Greensboro News, Houston Chronicle, Knoxville News-Sentinel, Louisville Courier-Journal, Lynchburg News and Advance, Memphis Commercial Appeal, Miami Herald, Nashville Banner, Norfolk Virginian-Pilot, Richmond Times-Dispatch, Roanoke Times, Savannah Morning News,* and *Shreveport Times.* FDRL, OF 857, file 'Straw Votes, 1936,' Tibby to McIntyre, 4 Nov. 1936.

84 Among the hundreds of AIPO surveys between 1935 and 1943, only a handful touched on race. There were four questions (Jan. 1937, Nov. 1937, Jan. 1938, Feb. 1940) on federal anti-lynching legislation; one (Oct. 1937) on whether Hugo Black should resign from the Supreme Court for prior KKK membership; one (March 1939) on Eleanor Roosevelt's resignation from the Daughters of the American Revolution for their refusal to allow Marion Anderson to sing in a DAR hall; one (June 1942) on blacks and whites serving together in the military; and one (July 1943) on the causes of the Detroit race riot. Gallup, ed., *The Gallup Poll,* 48, 75, 86, 209, 73, 142, 396; Cantril, ed., *Public Opinion, 1935–1946,* 151–2, 988; Converse, *Survey Research,* 312–13; Paul B. Sheatsley, 'White Attitudes toward the Negro,' *Daedalus,* 95, 1 (1966), 217.

85 Gallup, ed., *The Gallup Poll,* 403.

86 Glenn, 'Opportunities and Pitfalls,' I-36.

87 Maloney interview.

88 Richard Robbins, 'Charles S. Johnson,' in James E. Blackwell and Morris Janowitz, eds., *Black Sociologists: Historical and Contemporary Perspectives* (Chicago: University of Chicago Press, 1974), 83; Ralph J. Bunche, *The Political Status of the Negro in the Age of FDR* (Chicago: University of Chicago Press, 1973), preface; Ben Keppel, *The Work of Democracy: Ralph Bunche, Kenneth B. Clark, Lorraine Hansberry, and the Cultural Politics of Race* (Cambridge: Harvard University Press, 1995); Martin Bulmar, Kevin Bales, and Kathryn Kish Sklar, eds., *The Social Survey in Historical Perspective, 1880–1940* (Cambridge: Cambridge University Press, 1991) xviii. On a more general note, see Patricia Sullivan, *Days of Hope: Race and Democracy in the New Deal Era* (Chapel Hill: University of North Carolina Press, 1996).

89 Myrdal, *An American Dilemma,* 439, 508; Weatherford and Johnson, *Race Relations,* 421.

90 Myrdal, *An America Dilemma,* 1077, 438.

91 Morain, *Prairie Grass Roots,* 42, 37.

92 Carl N. Degler, *In Search of Human Nature: The Decline and Revival of Darwinism in American Social Thought* (New York: Oxford University Press, 1991).

93 Cantril, ed., *Public Opinion,* 988.

94 Cantril, *Gauging Public Opinion,* 148–9.

95 Ibid., 110, 112, 140–1.

96 Gallup testimony, *Hearings before the Committee to Investigate Campaign* (28 Dec. 1944), 1276.

97 Gallup, *A Guide to Public Opinion Polls*, 72–3; see also Gallup and Rae, *Pulse of Democracy*, 239.

98 In 1950 this cohort made up 63.9 per cent of the census but only 52.4 per cent of AIPO samples. In 1960 the respective figures were 56.3 and 48.2 per cent. Glenn, 'Opportunities and Pitfalls,' I-36. Similar forms of sample bias are found in contemporary Gallup polling in less developed countries. A 1995 international Gallup survey of eighteen countries on personal and governmental satisfaction noted that in Chile, India, and Mexico only the urban population was surveyed 'because of the difficulty of reaching a sample of all people.' In India, 'the sample was further restricted to people in middle-class (or higher) neighbourhoods.' 'The International Gallup Poll Report,' *Gallup Poll* (Toronto), 28 June 1995, 9.

99 Daniel Katz, 'Do Interviewers Bias Poll Results?' *Public Opinion Quarterly*, 6, 2 (Summer 1942), 248–68; see also Katz and Cantril, 'Public Opinion Polls,' *Sociometry*, 1, 1 (July–Oct. 1937), 169; and Cantril, *Gauging Public Opinion*, 77, 118.

100 Arthur Kornhauser, 'Are Public Opinion Polls Fair to Organized Labor?' *Public Opinion Quarterly*, 10, 4 (Winter 1946), 484–7, 499. After the 1936 election, when most newspapers backed Landon, books appeared attacking the daily press for anti-liberal bias and pro-business sympathies. See George Seldes, *Lords of the Press* (New York: Julian Messner, 1938); and Harold L. Ickes, *America's House of Lords: An Inquiry into the Freedom of the Press* (New York: Harcourt, Brace, 1939), esp. 17–20.

101 For examples see, Gallup, ed., *The Gallup Poll*, 52, 55, 158, 303, 365, 418–20, 447–8.

102 On sit-down strikes, see AIPO columns, 'Public Favors G.M.C. in American Institute Poll on Sit-Down Strike Stand,' *Cleveland Plain Dealer* (CPD), 7 Feb. 1937, 1; 'Public Opinion Condemns Sit-Down Strikes 3 to 2 in National Opinion Poll,' *CPD*, 21 March 1937, 1; 'Remove Sit-Down Strikers by Force if Necessary, Is Majority Opinion in Poll,' *CPD*, 18 April 1937, 1; 'Sympathy of U.S. Voters for Unions Shows Decline since Big Strikes Began,' *CPD*, 4 July 1937, 1.

103 Gallup, ed. *The Gallup Poll*, 159, 365.

104 Gallup, 'Public Opinion Condemns Sit-Down Strikes,' 28.

105 David P. Thelen, 'The Public against the Historians: The Gallup Poll, 1935–1971,' *Reviews in American History*, 4, 4 (Dec. 1976), 614–18. Kornhauser writes: '[There is] no dearth of questions on unions' interference with war-

time production, but not one on management's hoarding of labor or its self-interested delays in accepting government contracts. [There are] questions on whether labor leaders are "absolutely" honest, but not whether business-men are; on unions' blame for strikes but not on employers' blame for sub-standard wages or for unsafe conditions in coal mines.' 'Are Public Opinion Polls Fair to Organized Labor?' 498.

106 Cantril, ed., *Public Opinion*, 136.

107 O'Malley, 'Black Beans and White Beans,' 24, 22; Cantril, ed., *Public Opinion*, 920. On this general point, survey researcher Albert Blankenship wrote in 1943: 'The very fact that the Gallup poll is subscribed to and paid for by newspapers means that polls have to have material generally acceptable to the newspapers, or they would never have subscribed to it in the first place.' *Consumer and Opinion Research: The Questionnaire Technique* (New York: Harper and Brothers, 1943), 227. For a contemporary attack on news-paper publishers' increasing role as 'spokesmen for special interests,' see Harold L. Ickes, *America's House of Lords: An Inquiry into the Freedom of the Press* (New York: Harcourt, Brace, 1939), esp. 19, 163–4.

108 Gallup and Rae, *Pulse of Democracy*, 169; Gallup, 'We, the People, Are Like This,' *New York Times Magazine*, 8 June 1941, 24.

109 See Gallup and Rae, *Pulse of Democracy*, 246–56; and Gallup's *Public Opinion in a Democracy*, 11–12; *Guide to Public Opinion Polls*, 81–5; 'Putting Public Opinion to Work,' *Scribner's*, Nov. 1936, 39.

110 Leonard Doob, *Public Opinion and Propaganda* (Hamden, Conn.: Archon, 1948), 168. For examples, see Henry T. Moore, 'The Comparative Influence of Majority and Expert Opinion,' *American Journal of Psychology*, 31 (1921), 16–20; David Wheeler and Jordan Howard, 'Change of Individual Opinion to Accord with Group Opinion,' *Journal of Abnormal and Social Psychology*, 24 (1929), 203–6; Clare H. Marple, 'The Comparative Susceptibility of Three Age Levels to the Suggestion of Groups vs. Expert Opinion,' *Journal of Social Psychology*, 4 (1933), 176–86.

111 Winston Allard, 'A Test of Propaganda Values in Public Opinion Surveys,' *Social Forces*, 20, 2 (Dec. 1941), 213.

112 Harwood Childs, 'Rule by Public Opinion,' *Atlantic Monthly*, June 1936, 763.

113 Walter M. Pierce, 'Climbing on the Bandwagon,' *Public Opinion Quarterly*, 4, 2 (June 1940), 241–2; George F. Lewis, Jr, 'The Congressmen Look at the Polls,' *Public Opinion Quarterly*, 4, 2 (June 1940), 230.

114 James A. Farley, *Jim Farley's Story: The Roosevelt Years* (New York: McGraw-Hill, 1948), 79, 232, 330.

115 James MacGregor Burns, *Roosevelt: The Lion and the Fox* (New York: Har-court, Brace, 1956), 445.

116 Paul Hutchison, 'Who Makes Public Opinion?' *Survey Graphic*, 28, 6 (June 1939), 374; Lee, *Daily Newspaper in America*, 599. Two early classics of polling criticism, published shortly after this study's time period, are Herbert Blumer, 'Public Opinion and Public Opinion Polling,' *American Sociological Review*, 13, 5 (Oct. 1948), 542–54, and Lindsay Rogers, *The Pollsters: Public Opinion, Politics and Democratic Leadership* (New York: Alfred A. Knopf, 1949).

117 Significantly, all three of Gallup's undersampled constituencies – women, African Americans, low socio-economic groups – voted disproportionately Democratic. Harvard Sitkoff, *A New Deal for Blacks: The Emergence of Civil Rights as a National Issue*, vol. 1: *The Depression Decade* (New York: Oxford University Press, 1978), 95. In AIPO pre-election polling in 1944, 53 per cent of women favoured Roosevelt, compared to 48 per cent of men. FDRL, PSF 157, file 'Public Opinion Polls, 1942–44,' Cantril to Niles, 12 July 1944.

118 During the early 1970s, Gallup executives secretly passed on advance poll results to Nixon administration officials. This fact, among others, prompted Lawrence R. Jacobs and Robert T. Shapiro to conclude that 'Gallup's optimistic expectations that opinion surveys would only serve to boost government responsiveness' to ordinary citizens was 'undermined.' 'Presidential Manipulation of Polls and Public Opinion: The Nixon Administration and the Pollsters,' *Political Science Quarterly*, 110, 4 (1995–6), 520.

119 Maloney interview; Irving Crespi interview, Princeton, NJ, 25 Feb. 1994; see also O'Malley, 'Black Beans,' 20; Benjamin Ginzburg, 'Dr. Gallup on the Mat,' *Nation*, 16 Dec. 1944, 737; Gallup testimony, *Hearings before the Committee to Investigate Campaign Expenditures*, 1287; Richard W. Steele, 'The Pulse of the People: Franklin D. Roosevelt and the Gauging of American Public Opinion,' *Journal of Contemporary History*, 9, 4 (Oct. 1974), 208; Michael Wheeler, *Lies, Damn Lies, and Statistics: The Manipulation of Public Opinion in America* (New York: Liveright, 1976), 41–2.

120 *Hearings before the Committee*, 1270–1, 1294; Converse, *Survey Research*, 207–11.

121 On the history of sampling methods, see Converse, *Survey Research*, esp. 202–7; William Kruskal and Frederick Mosteller, 'Representative Sampling, IV: The History of the Concept in Statistics, 1895–1939,' *International Statistical Review*, 48 (1980), 188–91; Archibald Crossley, 'Theory and Application of Representative Sampling as Applied to Marketing,' *Journal of Marketing*, 5, 4 (April 1941), 456–61; Alain Desrosières, 'The Part in Relation to the Whole: How to Generalise? The Prehistory of Representative Sampling,' in Bulmar et al., *The Social Survey in Historical Perspective*, 217–44; and Frederick F. Stephan, 'History of the Uses of Modern Sampling Procedures,' *Journal of*

the American Statistical Association, 43 (March 1948), 12–39. For a criticism of the AIPO's use of quota sampling, see Dorwin Cartwright's review of Gallup's book, *A Guide to Public Opinion Polls*, in *Journal of Consulting Psychology*, 9, 4 (July–Aug. 1945), 201–2.

122 Sample bias was not the only Achilles' Heel for Gallup and fellow pollsters Crossley and Roper. A last-minute voter shift to Truman was missed by the polls. They also wrongly projected voter turnout. See Frederick Mosteller, Herbert Hyman, Philip J. McCarthy, Eli S. Marks, and David B. Truman, *The Pre-Election Polls of 1948: Report of the Committee on Analysis of Pre-Election Polls and Forecasts* (New York: Social Science Research Council, 1949).

123 Warren Susman, *Culture as History: The Transformation of American Society in the Twentieth Century* (New York: Pantheon, 1984) 158.

124 On the technocratic dimension of American social reform between 1900 and 1939, see John M. Jordan, *Machine-Age Ideology: Social Engineering and American Liberalism, 1911–1939* (Chapel Hill: University of North Carolina Press, 1994).

125 Susan Herbst, *Numbered Voices: How Opinion Polling Has Shaped American Politics* (Chicago: University of Chicago Press, 1993), 38. See also Sidney Verba, 'The Citizen as Respondent: Sample Surveys and American Democracy,' *American Political Science Review*, 90, 1 (March 1996), 3.

126 For examples, see Benjamin Ginsberg, *The Captive Public: How Mass Opinion Promotes State Power* (New York: Basic Books, 1986); John S. Dryzek, 'The Mismeasure of Political Man,' *Journal of Politics*, 50, 3 (Aug. 1988), 705–25; Christopher Hitchens, 'Voting in the Passive Voice,' *Harper's*, April 1992, 45–52; and Charles T. Salmon and Theodore L. Glasser, 'The Politics of Polling and the Limits of Consent,' in Glasser and Salmon, eds., *Public Opinion and the Communication of Consent* (New York: Guilford Press, 1995), 437–58.

3: Polling Citizens

1 National Archives of Canada (NAC), CCF Papers, MG 28 IV-I, vol. 157, 'Gallup Polls, 1942–45,' CIPO pamphlet, 'Polling Public Opinion,' circa 1945.

2 George Gallup, 'Reporting Public Opinion in Five Nations,' *Public Opinion Quarterly*, 6, 3 (Fall 1942), 431–3; Robert M. Worcester, 'Political Opinion Polling in Great Britain,' in Worcester, ed., *Political Opinion Polling: An International Review* (London: Macmillan, 1983), 61–3; George Gallup and Saul Forbes Rae, *The Pulse of Democracy: The Public-Opinion Poll and How It Works* (New York: Simon and Schuster, 1940), 4–5; L'Institut Français d'Opinion Publique, *L'Institut Français d'Opinion Publique* (Paris: Imprimerie Le Chancelier, 1947), 3; Jean Stoetzel, 'Political Opinion Polling in France,' in Worcester,

ed., *Political Opinion*, 21; Worcester, 'The Internationalization of Public Opinion Research,' *Public Opinion Quarterly*, 51, special issue (1987), S79–S85.

3 Gallup, 'Reporting Public Opinion in Five Nations,' 429. By 1945, Gallup affiliates were also established in Sweden, Denmark, and Finland.

4 Interviews with the Honourable Bob Rae, Toronto, 3 June 1993, 8 Nov. 1995.

5 P.M. Richards, 'He Feels the Public Pulse,' *Saturday Night*, 5 Oct. 1940, 18.

6 NAC, W.L.M. King Papers, MG 26 J 1, vol. 283, C-4566, Benson to King, 20 Aug. 1940.

7 Gallup, 'Reporting Public Opinion in Five Nations,' 433; A.B. Blankenship, Chuck Chakrapani, and W. Harold Poole, *A History of Marketing Research in Canada* (Toronto: Professional Marketing Research Society, 1985), 35.

8 King Papers, vol. 299, C-4860, Armstrong to King, 14 Oct. 1941.

9 King Papers, vol. 326, C225679–83, Rae to Robertson, 28 Nov. 1941.

10 NAC, CCF Papers, vol. 157, file 'Gallup Polls 1942–45,' CIPO brochure, 'Polling Public Opinion,' circa 1945. The CIPO conducted three national surveys in November and December 1941, eleven in 1942, ten in 1943, ten in 1944, and sixteen in 1945. Gallup Canada (GC), Toronto, CIPO questionnaires, 1941–5.

11 Gallup, 'Reporting Public Opinion in Five Nations,' 433. The following dailies subscribed to the CIPO: *Calgary Herald, Edmonton Journal, Galt Reporter, Halifax Herald, Hamilton Spectator, Kingston Whig-Standard, La Presse, L'Action Catholique, Montreal Daily Star, Niagara Falls Review, Ottawa Evening Citizen, Prince Albert Herald, Regina Leader-Post, St. Catharines Standard, St. John Times-Globe, St. Thomas Times-Journal, Sarnia Canadian Observer, Saskatoon Star Phoenix, Sault Ste. Marie Star, Stratford Beacon-Herald, Toronto Star, Vancouver Daily Province, Victoria Daily Times, Welland-Port Colborne Tribune, Windsor Star, Winnipeg Tribune*, and *Woodstock Sentinel-Review.*

12 Duke University, Special Collections Library, J. Walter Thompson Papers (JWT), box 28, file 'Porter, Arthur, 1957–59,' Porter bio., 24 Jan. 1957.

13 GC, 'A History of Gallup Canada,' in-house history, circa 1988, and CIPO questionnaires, 1941–2; Blankenship et al., *History of Marketing Research*, 35; H.T. Stanner, 'Gallup Poll Comes to Canada,' *Canadian Business*, Dec. 1941, 36–7, 100; Wilfrid Sanders, 'How Good Is the Canadian Gallup Poll?' *Public Affairs*, 6, 6 (1943), 136–7; Gallup, 'Reporting Public Opinion in Five Nations,' 433–4; King Papers, vol. 326, 225679–83, Rae to Robertson, 28 Nov. 1941.

14 WIB, vol. 13, file 8–7–B, Ketchum to Boyd, 5 May 1944; Blankenship et al., *History of Marketing Research*, 35; 'The Gallup Polls Are Impartial,' *Toronto Daily Star*, 18 June 1943, 6.

15 Archives of Ontario (AO), Maclean-Hunter Papers, vol. 403, file 'Surveys-Opinion-General,' Irwin to Moore, 27 Nov. 1941.

16 'A.C.A. to Meet in Toronto,' *Canadian Advertising*, fourth quarter, 1941, 26. For an earlier article on Gallup's comic-strip-advertising research, see Frank E. Dowsett, 'Talking Seriously about Humor in Advertising,' *Canadian Advertising*, July 1938, 19–21.

17 'To Conscript or Not, That's Canada's Question – Gallup,' *Toronto Daily Star*, 29 Nov. 1941, 21.

18 'Sees Publication of Polls Contribution to Democracy,' *Toronto Daily Star*, 29 Nov. 1941, 2. Throughout the war, CIPO officials repeatedly used terms like 'scientific,' 'non-partisan,' and 'objective' to describe the work of the institute. See Wilfrid Sanders, *Jack and Jacques: A Scientific Approach to the Study of French and Non-French Thought in Canada* (Toronto: Ryerson Press, 1943), 1; Arthur Porter, 'After Victory, What ... ?' *Canadian Business*, Dec. 1942, 95–6; Sanders, 'How Good Is the Canadian Gallup Poll?' 137.

19 Seymour Martin Lipset, *Continental Divide: The Values and Institutions of the United States and Canada* (New York: Routledge, 1990), xiii, 30. For a recent work on the left- and right-wing varieties of American populism, see Michael Kazin, *The Populist Persuasion: An American History* (New York: Basic Books, 1995).

20 James Bryce, *Modern Democracies*, vol. 2 (New York: Macmillan, 1921), 112. On the relationship between American culture and politics and the development and proliferation of polling in the United States, see Sidney Verba, 'The Citizen as Respondent: Sample Surveys and American Democracy, Presidential Address, American Political Science Association, 1995,' *American Political Science Review* 90, 1 (March 1996), 6–7.

21 Lipset, *Continental Divide* 8, 14; Carl Berger, *The Sense of Power: Studies in the Ideas of Canadian Imperialism, 1867–1914* (Toronto: University of Toronto Press, 1970), 203–5; H. McD. Clokie, *Canadian Government and Politics* (Toronto: Longmans, Green and Co., 1944), 97–9; Robert MacGregor Dawson, *The Government of Canada* (Toronto: University of Toronto Press, 1948), 48; Barry Ferguson, *Remaking Liberalism: The Intellectual Legacy of Adam Shortt, O.D. Skelton, W.C. Clark, and W.A. Mackintosh, 1890-1925* (Montreal and Kingston: McGill-Queen's University Press, 1993), 155; J. Patrick Boyer, *Lawmaking by the People: Referendums and Plebiscites in Canada* (Toronto: Butterworths, 1982), 39–40.

22 William Mishler, *Political Participation in Canada: Prospects for Democratic Citizenship* (Toronto: Macmillan, 1979), 25; W.L. Morton, 'The Extension of the Franchise in Canada: A Study in Democratic Nationalism,' *Canadian Historical Association, Historical Papers* (1943), 73; Bryce, *Modern Democracies*, vol. 1 (New York: Macmillan, 1921), 495. For related commentary, see A.R.M. Lower, 'The Origins of Democracy in Canada,' *Canadian Historical Associa-*

tion, Historical Papers (1930), 70; and Alexander Brady, *Democracy in the Dominions* 3rd edition (Toronto: University of Toronto Press, 1958), 42.

23 Prairie politics from the early 1900s to World War Two, as David Laycock documents, were infused with a wide array of agrarian populist ideas and programs, many with American origins. Populist sentiment also surfaced in Canadian cities, as seen with the campaigns to regulate private utilities. These early 1900s efforts, dubbed 'civic populism' by Armstrong and Nelles, pitted local public officials and community groups against the formidable utility companies and their big business allies. David Laycock, *Populism and Democratic Thought in the Canadian Prairies, 1910–1945* (Toronto: University of Toronto Press, 1990); Christopher Armstrong and H.V. Nelles, *Monopoly's Moment: The Organization and Regulation of Canadian Utilities, 1830–1930* (Philadelphia: Temple University Press, 1986), 145, 148, 151.

24 Gunnar Myrdal, *An American Dilemma: The Negro Problem and Modern Democracy* (New York: Harper and Bros., 1944), 3–9; Bryce, *Modern Democracies*, 1: 496.

25 The three major works on Canadian democracy and politics published in the 1940s contain no index citations for populism or popular sovereignty. Corry's study has three brief page references for public opinion. None of these works discuss public opinion polls. Clokie, *Canadian Government and Politics*; J.A. Corry, *Democratic Government and Politics* (Toronto: University of Toronto Press, 1946); and Dawson, *The Government of Canada*.

26 Canada, *Debates of the House of Commons*, 24 Feb. 1939, 1307–8, cited in Dawson, *The Government of Canada*, 374, 359. On representative democracy in Canada, see Allan Kornberg, William Mishler, and Harold D. Clarke, *Representative Democracy in the Canadian Provinces* (Scarborough: Prentice-Hall, 1982).

27 For examples, see 'He's Ready to Take It,' *Maclean's Magazine*, 1 Jan. 1943, 12, 29–30; 'American Opinion Swinging from Isolationism,' *Saturday Night*, 3 July 1943, 10; 'Pro-Votes and Con-Votes,' *Saturday Night*, 21 Aug. 1943, 29; 'How Good Is the Canadian Gallup Poll?' 136–9; What Canadians Don't Know,' *Maclean's Magazine*, 15 Aug. 1945, 11, 58.

28 Cassandra Sanders, private collection, Toronto; 'Background notes, re Wilfrid Sanders,' n.d.; Blankenship et al., *History of Marketing Research*, 35.

29 'Public Opinion Poll Speeds Democratic War Processes,' *Toronto Daily Star*, 19 Dec. 1941, sec. II, 26.

30 'Big Majority behind "Ceiling" Is Surprise,' *Toronto Daily Star*, 3 Dec. 1941, sec. II, 1; 'Canada's War Effort Satisfied 61 Per Cent on Eve of Jap Attack,' *Toronto Star*, 13 Dec. 1941, sec. II, 1; 'Let Government Pick Jobs 72 P.C. of Canadians Say,' *Toronto Star*, 20 Dec. 1941, 3.

31 GC, CIPO releases, 14 Jan. 1942; 21 Jan. 1941; 28 Jan. 1941; 11 Feb. 1941; 15 April, 1942; 7 March 1941. Sanders, 'He's Ready to Take It,' 12.

32 On the 1942 conscription crisis, see J.L. Granatstein, *Canada's War: The Politics of the Mackenzie King Government, 1939–1945* (Toronto: Oxford University Press, 1975), 201–48; Granatstein and J.M. Hitsman, *Broken Promises: A History of Conscription in Canada* (Toronto: Oxford University Press, 1977), 133–84; C.P. Stacey, *Arms, Men and Governments: The War Policies of Canada, 1939–1945* (Ottawa: Queen's Printer, 1970), 399–402.

33 The AIPO had previously done election forecasts for state referenda.

34 GC, CIPO releases, 28 April 1942; 29 Jan. 1942.

35 Ibid., 21 March 1942; 4 April 1942. Also, college-educated respondents outside Quebec favoured the Yes side by an 80–20 margin, compared to 60–40 support among those with grade 8 education or less. CIPO release, 18 April 1942.

36 GC, CIPO questionnaires, Dec. 1941 to Dec. 1942; CIPO releases, Feb. to April 1942; Sanders to institute editors and promotion managers, 13 April 1942; CIPO releases, 18 April 1942; 25 April 1942.

37 In 1940 Gallup and Saul Rae wrote: 'The goal of present-day surveys is to keep within three to four percentage points of the correct division of the total vote.' *The Pulse of Democracy*, 88. See also Richards, 'He Feels the Public Pulse,' 18; and Sanders, 'He's Ready to Take It,' 30.

38 GC, CIPO releases 28 April 1942, 29 April 1942.

39 *Canada Gazette*, 27 June 1942, 5461. The CIPO later reported in 1945 that its prediction error for the plebiscite had been 5 per cent. GC, CIPO release, 29 May 1945; CCF Papers, vol. 157, 'Gallup Polls, 1942–1945,' CIPO brochure, 'Polling Public Opinion,' ca. 1945.

40 The first CIPO survey available in data form, from May 1945, undersampled rural and small-town residents. Areas with fewer than ten thousand inhabitants constituted 51 per cent of the CIPO sample, compared to 62 per cent of the 1941 census. Conversely, cities with more than one hundred thousand residents totalled 31 per cent of the sample, but only 23 per cent of the census population. Further accentuating this discrepancy were higher rates of rural than urban voting between 1925 and 1945. York University, Institute for Social Research (ISR), CIPO survey #142, May 1945; *Canada Year Book, 1943–44* (Ottawa: Dominion Bureau of Statistics, 1944), 118; Howard A. Scarrow, 'Patterns of Voter Turnout in Canada,' in John C. Courtney, ed., *Voting in Canada* (Scarborough: Prentice-Hall, 1967), 108–9.

41 Granatstein and Hitsman, *Broken Promises*, 171.

42 GC, CIPO release, 6 May 1942; *Canada Gazette*, 27 June 1942, 5461.

43 GC, Porter memo to newspaper subscribers, 7 May 1942.

44 The CIPO did not attempt vote forecasts in 1944 for the Saskatchewan,

Alberta, and New Brunswick elections because these provinces' small populations would incur high levels of sampling error. Ontario and Quebec were large enough to remain within a 4 per cent margin of error. GC, Special Release, 'Gallup Poll States Policy on Elections,' 29 July 1944.

45 GC, CIPO releases, 10 July 1943, 24 July 1943, 3 Aug. 1943, 5 Aug. 1943. Howard A. Scarrow, *Canada Votes: A Handbook of Federal and Provincial Election Data* (New Orleans: Hauser Press, 1962), 211. The CIPO election figures provided on 5 August 1943, and based on near-complete returns, differ marginally from those provided by Scarrow, but the 2.5 per cent error remained unchanged.

46 See 'An Accurate Forecast,' *Vancouver Daily–Province*, 5 Aug. 1943; 'In the "Target Area,"' *Victoria Daily Times*, 6 Aug. 1943, and 'The Gallup Poll,' *St. Catharines Standard*, 5 Aug. 1943; NAC, Wartime Information Board (WIB), RG 36 series 31, vol. 13, file 8–7–A, Porter to Ketchum, 11 Aug. 1943; 'Gallup Poll Scores Again,' *Saskatoon Star-Phoenix*, 7 Aug. 1943.

47 GC, CIPO release, 9 Aug. 1944.

48 GC, CIPO questionnaires, 20 April 1945 through 1 June 1945.

49 GC, CIPO releases, 12 June 1945; 29 May 1945. These findings call into question Mildred A. Schwartz's assertion that 'the record of the [CIPO] in predicting election results has been good. It was only in the election of 1957, when the Institute underestimated the Conservative share of the popular vote by 5 percent, that its figures differed appreciably from the results.' *Public Opinion and Canadian Identity* (Scarborough: Fitzhenry and Whiteside, 1967), 56. In an analysis of CIPO election forecasting from 1945 to 1974, Hugh Whalen concluded that the Gallup Poll had 'not achieved an outstanding record of accuracy in the prediction of Canadian election outcomes.' Whalen, 'The Perils of Polling,' in Paul W. Fox, ed., *Politics: Canada*, (4th edition) (Toronto: McGraw-Hill, 1977), 195.

50 There is no complete compendium of CIPO polls prior to the 1950s. Scattered wartime CIPO polls are found in Hadley Cantril, ed., *Public Opinion, 1935–1946* (Princeton: Princeton University Press, 1951), and Schwartz, *Public Opinion and Canadian Identity*. CIPO results also appeared from 1942 to 1945 in 'Gallup and Fortune Polls,' 'Public Opinion Polls,' and 'The Quarter's Polls' – regular features of *Public Opinion Quarterly*. For opinion surveys on women in wartime industries and the armed forces, see Diane G. Forestell, 'The Necessity of Sacrifice for the Nation at War: Women's Labour Force Participation, 1939–1946,' *Histoire sociale/Social History*, 22 (Nov. 1989), 333–48. On wartime opinions of Germany, see Paul Létourneau, 'Evaluation Canadienne des Perspectives Ouvertes à l'Allemagne, 1943–1945,' *Guerres Mondiales et Conflits Contemporains*, 157 (Jan. 1990), 49–66.

51 GC, Porter to newspaper subscribers, 5 Aug. 1942; CIPO releases, 15 Aug. 1942, 22 Aug. 1942; 'Neutral, If Not in Empire Say Most French-Canadians,' *Toronto Daily Star*, 19 Aug. 1942, 9. See also 'What French Canada Thinks,' *Canadian Business*, Dec. 1942, 35.

52 Sanders, *Jack and Jacques: A Scientific Approach to the Study of French and Non-French Thought in Canada* (Toronto: Ryerson Press, 1943), 3. This work was recently reissued in French with an introduction by Claude Beauregard, Edwidge Munn, and Béatrice Richard, *Jack et Jacques* (Montreal: Comeau et Nadeau, 1996). See also Sanders, 'Canada Looks toward Postwar,' *Public Opinion Quarterly*, 8, 4 (Winter 1944–5), 523–8. On public opinion and French-English relations in Canada, see Schwartz, *Public Opinion and Canadian Identity*, 83–6.

53 Guy Lachapelle also takes up some of these wartime disparities. His analysis, unfortunately, is marred by numerous factual errors. Gallup's decision to found a Canadian affiliate did not at all 'émane directement du bureau du premier ministre King,' but from AIPO and Canadian newspaper officials. Saul Rae was neither Gallup's student nor his 'bras droit'; his PhD came from the London School of Economics and his business involvement with Gallup while in Princeton was not extensive. Wilfrid Sanders was not of American origin, but was born in South Africa and emigrated to Canada as a toddler. See 'La Guerre de 1939–1945 dans l'Opinion Publique: Comparaison entre les Attitudes des Canadiens Français et des Canadiens Anglais,' *Bulletin d'Histoire Politique*, 3, 4 (spring 1995), 202–3.

54 GC, CIPO releases, 2 Sept. 1942, 26 Aug. 1942, 24 Oct. 1942, 27 Jan. 1943, 13 Feb. 1943, 14 July 43. Issues where French and English Canadian views were in tandem include outlawing strikes in war industries, support for labour unions, opposition to titles for national service, Senate abolition, and making English a compulsory subject in all French elementary grades. Sanders, *Jack and Jacques*, 29, 30, 32, 45.

55 MacLennan, *Two Solitudes* (Toronto: Macmillan, 1945).

56 GC, CIPO release, 29 Sept. 1943. The results were CCF 29 per cent, Liberals 28 per cent, and Progressive-Conservatives 28 per cent.

57 On the King government's response to this phenomenon, see Granatstein, *Canada's War*, 249–93; and Doug Owram, *The Government Generation: Canadian Intellectuals and the State, 1900–1945* (Toronto: University of Toronto Press, 1986), 254–317.

58 GC, CIPO releases, 19 May 1943, 22 May 1943, 26 May 1943, 29 May 1943; 8 April 1942, 22 May 1943, 8 April 1944, 12 April 1944. All percentages in the rest of the paragraph are for decided respondents.

59 In October 1944 the CIPO reported that 29 per cent believed family allow-

ances to be a 'political bribe,' 34 per cent held them a 'necessary law,' and 16 per cent, perhaps most astutely, termed them a combination of bribe and necessity. GC, releases, 20 Oct. 1943, 2 Aug. 1944, 14 Oct. 1944, 30 May 1945.

60 GC, CIPO release, 29 May 1943, 17 July 1943, 19 May 1943. In July 1943, Ottawa raised the monthly pension to $25. Owram, *The Government Generation*, 299.

61 GC, CIPO releases, 27 Feb. 1943, 31 July 1943, 2 Oct. 1943.

62 The results were: government ownership (33 per cent); government ownership under other party (6 per cent); private management (47 per cent); undecided (14 per cent). GC, CIPO release, 18 Dec. 1943.

63 The results came in at: government ownership (61 per cent); private ownership (27 per cent); undecided (12 per cent). GC, CIPO release, 29 Dec. 1943.

64 The results were: approving nationalization (28 per cent), disapprove (46 per cent), undecided (26 per cent). GC, CIPO release, 29 April 1944.

65 Twenty-three per cent favoured government ownership, 66 per cent were opposed, and 11 per cent remained undecided. GC, CIPO release, 3 May 1944.

66 The results were: yes (63 per cent), no (23 per cent), undecided (14 per cent). GC, CIPO release, 17 Dec. 1941.

67 The complete figures were: yes (60 per cent), no (25 per cent), undecided (15 per cent). GC, CIPO release, 10 April 1943.

68 GC, CIPO releases, 8 Dec. 1943, 30 Jan. 1943, 10 April 1943, 22 Dec. 1941, 20 Jan. 1942, 9 Feb. 1942, 16 March 1942, 25 Jan. 1943, 17 May 1943, 23 Aug. 1943, 5 June 1944, 22 Jan. 1945. For other Canadian labour polls, see releases for 18 Aug. 1943, 23 Oct. 1943, 11 Dec. 1943, 16 Aug. 1944.

69 The Southam papers were the *Calgary Herald, Edmonton Journal, Hamilton Spectator, Ottawa Evening Citizen, Vancouver Daily Province, Victoria Daily Times,* and *Winnipeg Tribune.* The two Sifton papers were the *Regina Leader-Post* and *Saskatoon Star Phoenix.* The Thompson papers, acquired in 1944, were the *Galt Reporter, Sarnia Canadian Observer, Welland-Port Colborne Tribune,* and *Woodstock Sentinel-Review.* W.A. Craick, *A History of Canadian Journalism,* vol. 2 (Toronto: Ontario Publishing Co., 1959), 293.

70 GC, CIPO questionnaires, 28 Jan. 1942, 21 Feb. 1942, 30 Nov. 1942.

71 The inflation argument was disingenuous. From August 1939 to October 1941 (before the CIPO's formation), the cost of living rose 17.8 per cent. But from October 1941 until April 1945 it rose only 2.8 per cent, owing to wage and price controls and rationing. Granatstein, *Canada's War,* 186.

72 GC, 'A History of Gallup Canada,' 4; Blankenship et al., *Marketing Research in Canada,* 35. The BIPO similarly began commercial polling in the 1940s. Henry

Durant, the BIPO's first director, later recounted: 'People constantly asked us to put questions on our regular surveys and at the beginning I was stupid enough to regard these as a nuisance: then I suddenly realised that this was a beautiful way of making money. It grew and soon had its own Omnibus survey: today [1979] it's one of the things that researchers live off.' Worcester, 'Political Opinion Polling in Great Britain,' in Worcester, ed., *Political Opinion Polling*, 63.

73 WIB, vol. 13, file 8–7–A, Porter to Ketchum, 27 Jan. 1943; Blankenship et al., *Marketing Research in Canada*, 35. For advertising trade press coverage of Gallup's market research practices, see 'Gallup "Measures" Advertising,' *Canadian Advertising*, fourth quarter 1943, 9–11.

74 GC, COC questionnaires, 15 Dec. 1942, 26 April 1942, 10 Sept. 1943, 3 Nov. 1944; CIPO releases 20 Nov. 1943, 11 Dec. 1943; interview with Clara Hatton, Toronto, 19 June 1995; WIB, vol. 13, file 8–7–C, Ketchum to Boyd, 5 May 1944.

75 GC, Sanders memo to newspaper editors, 12 March 1943; CIPO release 12 March 1943.

76 GC, CIPO questionnaire, 12 Feb. 1943; CIPO release, 12 March 1943. (Emphasis added.)

77 GC, CIPO questionnaires, 29 Sept. 1942, 7 July 1944, 3 Nov. 1944, 23 March 1945; CIPO releases, 19 Dec. 1942, 23 Dec. 1942, 20 Sept. 1944, 24 Jan. 1945, 30 June 1945; John Kendle, *John Bracken: A Political Biography* (Toronto: University of Toronto Press, 1979), 218.

78 GC, CIPO release, 29 May 1945; Institute for Social Research (ISR), CIPO survey #142, May 1945.

79 For the 1917 dominion election, only the immediate female relatives of armed forces personnel were given the vote. On female suffrage, see Catherine Lyle Cleverdon, *The Woman Suffrage Movement in Canada* (Toronto: University of Toronto Press, 1950); and Carol Lee Bacchi, *Liberation Deferred? The Ideas of the English-Canadian Suffragists, 1877–1918* (Toronto: University of Toronto Press, 1983).

80 Scarrow, 'Patterns of Voter Turnout in Canada,' 105; and Munroe Eagles, 'Voting and Non-Voting in Canadian Federal Elections,' in Herman Bakvis, ed., *Voter Turnout in Canada* (Toronto: Dundurn Press, 1991), 6–7.

81 For examples, see Mishler, *Political Participation in Canada*, 29; and Scarrow, 'Patterns of Voter Turnout,' 104. A voter survey done after the 1965 general election, admittedly twenty years after our time period, found just 3 per cent more men than women had voted. Canada, *Report of the Royal Commission on the Status of Women* (Ottawa: Queen's Printer, 1970), 353.

82 In 1904 and 1908 the respective voter participation rates were 72 and 70 per cent. In 1930, 1935, and 1945, the rates were 74, 74, and 75 per cent. In 1940,

because of an election-day winter blizzard, the voting rate dipped to 70 per cent. Scarrow, 'Patterns of Voter Turnout,' 105. See also Cleverdon, *The Woman Suffrage Movement in Canada*, 8–9.

83 GC, CIPO releases, 18 March 1942, 28 March 1942, 13 June 1942, 17 Feb. 1943, 4 Sept. 1943, 19 April 1944, 25 April 1945, 23 May 1945; Sanders, *Jack and Jacques*, 2.

84 'Big Majority behind "Ceiling" Is Surprise,' *Toronto Daily Star*, 3 Dec. 1941, sec. II, 1; GC, CIPO releases, 6 Jan. 1943, 26 May 1943, 29 May 1943, 14 Feb. 1944, 10 Oct. 1942, 26 Feb. 1944. Another male-female dichotomous example is found in a 25 September 1943 release on price-and-wage controls: 'the ratio of support is the same with men (who come into direct contact with wage control) and women (who come in direct contact with price control).'

85 Canada, *Canada Year Book, 1946* (Ottawa: King's Printer, 1946), 120; M.C. Urquhart and K.A.H. Buckley, eds., *Historical Statistics of Canada* (Toronto: Macmillan, 1965), 559.

86 For this question, the interviewer's instructions were 'If housewife or student, record occupation of head of family. If retired or unemployed, record former occupation.' GC, CIPO questionnaire, 25 May 1945; ISR, CIPO survey #142, May 1945.

87 Canada, *Canada Year Book, 1946*, 1067.

88 The comparative figures for the June 1945 survey were virtually identical: English (71.0 per cent), French (11.5 per cent), Bilingual (17.5 per cent). ISR, CIPO survey #143, June 1945.

89 Canada, *Canada Year Book, 1943–44* (Ottawa: King's Printer, 1944), 136–7.

90 WIB, vol. 13, file 8–7–B, Estall to Morris, 21 May 1945, Morris to Estall, 26 June 1945.

91 *Canada Year Book, 1943–44*, 136.

92 Ibid., Everett C. Hughes, *French Canada in Transition* (Chicago: University of Chicago Press, 1943), 46–64, 202–6; E. Jacques Brazeau, 'Language Differences and Occupational Experience,' *Canadian Journal of Economics and Political Science*, 24, 4 (Nov. 1958), 532–40.

93 WIB, vol. 13, file 8–7–A, Ketchum to Porter, 9 Feb. 1944; Morris to Ketchum, 14 Feb. 1944; King Papers, vol. 326, C225679–83, Rae to Robertson, 28 Nov. 1941.

94 WIB, vol. 13, file 8–7–B, Estall to Morris, 13 July 1945; Ketchum to Morris, 16 Sept. 1944; Estall to Morris, 21 May 1945.

95 Interview with Clara Hatton, Toronto, 19 June 1995.

96 NAC, Wartime Prices and Trade Board, RG 64, vol. 1460, file A-10–9–23, McDonald to Gibson, 14 July 1945.

97 For examples, see Porter, 'After Victory, What ... ?' *Canadian Business*, Dec. 1942, 68–9, 94–6; Gallup, 'Reporting Public Opinion in Five Nations,' 429–36;

Sanders, 'He's Ready to Take It,' 12, 29–30; Sanders, 'How Good Is the Canadian Gallup Poll?' 138–9; Gallup, 'What Do They Think?' *Maclean's Magazine*, 1 June 1944, 16, 26–7. See also Elmo Roper, 'Public Opinion Survey Seen Aid to Democracy of the Common Man,' *Montreal Gazette*, 1 Dec. 1944.

 98 Lucy Van Gogh, 'The Gallup Poll System Has Its Limitations,' *Saturday Night*, 29 Nov. 1941, 9. BIPO director Henry Durant also concurred that the British were less 'poll conscious' than the Americans, and less supportive of unchecked popular opinion as a governing force. Gallup, 'Reporting Public Opinion in Five Nations,' 432.

 99 H.T. Stanner, 'Gallup Poll Comes to Canada,' *Canadian Business*, Dec. 1941, 37; Clarissa Duff, 'Opinion Moulds Our Future,' *Saturday Night*, 25 Sept. 1943, 16.

100 For examples of highbrow contempt for the civic competence of 'lower element' voters in the early 1900s, see Owram, *Government Generation*, 43–4.

101 NAC, J.W. Dafoe Papers, MG 30 D45, vol. M-80, Harvey to King, 8 June 1943; King Papers, C-7038, Harvey to Macdonald, 6 July 1943 (original emphasis).

102 The poll was originally scheduled for release on 3 April, but after several member newspapers 'objected quite strenuously' to its findings, the advisory board and the CIPO moved to kill it. One member paper, the *Windsor Star*, missed the cancellation notice and published the poll, and these results later received wide dissemination. The Board of Advisors then decided to rerelease the poll to all member newspapers. GC, Sanders memo to member newspapers, 15 June 1943; CIPO release 15 June 1943.

103 Canada, *Debates of the House of Commons*, 16 June 1943, 3698; 22 June 1943, 3882; 16 March 1944, 1510.

104 R.H. Coats, 'The Social Sciences and Public Administration,' *Canadian Journal of Economics and Political Science*, 11, 4 (Nov. 1945), 506; 'The Nonsense and Danger of the "Gallup Poll,"' *Ottawa Journal*, 4 June 1945. Similarly, nine years earlier, a *Journal* editorial informed readers that it would be a 'sorry day when [newspapers] had to follow willy nilly the "man on the street" able to think only as his neighbors think and those neighbors unable or unwilling to base their conclusions on reliable information.' *Ottawa Journal*, 21 Nov. 1936.

105 Canadian Daily Newspaper Association (CDNA), Toronto, 'Report of CDNA Annual Meeting,' 12–13 April 1945, 7, 48; 4–5 April 1946, x.

106 Robert Bothwell and John English, 'The View from Inside Out: Canadian Diplomats and Their Public,' *International Journal* 39, 1 (Winter 1983–4), 61.

107 Porter, 'After Victory, What ... ?' 96; and Sanders, *Jack and Jacques*, 1.

4: Mobilizing Popular Consent

1 Elmo Roper, 'Sampling Public Opinion,' *Journal of the American Statistical Association* (1940), 332-3; cited in Doug Owram, *The Government Generation: Canadian Intellectuals and the State, 1900–1945* (Toronto: University of Toronto Press, 1986), 260; Wilfrid Sanders, *Jack and Jacques: A Scientific Approach to the Study of French and Non-French Thought in Canada* (Toronto: Ryerson Press, 1943), 1.

2 Keenleyside had earned a PhD in history from Clark University, and had had brief teaching stints at Penn State, Brown, and Syracuse universities in the 1920s.

3 National Archives of Canada (NAC), Wartime Information Board (WIB), RG 36, series 31, vol. 25, file 34–628 pt. II, Webster et al. to Keenleyside, 25 Aug. 1939.

4 On World War One, see Jeff Keshen, *Propaganda and Censorship during Canada's Great War* (Edmonton: University of Alberta Press, 1996).

5 University of Toronto Archives (UTA), J.D. Ketchum Papers, B74–0072, file, 'Ketchum and Williams, 1939 memos,' 'Memorandum on War Censorship and Propaganda in Canada from a Psychological Point of View,' Oct. 1939.

6 UTA, Ketchum Papers, file 'Biographical sketches, c.v.' Ketchum c.v., ca. 1958.

7 In December 1940, Webster and other psychologists, including Henry Link, established Opinion Surveys Limited to conduct consumer and public opinion polls. However, soon afterwards, Webster joined the staff of the Canadian Army's Directorate of Special Surveys. Consequently, Opinion Surveys remained mostly dormant during the war. *Bulletin of the Canadian Psychological Association* (BCPA), 1 (1940–1), 6, 14; *BCPA*, 1 (Feb. 1941), 24; *BCPA* 2, 3 (Oct. 1942), 27.

8 Ketchum Papers, file 'Wartime Information Board Public Opinion Report,' Ketchum memos, 'Attitudes of 200 Students Towards the War, Nov. 1942,' and 'Morale Level of 166 University Students in April, 1942'; J.D. Ketchum, 'Morale in Canada,' in Goodwin Watson, ed., *Civilian Morale: Second Yearbook of the Society for the Psychological Study of Social Issues* (Boston: Houghton, Mifflin, 1942), 249, 259–61.

9 Hans E. Skott, 'Attitude Research in the Department of Agriculture,' *Public Opinion Quarterly,* 7, 2 (Summer 1943), 283; Jean M. Converse, *Survey Research in the United States: Roots and Emergences 1890–1960* (Berkeley: University of California Press, 1987), 157; Seymour Sudman and Norman M. Bradburn, 'The Organizational Growth of Public Opinion Research in the United States,' *Public Opinion Quarterly,* 51, special issue (1987), S67–S68.

10 Converse, *Survey Research*, 133–44, 212–13. Paul Lazarsfeld, Bernard Berelson, and Hazel Guidet, *The People's Choice* (New York: Columbia University Press, 1944).

11 Converse, *Survey Research*, 144–53, 380, 154–5, 134, 272.

12 On Cantril's polling work for Roosevelt, see Cantril, *The Human Dimension: Experiences in Policy Research* (New Brunswick, NJ: Rutgers University Press, 1967), 35–64; Richard W. Steele, 'The Pulse of the People: Franklin D. Roosevelt and the Gauging of American Public Opinion,' *Journal of Contemporary History*, 9, 4 (Oct. 1974), 208–12; Ellen Herman, *The Romance of American Psychology: Political Culture in the Age of Experts* (Berkeley: University of California, 1995), 54–5; Converse, *Survey Research*, 152–4.

13 Ibid., 258.

14 Mary J. Wright, 'CPA: The First Ten Years,' *Canadian Psychologist*, 15, 2 (April 1974), 112. This figure questions Barry Ferguson and Doug Owram's contention that only twenty-eight psychologists, sociologists, and geographers held positions in English-speaking Canadian universities in 1939. 'Social Scientists and Public Policy from the 1920s through World War II,' *Journal of Canadian Studies*, 15, 4 (Winter 1980–1), 4.

15 Mary J. Wright and C. Roger Myers, *History of Academic Psychology in Canada* (Toronto: C.J. Hogrefe, 1982), 15–16, 81–5; C.R. Myers, 'Notes on the History of Psychology in Canada,' *Canadian Psychologist*, 6a, 1 (Jan. 1965), 4–13; Karl S. Bernhardt, 'Canadian Psychology – Past, Present and Future,' *Canadian Journal of Psychology*, 1, 2 (June 1947), 51–2; Robert B. MacLeod, *Psychology in Canadian Universities and Colleges* (Ottawa: Canadian Social Science Research Council, 1955), 10–15.

16 Wright, 'CPA: The First Ten Years,' 114. It is noteworthy that the proposed close association between the CPA and federal officials was not adopted by the Canadian Social Science Research Council when it was founded in 1940. The council promoted basic over applied research and opposed funding from government sources. Consequently, psychologists played minor roles in the council's hierarchy and internal affairs. Donald Fisher, *The Social Sciences in Canada: Fifty Years of National Activity by the Social Science Federation of Canada* (Waterloo: Wilfrid Laurier University Press, 1991), 10–13.

17 McNaughton left the National Research Council on 18 October 1939 to become 'Inspector-General of Units of the 1st Canadian Division.' John Swettenham, *McNaughton*, vol. 2, *1939–1943* (Toronto: Ryerson, 1969), 6.

18 Psychologists closely involved in these efforts included E.A. Bott and C.R. Myers of the University of Toronto and N.W. Morton of McGill. Wright and Myers, *History of Academic Psychology in Canada*, 55–7; Terry Copp and Bill McAndrew, *Battle Exhaustion: Soldiers and Psychiatrists in the Canadian Army*,

1939–1945 (Montreal and Kingston: McGill-Queen's University Press, 1990), 12, 28; Wright, 'CPA: The First Ten Years,' 115–18.

19 The two other psychologists were R.B. Liddy of the University of Western Ontario and J.S.A. Bois of the University of Montreal. NAC, WIB, vol. 12, file 8–2–2 pt.1, Lash to Ketchum, 12 Nov. 1941.

20 In addition to Ketchum, the original committee members were R.D. Wallace, principal of Queen's University; R.B. Liddy, a University of Western Ontario psychology professor; Jean-Charles Harvey, editor of *Le Jour*; Huet Massue, a public relations executive at Shawinigan Water and Power Co.; W.S. Thompson, director of public relations at Canadian National Railways; Grace Hyndman of General Engineering Co.; and J.S.A. Bois. WIB, vol. 12, file 8–2–2 pt. 1, 'Order-in-Council authorizing Committee on Morale,' 8 June 1942.

21 Ketchum, 'Psychology and Wartime Information,' *Bulletin of the Canadian Psychological Association* 3, 2 (April 1943), 20–1.

22 WIB, vol. 12, 8–2–2 pt. 2, Bois memo, 'Notes on the Committee for Civilian Morale (First Meeting),' n.d.; Committee on Morale meeting, 19 June 1942; Ketchum memo, 'Civilian Morale in Canada,' 31 March 1942; William R. Young, 'Academics and Social Scientists versus the Press: The Policies of the Bureau of Public Information and the Wartime Information Board, 1939 to 1945,' *Historical Papers* (1978), 226–7.

23 On the American government's wartime use of opinion polling, see Steele, 'The Pulse of the People,' 195–216; Harold F. Gosnell and Moyca C. David, 'Public Opinion Research in Government,' *American Political Science Review,* 43, 3 (June 1949), 564–72; Allan M. Winkler, *The Politics of Propaganda: The Office of War Information, 1942–1945* (New Haven: Yale University Press, 1978); Jean M. Converse, *Survey Research,* 162–236; Michael Leigh, *Mobilizing Consent: Public Opinion and American Foreign Policy* (Westport, Conn.: Greenwood Press, 1976).

24 Ketchum, 'Psychology and Wartime Information,' 23.

25 WIB, vol. 12, file 8–2–2 pt. 2, Committee on Morale Meeting, 8 Sept. 1942; Young, 'Academics and Social Scientists,' 227–8; William R. Young, 'Making the Truth Graphic: The Canadian Government's Home Front Information Structure and Programme during World War II' (PhD dissertation, University of British Columbia, 1978), 45. On Ketchum's career, see Wright and Myers, *History of Academic Psychology in Canada,* 87–8; and obituaries in *O.P.A. Quarterly,* 15, 2 (June 1962), 54–5, and *Globe and Mail,* 25 April 1962, 33.

26 UTA, Ketchum Papers, file '(Radio) What is morale?,' various Ketchum speeches and listeners' correspondence with Ketchum; Rice to Ketchum, 31 March 1942; file, 'War's Third Dimension,' Ketchum speech to Royal Canadian Institute, 24 Jan. 1942.

27 NAC, King Papers, MG 26 J4, vol. 326, C225679–83, Rae to Robertson, 28 Nov. 1941.

28 Robert Bothwell and John English, 'The View from Inside Out: Canadian Diplomats and Their Public,' *International Journal*, 39 (Winter 1983–4), 62. A careful reading of the unpublished King diary between 1941 and 1945 reveals almost no polling references. This is mildly ironic, in light of King's early career as deputy minister of labour, when, Doug Owram contends, 'he seemed to represent the potential for more scientific ... government under the guidance of knowledgeable and rational men.' Such a technocratic orientation, albeit forty years earlier, might normally suggest a stronger embrace of techniques like opinion polling. *Government Generation*, 68.

29 NAC, Mackenzie King Papers, MG 26 J 13, King Diary, 27 Feb. 1942; King Papers, MG 26 J 1, vol. 331, 282985–91, Porter to Turnbull, 30 March 1942; Turnbull to Porter, 3 June 1942; Porter to Turnbull, 5 June 1942; Turnbull to Porter, 6 June 1942; Porter to Turnbull, 8 June 1942. On Ottawa's generally unsuccessful information campaigns aimed at French Canadians, see Young, 'Making the Truth Graphic,' 197–214.

30 NAC, Claxton Papers, MG 32 B 5, vol. 253, 'Claxton memoirs,' 549–55; David Jay Bercuson, *True Patriot: The Life of Brooke Claxton, 1898–1960* (Toronto: University of Toronto Press, 1993), 98.

31 Claxton Papers, vol. 179, file 'Information and Morale in War,' Claxton address to CPSA, 23 May 1941; NAC, Privy Council Office (PCO), RG 2, vol. 15, file D-27–6, Claxton to King, 29 May 1942; Bercuson, *True Patriot*, 103.

32 King Papers, vol. 331, 282992, Rae to N. Robertson, 8 June 1942. Cantril had some previous experience with small-scale polling in Canada. During the plebiscite campaign, Cantril tested clandestine polling methods intended for later use in Axis-occupied countries. Two OPOR interviewers – an American of French descent and a Princeton graduate student – interviewed 207 people in Quebec and Ontario employing a quota sample method. No visible questionnaires were used. Instead, the interviewers memorized questions in advance, presented them to respondents in casual conversation, and recorded answers after the person had left. The survey took place a week before the plebiscite, and its results were off by just 4.5 per cent of the actual vote, a slightly better showing than the CIPO forecast. See Hadley Cantril, *Gauging Public Opinion* (Princeton: Princeton University Press, 1944), 151–6; and Cantril, *The Human Dimension*, 27.

33 King Papers, vol. 331, 282994, Turnbull to Porter, 26 June 1942; Claire Hoy, *Margin of Error: Pollsters and the Manipulation of Canadian Politics* (Toronto: Key Porter Books, 1989), 15. Cantril's involvement with polling done for the Liberal party is discussed in the next chapter.

34 Saul Rae helped draft the questions. King Papers, vol. 331, 282993–5, Porter to Turnbull, 19 June 1942; Porter to Turnbull, 27 June 1942.

35 Gallup Canada (GC), CIPO French and English questionnaires, 7 July 1942; PCO, vol. 15, file D-27–6, Claxton to King, 29 May 1942.

36 King Papers, vol. 331, 283001–2, Turnbull to Porter, 20 Aug. 1942 (emphasis added); Porter to King, 18 Aug. 1942; 'A Confidential Report of a Recent Survey of Public Opinion among French Canadians in the Province of Quebec,' 18 Aug. 1942. Officials were probably dismayed to learn that a thin plurality of French Canadians chose Pétain over de Gaulle as having done the most for the French people, and that among French Canadians familiar with Chalout, 74 per cent held favourable impressions of him.

37 Male youths made up 92 per cent of respondents. Deliberately underrepresented were working-class francophones. Business and professional classes formed 48 per cent of the sample, farmers 30 per cent, and 'hommes de métier' 22 per cent. Lévesque, *Entrez donc. Analyse du comportement familial de la population de langue française au Canada* (Montreal: Les Informations Albert Lévesque, 1944), 15–16.

38 On the history of social surveys, see Martin Bulmar, Kevin Bales, and Kathryn Kish Sklar, eds., *The Social Survey in Historical Perspective, 1880–1940* (Cambridge: Cambridge University Press, 1991).

39 Lévesque had earlier worked with the Psychological Institute to acquire applied psychological techniques for social research. This survey, unfortunately, proved a financial disaster, and 'Les Informations Albert Lévesque' shut down in 1944. Claire Lévesque, 'Albert Lévesque, mon père,' in Jacques Michon, ed., *L'Édition littéraire en quête d'autonomie* (Sainte-Foy: Presses de l'université Laval, 1994), 143–4.

40 WIB, vol. 12, file 8–2–2 pt. 2, Committee on Civilian Morale meeting, 19 June 1942; NAC, Department of External Affairs (DEA), RG 25 (int. 127), vol. 2877, file 1989–40, Lévesque to Irving, 3 Aug. 1942, 'Statistiques sur les habitudes de lectures de la jeunesse étudiante,' and 'Analyse de cinq périodiques préférés de la jeunesse étudiante de langue française,' 3 Sept. 1942; Ketchum to Rae, 22 March 1943.

41 According to the table of probable error in Gallup and Rae, an eighty-four-person sample would have an error margin of about 15 per cent. *Pulse of Democracy: The Public-Opinion Poll and How It Works* (New York: Simon and Schuster, 1940), 70.

42 DEA, vol. 2877, file 1989–40, 'Quebec and the Present War: A Study of Public Opinion,' July 1942.

43 WIB, vol. 13, file 8–7–A, Porter to Lash, 20 Aug. 1942; Lash to Porter, 26 Aug. 1942; Porter to Vining, 27 Aug. 1942; Sanders to Vining, 14 Sept. 1942; Porter

to Vining, 8 Oct. 1942. Porter had also written Stephen Early, Franklin Roosevelt's secretary, asking if he wanted regular CIPO reports. Early declined, citing the polls' availability in American newspapers. Franklin D. Roosevelt Library, Official File 857, file 'Gallup Poll, 1938–1944,' Porter to Early, 5 June 1942; Early to Porter, 9 June 1942.

44 WIB, vol. 13, file 8–7–A, Ketchum to Porter, 30 Sept. 1942; Porter to Ketchum, 5 Oct. 1942; Ketchum to Porter, 14 Oct. 1942; Porter to Ketchum, 28 Oct. 1942; Ketchum to Porter, 30 Oct. 1942; Porter to Ketchum, 2 Nov. 1942; Ketchum to Porter, 4 Nov. 1942.

45 See Young, 'Making the Truth Graphic,' 181–6; and John A. Irving, 'The Psychological Analysis of Wartime Rumor Patterns in Canada,' *Bulletin of the Canadian Psychological Association*, 3, 3 (Oct. 1943), 40–4. The CIPO would on occasion forward to the WIB lists of rumours picked up by interviewers. Some of the rumours making the rounds in mid-January were that U-boats were patrolling in the St Lawrence, that the royal family would soon move to Canada, that all non-essential university faculty members would soon be let go, and that civil servants were not paying taxes. WIB, vol. 13, file 8–7–A, Porter to Ketchum, 27 Jan. 1943; Ketchum to Porter, 2 March 1943.

46 GC, CIPO questionnaire, 15 Dec. 1942.

47 WIB, vol. 13, file 8–7–A, Ketchum to Porter, 17 Dec. 1942; Dunton to Porter, 7 Jan. 1943; Ketchum to Porter, 5 Jan. 1943.

48 WIB, vol. 13, 8–7–A, Ketchum to Porter, 9 Feb. 1943.

49 For example, Ketchum and Davidson Dunton requested multiple breakdowns for the institute's 13 March 1943 release on attitudes towards transferring powers from provincial to federal control. GC, CIPO release, 13 March 1943; WIB, vol. 13, file 8–7–A, Ketchum to Morris, 20 March 1943; Morris to Ketchum, 24 June 1943; Ketchum to Morris, 17 Aug. 1943; Ketchum to Morris, 21 March 1944; ibid., file 8–7–B, Ketchum to Morris, 7 Aug. 1944; Morris to Ketchum, 23 Aug. 1944; Morris to Ketchum, 19 Sept. 1944; Ketchum to Morris, 14 Dec. 1944; Porter to Ketchum, 26 Feb. 1945.

50 WIB, vol. 13, file 8–7–A, Porter to Ketchum, 6 Jan. 1943; Ketchum to Porter, 29 Jan. 1943; Porter to Ketchum, 18 Aug. 1943.

51 Ibid., Ketchum to Porter, 29 Jan. 1943.

52 PCO, vol. 12, Cabinet War Committee meetings, 21 Jan. 1943, 27 Jan. 1943; Young, 'Academics and Social Scientists,' 231–2; WIB, vol. 13, file 8–7–A, Ketchum to Porter, 13 Feb. 1943; DEA, vol. 2252, file 4310–40c pt. 1, WIB meeting, 22 Feb. 1943.

53 King Papers, vol. 376, file 3944, Heeney to King, 22 Feb. 1943; PCO, vol. 12, Cabinet War Committee meeting, 3 March 1943; DEA, vol. 2252, file 4310–40c pt. 1, Heeney to Grierson, 5 March 1943.

54 Young, 'Academics and Social Scientists,' 231.
55 Gary Evans, *John Grierson and the National Film Board: The Politics of Wartime Propaganda* (Toronto: University of Toronto Press, 1984), 28–9. For works on Grierson, labelled the 'father' of documentary cinema, see Jack C. Ellis, *John Grierson: A Guide to References and Resources* (Boston: G.K. Hall, 1986); James Beveridge, *John Grierson: Film Master* (New York: Macmillan, 1978); Forsyth Hardy, *Grierson on Documentary* (Berkeley: University of California Press, 1966); Hardy, *John Grierson: A Documentary Biography* (London: Faber and Faber, 1979); Elizabeth Sussex, *The Rise and Fall of British Documentary: The Story of the Film Movement Founded by John Grierson* (Berkeley: University of California Press, 1975); and Ian Aiken, *Film and Reform: John Grierson and the Documentary Film Movement* (London: Routledge, 1990).
56 Walter Lippmann, *Public Opinion* (New York: Macmillan, 1922), 11, 16; Lippmann, *The Phantom Public* (New York: Harcourt, Brace, 1925), 198–9.
57 Evans, *John Grierson*, 35.
58 Claxton Papers, vol. 148, file, 'Education # 4,' Grierson speech to Rockcliffe Home and School Club, 3 Nov. 1941. Claxton was highly enamoured of Grierson, who riled many government officials: 'If John Grierson is a dangerous character, it is high time we had more of them ... people who do things just as well as they can without thought of the political consequences, who are willing to throw up their job the second there is the least sign of interference from any improper source, who speak the truth in terms that ring around the world.' Ibid., vol. 44, file 'H.E. Kidd,' Claxton to Kidd, 18 June 1942.
59 On Grierson and the WIB, see Evans, *John Grierson*, 89–109; and Young, 'Making the Truth Graphic,' 51–60, 104–5.
60 WIB, vol. 13, file 8–7–A, Ketchum to Porter, 9 Feb. 1943, 13 Feb. 1943, 25 Feb. 1943, 2 March 1943; Porter to Ketchum, 2 March 1943.
61 Ibid., file 8–7–A, Ketchum to Porter, 8 March 1943; Porter to Ketchum, 9 March 1943; Ketchum to Porter, 14 April 1943; Porter to Ketchum, 15 May 1943; Ketchum to Porter, 18 May 1943.
62 Unfortunately, the survey questions and results are not found in the correspondence.
63 WIB, vol. 13, file 8–7–A, Sanders to Ketchum, 26 May 1943; Ketchum to Sanders, 28 June 1943; Sanders to Ketchum, 30 June 1943; Ketchum to Sanders, 7 July 1943; Ketchum to Porter, 18 Aug. 1943; Porter to Ketchum, 16 Nov. 1943.
64 GC, AIPO release, 22 Nov. 1943. In addition to the tax question, the column reported on whether Canada was more successful in controlling prices and whether it was doing its utmost to win the war. 'No opinion' responses, at 47 and 33 per cent respectively, were unusually high.
65 WIB, vol. 13, file 8–7–A, Ketchum to Porter, 13 March 1943; Porter to

Ketchum, 16 March 1943; GC, Canadian Opinion Company questionnaire, 26 April 1943.

66 DEA, vol. 2252, file 4310–40C pt. 2, 'Report on Activities of [WIB] Executive Personnel, May 10–June 12, 1943,' ca. June 1943.

67 WIB, vol. 13, file 8–7–A, Morris to Ketchum, 31 May, 1943.

68 NAC, Department of Labour, vol. 1, NFB meeting, 8 June 1943, cited in Evans, *John Grierson*, 108–9. Young, 'Making the Truth Graphic,' 224.

69 WIB, vol. 1, file 1–2–22, Ketchum memo 'W.I.B. and Canadian Statistics,' 1 Feb. 1944; Young, 'Making the Truth Graphic,' 65–6.

70 Donald Fisher, *The Social Sciences in Canada* (Waterloo: Wilfrid Laurier Press, 1991), 10–13. On Innis, see William Christian, ed., *The Idea File of Harold Adams Innis* (Toronto: University of Toronto Press, 1980); Michael Gauvreau, 'Baptist Religion and the Social Science of Harold Innis,' *Canadian Historical Review*, 76, 2 (June 1995), 161–204; and the special Innis issue of *Journal of Canadian Studies*, 12, 5 (Winter 1977). On the history of the social sciences in Canada, see Marlene Shore, *The Science of Social Redemption: McGill, the Chicago School, and the Origins of Social Research in Canada* (Toronto: University of Toronto Press, 1987); Barry Ferguson and Doug Owram, 'Social Scientists and Public Policy from the 1920s through World War II,' *Journal of Canadian Studies*, 15, 4 (Winter 1980–1), 3–17; Doug Owram, *The Government Generation: Canadian Intellectuals and the State 1900–1945* (Toronto: University of Toronto Press, 1986); and Barry Ferguson, *Remaking Liberalism: The Intellectual Legacy of Adam Shortt, O.D. Skelton, W.C. Clark and W.A. Mackintosh 1890–1925* (Montreal: McGill-Queen's University Press, 1993).

71 On this theme, see Yaron Ezrahi, *The Descent of Icarus: Science and the Transformation of Contemporary Democracy* (Cambridge: Harvard University Press, 1990).

72 WIB, vol. 13, file 8–7–A, Ketchum to Porter, 13 Sept. 1943.

73 M.C. Urquhart and K.A.H. Buckley, eds., *Historical Statistics of Canada* (Toronto: Macmillan, 1965), 14–15.

74 GC, CIPO releases, 25 Sept. 1943, 6 March 1943. See J.L. Granatstein, *Canada's War: The Politics of the Mackenzie King Government, 1939–1945* (Toronto: Oxford University Press, 1975), 182–3; and Pauline Jewett, 'The Wartime Prices and Trade Board: A Case Study in Canadian Public Administration' (PhD dissertation, Harvard University, 1950), 254.

75 Urquhart and Buckley, *Historical Statistics*, 298, 304. On the Great War experience with economic controls, see Robert Craig Brown and Ramsay Cook, *Canada, 1896–1921: A Nation Transformed* (Toronto: McClelland and Stewart, 1974), 228–49.

76 On Pickersgill's support for wartime controls, expressed in a mid-August

memo to King, see J.W. Pickersgill, *The Liberal Party* (Toronto: McClelland and Stewart, 1962), 32–3.

77 King Papers, vol. 341, 293397–401, Grierson to Pickersgill, 17 Sept. 1943; WIB, vol. 13, file 8–7–B, Dunton to Grierson, 21 Sept. 1943; ibid, file 8–7–A, Ketchum to Porter, 21 Sept. 1943 and 23 Sept. 1943. See also Young, 'Making the Truth Graphic,' 85; and Evans, *John Grierson*, 102–3.

78 For an account of this meeting, see Reginald Whitaker, *The Government Party: Organization and Financing the Liberal Party of Canada, 1930–1958* (Toronto: University of Toronto Press, 1977), 146–52.

79 PCO, RG 2 7C, vol. 12, Cabinet War Committee, 21 Oct. 1943; King Papers, vol. 376, file 3944, 'WIB Revised Estimates, 1943–44'.

80 Bercuson, *True Patriot*, 114.

81 Ketchum Papers, file 'Wartime Information Board,' Canadian Opinion Company survey, Oct. 1943.

82 GC, CIPO releases, 20 Nov. 1943, 22 Sept. 1943; WIB, vol. 13, file 8-7-A, Ketchum to Porter, 23 Sept. 1943.

83 Young, 'Academics and Social Scientists,' 235; Bercuson, *True Patriot*, 122–4, 135; WIB, vol. 8, file 2–14–1, Dunton to Claxton, 3 June 1943.

84 'Are you in favour of your province making any constitutional adjustment to enable the Dominion to adopt the measures after the war necessary to control inflation and produce maximum employment?' Claxton Papers, vol. 140, file DP-4–3, Claxton to Ketchum, 3 March 1944.

85 The question was: 'Do you think the problem of making plans to provide jobs for everyone after the war should be up to the Federal government in Ottawa or up to the government in each of the provinces?' The results were: federal (38 per cent); provincial (21 per cent); both (36 per cent); neither (1 per cent); undecided (4 per cent). GC, CIPO questionnaire, 3 March 1944; WIB, vol. 13, file 8-7-B Ketchum to Porter, 4 March 1944. Claxton Papers, vol. 140 file DP-4-3, Ketchum to Claxton, 31 March 1944; Claxton to Skelton, 3 April 1944.

86 WIB vol. 13, file 8-7-B, Ketchum to Morris, 4 March 1944; King Papers, vol. 362, 313757–61, Ketchum to Turnbull, 6 April 1944. Forty-seven per cent picked the independent option, 46 per cent the imperial one, and 7 per cent were undecided. GC, CIPO release, 25 March 1944, CIPO questionnaire, 21 April 1944; WIB, vol. 13, file 8-7-B, Claxton to Dunton, 30 March 1944; Ketchum to Porter, 30 March 1944; Dunton to Claxton, 5 April 1944; Ketchum to Porter, 24 April 1944; Porter to Ketchum, 26 April 1944; Ketchum to Porter, 28 April 1944.

87 GC, CIPO release, 17 May 1944. The questions were 1) 'Do you think the Dominions and Britain should send delegates to an Empire Council to try to

plan how they will deal with other countries in the world?' 2) 'If this were done do you think Canada and the other British nations should agree to deal with other countries in whatever way the majority of such a council decides, or do you think Canada should be free to act herself?'

88 WIB, vol. 4, files 1-3-26 and 1-3-27, WIB Monthly Reports, July and August 1945; WIB, vol. 13, file 8-7-B, Estall to Morris, 21 Aug. 1945. H.E. Kidd, an advertiser and Liberal partisan, praised Claxton's political handling of the conference: 'Public opinion is being prepared skilfully and here I see your hand and influence at work.' Claxton Papers, vol. 44, file 'Kidd, H.E.,' Kidd to Claxton, 3 Aug. 1945. For an overview of the conference, see Doug Owram, *The Government Generation*, 318–26.

89 On the NSS, see C.P. Stacey, *Arms, Men and Governments: The War Policies of Canada, 1939–1945* (Ottawa: Queen's Printer, 1970), 124–5, 406–13.

90 WIB, vol. 13, file 8-7-B, Grierson to Davis, 16 Sept. 1943; Grierson to Mac-Namara, 14 Oct. 1943; Gallup to Grierson, 15 Oct. 1943; MacNamara to Grierson, 25 Oct. 1943; Dunton to MacNamara, 23 March 1944; MacNamara to Dunton, 23 March 1944.

91 Ibid., Dunton to Local Draft Board no. 13, Fort Lee, NJ, 23 Feb. 1944; Ketchum to Dunton, 21 March 44; Ketchum to Porter, 23 March 1944; Sanders to Ketchum, 28 Dec. 1944; Dunton to Local Draft Board no. 13, Fort Lee, NJ, 19 Feb. 1945.

92 Ibid., file 8-7-C 'COC Survey Bills,' June 1943 to July 1945.

93 Ibid., file 8-7-B, Ketchum to Sanders, 12 Sept. 1944; Ketchum to Sanders, 14 Sept. 1944; Ketchum to Morris, 14 Dec. 1944; Ketchum to Porter, 19 March 1945; Estall to Sanders, 28 June 1945; Morris to Estall, 29 June 1945; Ketchum to Sanders, 15 Nov. 1944; Porter to Ketchum, 26 Feb. 1945; Ketchum to Morris, 26 Sept. 1944.

94 From January 1944 until May 1945 private and public CIPO poll results were included in these cabinet memoranda on the following dates: 14 Feb. 1944; 21 Feb. 1944; 28 Feb. 1944; 20 March 1944; 10 April 1944; 17 April 1944; 1 May 1944; 15 May 1944; 22 May 1944; 5 June 1944; 19 June 1944; 18 July 1944; 31 July 1944; 7 Aug. 1944; 14 Aug. 1944; 28 Aug. 1944; 11 Sept. 1944; 16 Oct. 1944; 13 Nov. 1944; 8 Jan. 1945; 22 Jan. 1945; 12 Feb. 1945; 19 March 1945; 26 March 1945; 23 April 1945; 30 April 1945; and 14 May 1945. King Papers, vol. 376, file 3944.

95 WIB, vol. 3, file 1-3-1, WIB Monthly Report (Reports Branch), Oct. 1943; ibid., vol. 2, file 1-3-1, WIB Monthly Report (Reports Branch), Nov. 1943, March 1944; WIB, vol. 13, file 8-7-B, Estall to Morris, 24 Aug. 1944.

96 WIB, vol. 2, file 1-3-1, WIB Monthly Report (Reports Branch), June 1944, December 1944; ibid., vol. 3, file 1-3-1, WIB Monthly Reports, Jan. and Feb.

1945; ibid., vol. 4, file 1-3-25, WIB Monthly Reports (March 1945) and WIB Report for April–May–June 1945; WIB, vol. 13, file 8-7-B, Ketchum to Sanders, 9 Nov. 1944.

97 For example, extensive polling on French Canadian attitudes towards the war did not change the fact that the WIB's French-language campaigns were generally poorly conceived and executed, often consisting of little more than English translations. See Young, 'Making the Truth Graphic,' 197–214.

98 Jeff Keshen, 'One for All or All for One: Government Controls, Black Marketing and the Limits of Patriotism, 1939–1947,' *Journal of Canadian Studies*, 29, 4 (Winter 1994–5), 111–12; Granatstein, *Canada's War*, 174–86. For other commentary on the WPTB, see K.W. Taylor, 'Canadian War-Time Price Controls, 1941–6,' *Canadian Journal of Economics and Political Science*, 13, 1 (Feb. 1947), 81–98; and Joseph Schull, *The Great Scot: A Biography of Donald Gordon* (Montreal: McGill-Queen's University Press, 1979), 51–116. See also, Ernest J. Spence, 'Canada's Wartime Prices and Trade Board, 1941–1947' (PhD dissertation, Northwestern University, 1947); Jewett, 'The Wartime Prices and Trade Board,' and Christopher Waddell, 'The Wartime Prices and Trade Board: Price Control in Canada During World War II' (PhD dissertation, York University, 1981); and Young, 'Making the Truth Graphic,' 229–51.

99 King Papers, vol. 331, 282987, Porter to Turnbull, 4 June 1942; 282992, Rae to Robertson, 8 June 1942. WIB vol. 13, file 8–7–A, Porter to Ketchum, 4 March 1943; Keshen, 'One For All,' 112; GC, CIPO questionnaires, 6 Nov. 1941, 3 Dec. 1941. Some of the questions, with results in parentheses, were: 'Have you heard or read about the new law which keeps prices and wages from going higher?' (yes 90 per cent, no 10 per cent); 'Do you have a clear idea of what this law involves so far as *you personally* are concerned?' (yes 55 per cent, no 45 per cent) 'Is there any particular thing about the new law that you would like to know more about?' (yes 40 per cent, no 60 per cent) 'If yes, then what?'

100 Fifty-nine per cent expected rationing for 'clothing, food and other materials.' GC, CIPO questionnaire, 24 Dec. 41.

101 GC, CIPO questionnaires, 28 Jan. 1942, 21 Feb. 1942, 7 March 1942, 11 April 1942, 30 Nov. 1942; WIB, vol. 13, file 8-7-A, Porter to Ketchum, 1 Dec. 1942; Waddell, 'The Wartime Prices and Trade Board,' 604–12.

102 GC, CIPO questionnaires, 12 Feb. 1943, 16 April 1943, 2 July 1943, 14 Jan. 1944. Almost every survey from 1943 until the war's end contained at least one question on rationing, conservation, or price and wage controls. GC, CIPO questionnaires, 1943 to 1945 passim.

103 NAC, WPTB, RG 64, vol. 1460, file A-10-9-23, Statistics Branch survey

results, 15 Feb. 1944; ibid., vol. 1536, 'Trends' (WPTB newsletter), 1–15 Oct. 1944, 15–31 Oct. 1944; Waddell, 'Wartime Prices and Trade Board,' 610–12. On discontentment with and evasion of WPTB measures, see Keshen, 'One for All.'

104 Converse, *Survey Research in the United States*, 91–2; Duke University, Special Collections Library, J. Walter Thompson Collection, reel 224, 'Report on a Questionnaire to Housewives Regarding Baking Powder,' Oct. 1934; reel 233, 'Garment Tag Survey,' Sept. 1936; Lazarsfeld et al., *The People's Choice*.

105 On the Women's Institutes, see Linda M. Ambrose, '"What are the Good of those Meetings Anyways?": Early Popularity of the Ontario Women's Institutes,' *Ontario History*, 87, 1 (March 1995), 1–20; and Ambrose, *For Home and Country: The Centennial History of the Women's Institutes in Ontario* (Erin, Ont.: Boston Mills Press, 1996).

106 Joseph Schull, *The Great Scot: A Biography of Donald Gordon* (Montreal: McGill-Queen's University Press, 1979), 66; see also Spence, 'Canada's Wartime Prices and Trade Board,' 268.

107 WPTB, vol. 1460, file A-10-9-23, Henry King memo, 'The Use of Preserves Coupons, and Consumer Panels, 1944,' Feb. 1945; memo 'Metal Household Appliances Survey,' 18 Aug. 1944.

108 See chapter 1. For a March 1945 survey on household goods, King emulated practices he had developed in the late 1920s with Cockfield, Brown. He secured the help of professors at McGill, University of Toronto, University of Western Ontario, University of British Columbia, University of Manitoba, and Regina College. University students were also used to conduct interviewing. WPTB, vol. 1460, file A-10-9-23, King to Donald Gordon, 21 Feb. 1945; McDonald memo, 'Summary Report on Supplies and Household Goods,' 28 March 1945.

109 WPTB, vol. 1460, file A-10-9-23, McDonald memos, 'Consumer Panel Surveys,' 30 Jan. 1945, and 'The Population Sample for Consumer Surveys,' 12 Feb. 1945; King memo, 'Consumer Panels,' 21 Feb. 1945; King memo, 'Consumer Panels,' 21 Feb. 1945; 'Consumer Questionnaire Analysis: Report No. 1,' 6 Sept. 1945; 'Consumer Questionnaire Analysis: Report No. 2,' 1 Oct. 1945; 'Consumer Questionnaire Analysis: Report No. 3,' 8 Feb. 1946.

110 Ibid., 'Consumer Questionnaire Analysis: Report No. 2,' 1 Oct. 1945.

111 Ibid., Parkinson to Gibson, 27 Jan. 1944. For similar views by postwar manufacturers towards female consumers, see Joy Parr, 'Shopping for a Good Stove: A Parable about Gender, Design, and the Market,' in Parr, ed., *A Diversity of Women: Ontario, 1945–1950* (Toronto: University of Toronto Press, 1995), 82, 84.

112 WPTB, vol. 1460, file A-10-9-23, 'A Nation-Wide Survey of Canadian Attitudes toward Wartime Ceilings and Rationing,' June 1944.

113 WPTB, vol. 1536, 'Report No. 1: Canadian Opinion in March, 1945,' 30 April 1945; 'Report No. 2: Canadian Opinion in May, 1945,' 7 July 1945.

114 Ibid., 'Report No. 3: Canadian Opinion in July, 1945,' 31 Aug. 1945; 'Report No. 3A: Resumé of Canadian Opinion on Rationing,' 1 Oct. 1945; Waddell, 'Wartime Prices and Trade Board,' 612–16.

115 Waddell, 'Wartime Prices and Trade Board,' 619.

116 Walter Lippmann, *A Preface to Morals* (New York: Macmillan, 1929), 283; John English, *The Decline of Politics: The Conservatives and the Party System* (Toronto: University of Toronto Press, 1977), 110.

117 For an excellent discussion of the wartime tension between bureaucratic rule – 'technocratic liberalism' – and individual freedom, see Owram, *The Government Generation*, 254–75.

118 James T. Kloppenberg, 'Democracy and Disenchantment: From Weber and Dewey to Habermas and Rorty,' in Dorothy Ross, ed., *Modernist Impulses in the Human Sciences, 1870–1930* (Baltimore: Johns Hopkins University Press, 1994), 79. On this theme, see especially John M. Jordan, *Machine-Age Ideology: Social Engineering and American Liberalism, 1911–1939* (Chapel Hill: University of North Carolina Press, 1994).

5: Pols and Polls

1 Spencer, 'We Went to the People,' *Canadian Forum*, 21 (April 1941), 23; F.W. Gross (Cockfield, Brown advertiser) in National Archives of Canada (NAC), H.E. Kidd Papers, MG 32 G9, vol. 21, file 1, Gross to Kidd, 24 March 1944; Gallup Canada (GC), Toronto, CIPO release, 29 May 1945.

2 Richard Gwyn, 'Ad-Men and Scientists Run This Election,' *Financial Post*, 28 April 1962, reprinted in Hugh G. Thorburn, ed., *Party Politics in Canada*, 2nd edition (Toronto: Prentice-Hall, 1967), 121–3.

3 Joseph Wearing, *Strained Relations: Canadian Parties and Voters* (Toronto: McClelland and Stewart, 1988), 91. On the 1962 election, see Wearing's *The L-Shaped Party: The Liberal Party of Canada, 1958–1980* (Toronto: McGraw-Hill, 1981), 33–42. On Liberal campaign management in the early 1960s, see Christina McCall-Newman, *Grits: An Intimate Portrait of the Liberal Party* (Toronto: Macmillan, 1982), and A.B. Blankenship, Chuck Chakrapani, W. Harold Poole, *A History of Marketing Research in Canada* (Toronto: Professional Marketing Research Society, 1985), 85.

4 The polling industry's generally short-sighted view of its own history is seen in Walker's statement that the 'public-opinion business emerged simulta-

neously over the past three decades [since the late 1950s] within academic circles as well as in the commercial world.' David C. Walker, 'Pollsters, Consultants, and Party Politics in Canada,' in Alain G. Gagnon and A. Brian Tanguay, eds., *Canadian Parties in Transition* (Scarborough: Nelson Canada, 1989), 387; Khayyam Zev Paltiel, 'Political Marketing, Party Finance and the Decline of Canadian Parties,' in ibid., 341. Paltiel does, however, note in passing that such polling 'activities [were] traceable to the 1940s.'

5 Robert Fulford glibly asserts that 'ever since [his] visitation, Louis Harris has occupied among Canadian pollsters a position equivalent to that of a major saint in the Roman Catholic Church.' See 'Election Frauds,' *Saturday Night*, Nov. 1992, 72. For other accounts locating the rise of electoral polling in the early 1960s, see Jeffrey Simpson, 'Pollstruck,' *Policy Options*, March 1987, 3–7; Fulford, 'This Brain for Hire,' *Saturday Night*, Dec. 1985, 33–4; Claire Hoy, *Margin of Error: Pollsters and the Manipulation of Canadian Politics* (Toronto: Key Porter, 1989), 21–2.

6 Walter L. Gordon, *A Political Memoir* (Toronto: McClelland and Stewart, 1977), 97–9; Keith Davey, *The Rainmaker: A Passion for Politics* (Toronto: Stoddart, 1986), 45–6.

7 For American historical works on this topic, see Larry J. Sabato, *The Rise of Political Consultants: New Ways of Winning Elections* (New York: Basic Books, 1981), and Robert B. Westbrook, 'Politics as Consumption: Managing the Modern American Election,' in Richard Wightman Fox and T.J. Jackson Lears, eds., *The Culture of Consumption: Critical Essays in American History, 1880–1980* (New York: Pantheon, 1983), 143–73. For contemporary works, see Gary A. Mauser, *Political Marketing: An Approach to Campaign Strategy* (New York: Praeger, 1983); Nicholas J. O'Shaughnessy, *The Phenomenon of Political Marketing* (London: Macmillan, 1990); and Philippe J. Maarek, *Political Marketing and Communication* (London: John Libbey and Co., 1995).

8 The *Canadian Periodical Index* (1938–47) lists Spencer as a pseudonym. No other 'Spencer' articles appear in the *CPI* before 1940 or after 1941. Nor is he mentioned in John Robert Colombo's *Colombo's Names and Nicknames* (Toronto: NC Press, 1978).

9 Spencer, 'Does It Sell the Stuff?' *Canadian Forum*, 20 (Oct. 1940), 215.

10 Spencer, 'Pardon Me, Madam, How Often Do You Take a Bath?' *Canadian Forum*, 20 (Dec. 1940), 274–6.

11 On the movement/party dualism, see Walter D. Young, *The Anatomy of a Party: The National CCF, 1932–1961* (Toronto: University of Toronto Press, 1969); Leo Zakuta, *A Protest Movement Becalmed: A Study of Change in the CCF* (Toronto: University of Toronto Press, 1964); and especially Alan Whitehorn,

Canadian Socialism: Essays on the CCF-NDP (Toronto: Oxford University Press, 1992), 18–34.

12 J.L. Granatstein and Peter Stevens, eds., *Forum: Canadian Life and Letters, 1920–1970: Selections from 'The Canadian Forum'* (Toronto: University of Toronto Press, 1972), xiv.

13 Spencer, 'We Went to the People,' *Canadian Forum*, 20 (Jan. 1941), 317; 'We Went to the People – IV,' *Canadian Forum*, 21 (April 1941), 22. (Original emphasis.)

14 Spencer, 'We Went to the People,' *Canadian Forum*, 20 (Jan. 1941), 318. Original emphasis. 'We Went to the People – II,' *Canadian Forum,* 20 (Feb. 1941), 348.

15 'We Went to the People – III,' *Canadian Forum*, 20 (March 1941), 379–82.

16 'We Went to the People,' *Canadian Forum*, 21 (April 1941), 20, 21, 24.

17 Two articles on advertising appeared in 1942, which attacked the 'unpardonable waste' of corporate advertising during wartime. C.D. Watt, 'The War and Advertising,' *Canadian Forum*, 22 (May 1942), 47–8; 'Advertising and the War,' *Canadian Forum*, 22 (Oct. 1942), 218–19.

18 Queen's University Archives, Ontario CCF/NDP Papers, Executive Minutes, 17 Jan. 1941, cited in J.T. Morley, *Secular Socialists: The CCF/NDP in Ontario, A Biography* (Kingston and Montreal: McGill-Queen's University Press, 1983), 46.

19 National Archives of Canada (NAC), CCF Papers, MG 28 IV-1, vol. 157, file 'Gallup Polls, 1942–45'; 'C.C.F. Vote Drawn Largely from Lower Income Group,' *Saskatoon Star-Phoenix*, 7 Aug. 1943; 'The Gallup Poll: How It Works in Measuring Public Opinion,' *Ottawa Citizen*, 8 June 1945.

20 CCF, vol. 157, file 'Gallup Polls 1942–45,' 'E.R.' to Rae, 14 Dec. 1942; 'Confidential Memorandum: "What the Poll Means to the CCF,"' circa April 1943.

21 Joan Sangster, *Dreams of Equality: Women on the Canadian Left, 1920–1950* (Toronto: McClelland and Stewart, 1989), 99, 105, 107, 195–7. Sangster also argues that a sizeable chasm separated CCF egalitarian rhetoric and the oftentimes secondary role women played in party affairs.

22 Young, *Anatomy of a Party,* 190. The CCF file entitled 'Party Research, 1946–57' contains no mention of polling. NAC, CCF papers, vol. 140.

23 Young, *Anatomy of a Party,* 179, 178, 45, 50; Whitehorn, *Canadian Socialism,* 44.

24 Maurice Duverger, *Political Parties* (New York: John Wiley and Sons, 1954); and Frederick C. Engelmann and Mildred A. Schwartz, *Political Parties and the Canadian Social Structure* (Scarborough: Prentice-Hall, 1967), 6–7, 134–6. For a useful overview of party organization in Canada, see Dan Azoulay, 'The Evolution of Party Organisation in Canada since 1900,' *Journal of Commonwealth and Comparative Politics*, 33, 2 (July 1995), 185–208.

25 Khayyam Zev Paltiel, *Political Party Financing in Canada* (Toronto: McGraw-Hill, 1970), 48–9; Zakuta, *A Protest Movement Becalmed*, 46; Morley, *Secular Socialists*, 101–3.
26 David Lewis and Frank Scott, *Make This Your Canada* (Toronto: Central Canada Publishing, 1943), 133–44; Frederick C. Engelmann, 'The Cooperative Commonwealth Federation of Canada: A Study of Membership Participation in Party Policy-Making' (PhD dissertation, Yale University, 1954); S.M. Lipset, *Agrarian Socialism: The Cooperative Commonwealth Federation in Saskatchewan* (Berkeley: University of California Press, 1950); Young, *Anatomy of a Party*, 164–75.
27 Walker, 'Pollsters, Consultants, and Party Politics in Canada,' 385. Similarly, Walker suggests that one reason for the federal NDP's belated start in opinion polling was its ties to organized labour: 'the trade unions have long been suspicious of polls and, within their organizations, have relied on the mythology of union democracy to legitimize their leadership. In this context, many unions have found it difficult to endorse the concept that a market research company, which normally deals with corporate clients, can, through the magic of polling, understand the working world better than the membership' (389).
28 On this point, see Paltiel, 'Political Marketing, Party Finance, and the Decline of Canadian Parties,' 334–5, and Walker, 'Pollsters, Consultants, and Party Politics in Canada,' 397. See also Stephen Kline, Rovin Deodat, Arlen Shwetz, and William Leiss, 'Political Broadcast Advertising in Canada,' in Frederick J. Fletcher, ed., *Election Broadcasting in Canada* (Toronto: Dundurn, 1991), 227.
29 For two brief advertising references, see Dean E. McHenry, *The Third Force in Canada: The Cooperative Commonwealth Federation, 1932–1948* (Berkeley: University of California Press, 1950), 58; and Gerald D. Caplan, *The Dilemma of Canadian Socialism: The CCF in Ontario* (Toronto: McClelland and Stewart, 1973), 113, 164–5. Caplan notes that CCF advertising in 1944 was done by a 'friendly professional advertising concern, the William Orr Advertising Company' (113). The party had hoped to raise $500,000 for the 1945 election, but only managed to secure $84,000.
30 Young, *Anatomy of a Party*, 200. Original emphasis.
31 Ibid., 200; Caplan, *Dilemma*, 164.
32 Caplan, *Dilemma*, 113.
33 For this, see the advertising trade magazines *Canadian Advertising* and *Marketing*.
34 Whitehorn, *Canadian Socialism*, 262; Caplan, *Dilemma*, 88.
35 NAC, National Liberal Federation (NLF) Papers, vol. 807, file 'Gallup Trends,' memo 'Trend of Popular Vote According to the Gallup Poll, 1942–1952,' n.d.

36 Young, *Anatomy of a Party*, 111; Paltiel, *Political Party Financing in Canada*, 51;
    Whitehorn, *Canadian Socialism*, 262; John English, 'Politics and the War:
    Aspects of the Canadian National Experience,' in Sydney Aster, ed., *The
    Second World War as a National Experience* (Ottawa: Canadian Committee for
    the History of the Second World War, 1981), 52–66. On Communist attacks on
    the CCF, see Young, *Anatomy of a Party*, 254–85.

37 Whitehorn, *Canadian Socialism*, 27; Caplan, *Dilemma*, 192; David Lewis, *The
    Good Fight: Political Memoirs, 1909–1958* (Toronto: Macmillan, 1981), 310–19;
    J.L. Granatstein, *The Politics of Survival: The Conservative Party of Canada, 1939–
    1945* (Toronto: University of Toronto Press, 1967), 187, 189. John English dis-
    counts the impact of Trestrail and Murray's propaganda on CCF fortunes,
    claiming that their activities reached high gear well after the CCF had begun
    dropping in the polls. He also argues that these propaganda efforts 'probably
    hurt the Grits as well as the CCF. Business, the polls showed clearly, was not
    very fond of Liberalism' between 1943 and 1945, and it solidly backed the
    Tories. The first point has some merit: most of the mass mailings from Trestrail
    and Murray occurred in early 1945. But these were preceded in 1943 and 1944
    by extensive publicity work, from Murray especially, providing newspapers,
    magazines, radios, and other media with anti-socialist material. English's sec-
    ond point misses the intent of anti-CCF propaganda. The target audiences
    were not 'business' people, who had largely avoided the CCF bandwagon, but
    the many recent CCF converts drawn from the ranks of farmers, blue-collar
    workers, and the middle class. English, 'Politics and the War,' 57.

38 'Gladstone Murray as a Point of Reference,' *Canadian Forum*, 23 (March 1944),
    270–2; Caplan, *Dilemma*, 123; University of Toronto, Thomas Fisher Rare
    Book Library (TFRBL), Kenny collection, pam-0364, Murray reprinted
    speech, 'Private Property a Guarantee of Freedom,' 14 Nov. 1944; Young,
    Anatomy of a Party, 204; Lewis, *The Good Fight*, 312.

39 Young, *Anatomy of a Party*, 200.

40 Lewis, *The Good Fight*, 318.

41 TFRBL, Kenny collection, pam-0436, 'Social Suicide,' 1945; Young, *Anatomy of
    a Party*, 203.

42 B.A. Trestrail, *Social Suicide* (Toronto: Public Information Association, 1945),
    3; Trestrail, *Stand Up and Be Counted* (Toronto: McClelland and Stewart, 1944),
    15 (original emphasis), 31. For David Lewis's reaction, see *The Good Fight*,
    315–17.

43 Trestrail, *Social Suicide*, 3.

44 Caplan, *Dilemma*, 160.

45 Trestrail, *Stand Up*, 12; GC, CIPO questionnaire 10 March 1944; CIPO release,
    3 May 1944.

46 Archives of Ontario (AO), Elliott Research Corporation Papers, finding aid 245, 'Historical Sketch'; vol. 53, file 245-20-0-2, 'A Third Study of Public Attitudes,' 17 May 1940; Ross A. Eaman, *Channels of Influence: CBC Audience Research and the Canadian Public* (Toronto: University of Toronto Press, 1994), 49–51.

47 Ibid., box 17, file 245-5-0-1, 'First Quarterly Survey of the Canadian Public's Attitude towards Business and Industry,' Oct. 1944. The poll sampled twelve hundred people in each of the Maritimes, Ontario, Quebec, the Prairies, and BC. The national results were weighted by population size, but the large regional samples afforded more accurate demographic breakdowns. The company also claimed that 10 per cent of questionnaires received from its 216 interviewers were rechecked by office staff as a quality control measure.

48 For early examples of public relations articles in Canada, see James A. Cowan, 'Public Relations,' *Canadian Advertising*, April 1939, 12–15, 22; Cowan, 'Again, Public Relations,' *Canadian Advertising*, Oct. 1939, 19–20, 46; C.E. Macdonald, 'Public Relations and Marketing,' in Jane McKee, ed., *Marketing Organization and Technique* (Toronto: University of Toronto Press, 1940), 76–82; James W. Young, 'What the Public Expects of the Business Man,' *Commerce Journal*, April 1943, 17–18; Hugh Mackenzie, 'Public Relations in a Post-War Economy,' *Quarterly Review of Commerce*, 11, 3 (1945), 127–36. A number of American books on public relations appeared before 1946. The early classic is Edward L. Bernays, *Crystallizing Public Opinion* (New York: Boni and Liveright, 1923 and 1934). See also Bronson Batchelor, *Profitable Public Relations* (New York: Harper and Bros, 1938); John Price Jones, *At the Bar of Public Opinion: A Brief for Public Relations* (New York: Inter-River Press, 1939); Milton Wright, *Public Relations for Business* (New York: McGraw-Hill, 1939); Verne Burnett, *You and Your Public: A Guide Book to the New Career – Public Relations* (New York: Harper and Bros, 1943); Theodore R. Sills, *Public Relations: Principles and Procedures* (Chicago: Richard D. Irwin, 1945); and Bernays, *Public Relations* (Boston: Bellman, 1945).

49 AO, Elliott Research, box 17, file 245-5-0-4, 'Public Attitudes towards Canadian Business and Industry,' Feb. 1945.

50 Ibid., 'First Quarterly Survey of the Canadian Public's Attitude towards Business and Industry,' Oct. 1944; 'Public Attitudes towards Canadian Business and Industry,' Feb. 1945.

51 See Lewis, *The Good Fight*, 311; Caplan, *Dilemma*, 132.

52 Caplan, *Dilemma*, 195; Lewis, *The Good Fight*, 316, 199.

53 The best study of the wartime Tories remains J.L. Granatstein, *The Politics of Survival: The Conservative Party of Canada, 1939–1945* (Toronto: University of Toronto Press, 1967). On the pre-war years, consult Larry A. Glassford, *Reac-*

tion and Reform: The Politics of the Conservative Party under R.B. Bennett, 1927–1938 (Toronto: University of Toronto Press, 1992). For an uneven account of the party's history from 1920 to 1949, see John R. Williams, *The Conservative Party of Canada, 1920–1949* (Durham: Duke University Press, 1956).

54 In each election an Independent Conservative was also elected. M.C. Urquhart and K.A.H. Buckley, eds., *Historical Statistics of Canada* (Toronto: Macmillan, 1965), 619.

55 Granatstein, *Politics of Survival*, 68.

56 Cited in ibid., 170 and John Kendle, *John Bracken: A Political Biography* (Toronto: University of Toronto Press, 1979), 203.

57 Kendle, *John Bracken*, 206.

58 Granatstein, *Politics of Survival*, 195; Williams, *The Conservative Party of Canada*, 153.

59 Ideology and party practices suggest that the Tories were less aligned with the cadre party ideal than the Liberals. Tory supporters, according to an Engelmann and Schwartz analysis of CIPO data between 1951 and 1962, exhibited marginally more internal cohesion on issues than did Liberals, but far less than CCF voters. The Conservative party had also held national conventions in 1927, 1938, and 1942 (compared to the Liberals' last such meeting in 1919), and the Dominion Progressive Conservative Association met annually from 1943 on. Williams, though, plays down the significance of these nominal displays of internal democracy, arguing that nearly all effective decision making remained in the hands of a small group of elected and appointed officials. Engelmann and Schwartz, *Political Parties and the Canadian Social Structure*, 207; Williams, *The Conservative Party of Canada*, 110–15.

60 NAC, Progressive Conservative Party Papers (PC), MG 28 IV-2, vol. 303, 'Canadian Institute of Public Opinion [CIPO] 1943–56,' untitled Brown memo, 30 June 1943; vol. 330, file 'CIPO, 1943–46'; vol. 303, 'CIPO 1943–56,' Morris to Brown. Scattered CIPO releases from March and June 1943 were also found in party records. Vol. 303, file 'CIPO, 1943–1956'; NAC, John Bracken Papers, MG 27 III C 16, vol. 42, file 'Organization – Dominion.'

61 PC, vol. 432, '"Public Opinion" Makes Its Bow,' *Public Opinion*, 31 Aug. 1943, 1; vol. 318, file 'Public Opinion: Readers' Views, 1943–1957,' Bird to Brown, 7 Sept. 1943.

62 PC, vol. 303, 'CIPO, 1943–56,' Sanders to Brown, 3 Aug. 1943; Morris to Brown, 4 April 1944; Brown to Morris, 10 April 1944. The CIPO poll on party standings, published on 29 March 1944 and showing a slight increase in overall Liberal support, contained no provincial breakdowns. GC, CIPO release, 29 March 1944.

63 Sanders, *Jack and Jacques: A Scientific Approach to the Study of French and Non-French Thought in Canada* (Toronto: Ryerson Press, 1943), 1.

64 PC, vol. 303, file 'CIPO, 1943–56,' Brown to Sanders, 12 July 1944; Sanders to Brown, 24 July 1944. During the 1953 federal election, Wilf Sanders and his sister, Byrne Hope Sanders, both CIPO directors, openly supported Margaret Aitken, the successful Tory candidate in York-Humber (Toronto). They even went so far as to conduct a pre-election poll in the riding. Incredibly, this was revealed soon after by Byrne Sanders in a publication. See Margaret Aitken (with Byrne Hope Sanders), *Hey Ma! I Did It* (Toronto: Clarke, Irwin, 1953), 106–8, 149; and Robert McAlpine Campbell, *Whee! the People* (Toronto: Bryant Press, n.d.), 7–8.

65 Granatstein, *Politics of Survival*, 157–8; NAC, Richard Bell Papers, MG 32 B 1, vol. 1, file 3 'Correspondence 1942–44,' Bell to H.R. Milner, 30 Dec. 1942; Milner to Bell, 4 Jan. 1943; Bracken Papers, vol. 41, file 'Report of the Annual Meeting of the Dominion Progressive Conservative Association' (DPCA), 4 March 1944; PC, vol. 316, file 'Publicity and Public Relations – Advisory Committee 1943–44'; vol. 317, file 'Publicity and Public Relations – Advisory Committee 1945–1953,' agenda for Publicity and Public Relations Committee meeting, 1 March 1945; and 'Report on Public Relations,' DPCA annual meeting, 2 March 1945. None of the party's files (vol. 358) on the 1945 election discuss opinion polls.

66 PC, vol. 309, file 'McKim Advertising Ltd,' E.P. Blenkarn to Charters, 6 April 1948; Charters to Blenkarn, 7 April 1948.

67 Reginald Whitaker, *The Government Party: Organizing and Financing the Liberal Party of Canada, 1930–1958* (Toronto: University of Toronto Press, 1977), 222. On the rise of modern, bureaucratic forms of government patronage, see David E. Smith, 'Patronage in Britain and Canada: An Historical Perspective,' *Journal of Canadian Studies*, 22, 2 (Summer 1987), 34–53; and Whitaker, 'Between Patronage and Bureaucracy: Democratic Politics in Transition,' *Journal of Canadian Studies*, 22, 2 (Summer 1987), 55–71.

68 H.E. Stephenson and Carlton McNaught, *The Story of Advertising in Canada: A Chronicle of Fifty Years* (Toronto: Ryerson Press, 1940). An ostensible 'general' history of Canadian advertising, its de facto purpose was to showcase the McKim record. No other advertisers are even mentioned.

69 A.B. Blankenship et al., *A History of Marketing Research in Canada*, 30–1.

70 The 'soap' line is Mackenzie King's, cited in Granatstein, *Politics of Survival*, 190–1; 'The Quarter's Polls,' *Public Opinion Quarterly*, 9, 3 (Fall 1945), 375.

71 King Papers, MG 26 J 13, King Diary, 9 Aug. 1943, 623.

72 See especially Granatstein, *Canada's War: The Politics of the Mackenzie King Government, 1939–1945* (Toronto: Oxford University Press, 1975), 382–418;

and Whitaker, *The Government Party*, 132–64, 222–8. On the impact of Ottawa mandarins in fashioning political policies, see Granatstein, *The Ottawa Men: The Civil Service Mandarins, 1935–1957* (Toronto: Oxford University Press, 1982), 214–18, and more generally Doug Owram, *The Government Generation: Canadian Intellectuals and the State* (Toronto: University of Toronto Press, 1986), 285–317.

73 David Bercuson, *True Patriot: The Life of Brooke Claxton, 1898–1960* (Toronto: University of Toronto Press, 1993), 122; Whitaker, *The Government Party*, 141. On the cadre party nature of the federal Liberals, see ibid., 405–7.

74 Ibid., 132–64, 216–34; Granatstein, 'Financing the Liberal Party, 1935–1945,' in Michael Cross and Robert Bothwell, eds., *Policy by Other Means: Essays in Honour of C.P. Stacey* (Toronto: Clarke, Irwin, 1972), 192–9.

75 NAC, H.E. Kidd Papers, MG 32 G9, vol. 1, file 1, 'Facts Re: H.E. Kidd,' 7 Sept. 1943; Kidd curriculum vitae, circa 1963; 'Canadian Advertising Agencies,' *Canadian Advertising*, July 1939, 149.

76 NAC, Brooke Claxton Papers, MG 32 B5, vol. 44, Kidd to Claxton, 16 March 1943, cited in Whitaker, *Government Party*, 226.

77 Bercuson, *True Patriot*, 92; Whitaker, *Government Party*, 226; Claxton Papers, vol. 28, file 'Election 1940,' Claxton to Fowler, 6 April 1940; Whitaker, *Government Party*, 227. For one such magazine example, see Carolyn Cox, 'First Parliamentary Assistant,' *Saturday Night*, 5 June 1943, 2. The extent of Kidd's close association with Claxton is playfully alluded to in one stanza of a 1942 poem written for Kidd by colleagues: 'Of thinkers, past and present then, / If we must name our pick, / In unison we'll name the guy / Who makes Brooke Claxton tick.' Kidd Papers, vol. 21, file 1, 'We Wouldn't Kidd Him,' 1942.

78 In December, Cockfield, Brown was informally invited to begin work on pre-election advertising, but the deal was not actually signed until 15 March 1944. Provincially run campaigns could use other advertisers, and the Canadian Advertising Agency was given charge of French advertising in Quebec. Kidd, vol. 4, file 3, Kidd to Hammond, 15 Sept. 1943; Fowler to N. Lambert, 21 Sept. 1943; Caverhill to Anderson, 23 Sept. 1943; ibid., file 4, Brown to Robertson, 14 April 1944. NLF, vol. 802, file 'Cockfield, Brown,' Brown to Robertson, 16 March 1944; Kidd to MacLean, 1 Sept. 1944.

79 On the mutually rewarding, though sometimes antagonistic, relationship between Cockfield, Brown's partisan work and federal government advertising contracts, see Whitaker, *Government Party*, 225–36.

80 Kidd Papers, vol. 1, file 8, Kidd to Claxton, 30 Sept. 1943. From March 1944 to the start of the 1945 election campaign, Cockfield, Brown performed nearly $2,600 of paid work in Claxton's riding. During the 1945 campaign, $2,750 of

Claxton's $5,109 in advertising spending was handled by Cockfield, Brown. Whitaker, *Government Party*, 228.

81 Kidd Papers, vol. 1, file 9, Poole to Claxton, 15 Feb. 1944; Claxton, vol. 44, file 'Kidd,' Kidd to Claxton, 9 May 1944; 'Report on Public Opinion Poll in Federal Constituency: St. Lawrence–St. George,' 2 May 1944.

82 Kidd Papers, vol. 4, file 4, Kidd to Anderson, 19 March 1944.

83 For example, see Gross's input during a December 1943 company meeting: 'Voters are divided into three groups: the staunch Liberal supporters; the large middle group who get their ideas from their newspapers and radio and are undecided which way to vote; and the third group who are loyal to an opposition party. The first group obviously can be left out and not much can be done about the third. Therefore let us attack the middle group. Print ads, not selling Joe Blotz, but selling the *idea* – what it is going to do for them, as workers in a plant, for instance. Sell, "Maintain production – it will help you!" Another thing, do not give political speeches on the radio – sell dramatized shows merchandising the idea. Instead of having political speeches at rallys [sic], etc., produce motion pictures carrying out the same merchandising angle. In the past, politicians have not done a merchandising job, which is actually what should be done.' Kidd Papers, vol. 4, file 3, 'Notes on Meeting re: National Liberal Organization,' 10 Dec. 1943.

84 Kidd Papers, vol. 21, file 1, Gross to Kidd, 24 March 1944.

85 Ibid., Cantril to Claxton, 4 April 1944. Original emphasis.

86 NLF Papers, vol. 603, file 'Public Opinion Survey 1944,' Kidd to Cantril, 3 June 1944.

87 Ibid., file 'Public Opinion Survey, 1944,' various tables; ibid., file 'Ontario Survey, 1944,' Poole to Kidd, 17 July 1944; Kidd to Cantril, 3 June 1944. Of $25,613 spent by the Liberals in the Saskatchewan election, more by 250 per cent than was spent in 1938, just $5,505 was handled by Cockfield, Brown. Whitaker, *Government Party*, 233, 463n50.

88 Kidd Papers, vol. 21, file 1, Waldo to Kidd, 23 May 1944.

89 Ibid., Cantril to Kidd, 8 June 1944; NLF, vol. 802, file 'Cockfield, Brown,' Kidd to MacLean, 1 Sept. 1944. On the Liberal party's difficulties raising campaign funds, see Whitaker, *Government Party*, 232–4; and Granatstein, 'Financing the Liberal Party, 1935–1945,' 194–5.

90 This polling project is mentioned briefly in Granatstein, *Canada's War*, 385, and Bercuson, *True Patriot*, 123.

91 Kidd Papers, vol. 4, file 4, Kidd to Anderson, 19 March 1944; ibid., vol. 21, file 1, Gross to Kidd, 24 March 1944; NLF, vol. 603, file 'Gallup and Opinions, 1944,' Poole to Anderson, 31 March 1944. The thirteen Toronto-area ridings were Greenwood, Broadview, Rosedale, Spadina, Trinity, Parkdale, St Paul's,

Davenport, High Park, York South, Danforth, York East, and Eglinton. The remaining twenty-nine were Brant, Brantford, Dufferin-Simcoe, Elgin, Essex East, Essex South, Essex West, Grey Bruce, Grey North, Halton, Hamilton East, Hamilton West, Huron North, Huron Perth, Kent, Lambton Kent, Lambton West, Lincoln, London, Middlesex East, Middlesex West, Norfolk, Oxford, Peel, Perth, Waterloo North, Waterloo South, Welland, and Wentworth. NLF Papers, vol. 603, file 'Ont. Survey 1944,' Kidd to Gardiner, 16 May 1944; Gardiner to Kidd, 16 May 1944; 'Summary of Report on Public Opinion in Federal Constituencies in Ontario,' 8 June 1944.

92 Constituency redistribution and riding name changes make an exact comparison of 1930 and 1940 seat differentials difficult. For these riding results, see Howard A. Scarrow, *Canada Votes: A Handbook of Federal and Provincial Election Data* (New Orleans: Hauser Press, 1962), 82–4, 111–13.

93 NLF Papers, vol. 603, file 'Gallup and Opinion Polls, 1944,' Poole to Anderson, 31 March 1944.

94 Ibid., Kidd to Gross, 11 April 1944; Gross to Kidd, 12 April 1944. Kidd, vol. 4, file 4, Brown to Robertson, 14 April 1944; Kidd to Poole, 8 June 1944; vol. 11, file 9, Poole to Kidd, 14 April 1944; file 'Ont. Survey 1944,' Poole to Kidd, 1 May 1944.

95 Ibid., Kidd to Gardiner, 2 May 1944; Poole to Kidd, 12 May 1944; Anderson to Kidd, 19 May 1944; Kidd to Gardiner, 16 May 1944; Gardiner to Kidd, 16 May 1944; Poole to Kidd, 22 May 1944; Anderson to Gross, 23 May 1944. A later Cockfield, Brown budget quote to a Liberal official involved a 25 per cent mark-up above survey costs. Ibid., Poole to Kidd, 17 July 1944; Kidd Papers, vol. 11, file 9, Kidd to Fogo, 18 July 1944.

96 Kidd Papers, vol. 21, file 6, Claxton to King, 28 June 1944; NLF, vol. 603, file, 'Ont. Survey 1944,' 'Summary of Report on Public Opinion Poll in Federal ... ' 8 June 1944; Kidd Papers, vol. 21, file 6, Claxton to King, 28 June 1944.

97 J.W. Pickersgill and D.F. Forster, eds., *The Mackenzie King Record*, vol. 2: *1944–1945* (Toronto: University of Toronto Press, 1972), 20–1.

98 NLF Papers, vol. 603, file 'Ont. Survey 1944,' Kidd to Poole, 21 June 1944; Poole to Kidd, 17 July 1944; Kidd to Poole, 20 July 1944. Kidd Papers, vol. 11, file 9, Kidd to Fogo, 18 July 1944.

99 Ibid., Graydon to Poole, 6 June 1944. These ridings, which came under the ministerialist direction of secretary of state Norman McLarty, were Brant, Brantford, Elgin, Essex East, Essex South, Essex West, Huron North, Huron Perth, Kent, Lambton Kent, Lambton West, London, Middlesex East, Middlesex West, Norfolk, Oxford, Perth, Waterloo North, and Waterloo South.

100 In July, Kidd again attempted to have Cantril visit Ottawa. Cantril's busy

teaching and White House consulting schedule prevented such a trip, but he did invite Kidd to visit him in Princeton. NLF, vol. 603, file 'Ont. Survey 1944,' Cantril to Kidd, 26 July 1944; Kidd to Cantril, 28 July 1944.

101 Pickersgill and Forster, eds., *The Mackenzie King Record*, 2: 21; Granatstein, *Canada's War*, 387–9.

102 Whitaker, *Government Party*, 233; Kidd Papers, vol. 1, file 9, Kidd to Claxton, 17 July 1944.

103 Whitaker, *Government Party*, 233.

104 NLF records (vols. 802–5) on the 1945 election do not discuss opinion polling.

105 Kidd Papers, vol. 4, file 4, 'The Pre-Election Campaign, 15 May–31 Aug. 1944,' ca. Sept. 1944; ibid., vol. 21, file 2, 'Report on Federal Election, 11 June 1945,' ca. June 1945.

106 Whitaker, *Government Party*, 159.

107 Ibid., 226.

Conclusion

1 James W. Carey, 'The Press, Public Opinion, and Public Discourse,' in Theodore L. Glasser and Charles T. Salmon, eds., *Public Opinion and the Communication of Consent* (New York: Guilford Press, 1995), 374.

2 National Archives of Canada (NAC), Mackenzie King Papers, MG 26 J 13, King Diary, 28 March 1938, 252.

3 University of Toronto Archives, J.D. Ketchum Papers, B74-0072, file 'U of T: Department of Extension,' brochure, 'An Evening Course in Public Relations,' 1947; file 'Addresses, Notes,' Ketchum's 'Public Relations Course' lecture, 20 Nov. 1947.

4 Archives of Ontario, Elliott Research Corporation Papers, box 33, file 245-11-0-30, 'Continuing Study of Public Attitudes towards Canadian Business and Industry,' 17 Nov. 1949.

5 NAC, Claxton Papers, vol. 179, file 'Information and Morale in War,' Claxton address to Canadian Political Science Association, 23 May 1941. On the subordination of public/democratic interests to state interests with respect to broadcasting in Canada, see Marc Raboy, *Missed Opportunities: The Story of Canada's Broadcasting Policy* (Montreal and Kingston: McGill-Queen's University Press, 1990).

6 For the links between opinion polling and Max Weber's concept of instrumental rationality, see Susan Herbst, *Numbered Voices: How Opinion Polling Has Shaped American Politics* (Chicago: University of Chicago Press, 1993), 12–20.

7 NAC, National Liberal Federation papers, vol. 603, file 'Public Opinion Polls,' Colwell to King, 18 June 1948 (emphasis added).

8 Harold A. Innis, 'Political Economy in the Modern State,' *Proceedings of the American Philosophical Society, 87,* 4 (Jan. 1944), 335; John M. Jordan, *Machine-Age Ideology: Social Engineering and American Liberalism, 1911–1939* (Chapel Hill: University of North Carolina Press, 1994), 229. John Ralston Saul in *The Unconscious Civilization* (Concord, Ont.: Anansi, 1995) presents a related, though less persuasive, critique of 'corporatist' denigration of democratic society. For a work on the tension between democratic ideals and the instrumental practices of academic political science, see David M. Ricci, *The Tragedy of Political Science: Politics, Scholarship, and Democracy* (New Haven: Yale University Press, 1984).

9 C.B. Macpherson, *The Life and Times of Liberal Democracy* (London: Oxford University Press, 1977), 77, 79.

Bibliography

Archival Sources

National Archives of Canada, Ottawa
Richard Bell Papers
John Bracken Papers
Brooke Claxton Papers
Cooperative Commonwealth Federation Papers
National Liberal Federation Papers
Progressive Conservative Party Papers
J.W. Dafoe Papers
H.E. Kidd Papers
Mackenzie King Papers
Department of External Affairs Records
Privy Council Office Records
Wartime Information Board Records
Wartime Prices and Trade Board Records

Archives of Ontario, Toronto
Elliott Research Corporation Papers
Maclean-Hunter Publishing Papers

Columbia University, Oral History Project, New York
George Gallup Interview, 15 March 1962

Franklin D. Roosevelt Library, Hyde Park, NY
Franklin D. Roosevelt Papers

Princeton University Archives, Princeton, NJ
Woodrow Wilson School of Public and International Affairs Records
Bruce and Beatrice Blackmar Gould Papers

Roper Center for Public Opinion Research, University of Connecticut, Storrs, Conn.
Elmo Roper Papers
1936–7 Composite Gallup Poll Data Set

Special Collections Library, Duke University, Durham, NC
J. Walter Thompson Papers

University of Toronto Archives, Toronto
J.D. Ketchum Papers

Thomas Fisher Rare Book Library, University of Toronto
Kenny Pamphlet Collection

Institute for Social Research, York University, Toronto
Canadian Institute of Public Opinion Data Set

Private Collections
Canadian Daily Newspaper Association, Toronto,
Canadian Facts, Limited, Toronto
Gallup Canada, Limited, Toronto
Cassandra Sanders Papers, Toronto
Shannon Sperry Papers, Toronto

Interviews

Irving Crespi, Princeton, NJ, 3 March 1994
Clara Hatton, Toronto, 19 June 1995
John F. Maloney, Chappaqua, NY, 23 April 1994
Paul Perry, Princeton, NJ, 7 Feb. 1994
Honourable Bob Rae, Toronto, 3 June 1993, 8 Nov. 1995

Canadian Government Publications

The Canada Gazette
Dominion Bureau of Statistics. *Canada Year Book* (1932–46) Ottawa, 1932

- *Census of Canada, 1931*, vols 10 and 11, *Merchandising and Services, Parts 1 and 2*. Ottawa, 1934
- *Consumer Market Data, 1931*. Ottawa, 1940
- *Consumer Market Data, 1941*. Ottawa, 1945.
- *Dominion Bureau of Statistics: History, Function, Organization*. Ottawa, 1952
- *Dominion Bureau of Statistics: Its Origins, Constitution and Organization*. Ottawa, 1935
- *Historical Catalogue of Dominion Bureau of Statistics Publications 1918-1960*. Ottawa, 1966

Parliament. House of Commons. *Debates*, 1942–5
Report of the Royal Commission on Newspapers. Ottawa, 1981
Report of the Royal Commission on Publications. Ottawa, 1961
Report of the Royal Commission on the Status of Women. Ottawa, 1970

United States Government Publications

Bureau of the Census. *Historical Statistics of the United States: Colonial Times to 1970, pt. 2*. Washington, 1975
House of Representatives. *Hearings before the Committee to Investigate Campaign Expenditures*. 78th Congress, 2nd session, H. Res 551, vol. 1031, pt. 12, 28 Dec. 1944

Dissertations

Gallup, George. 'An Objective Method for Determining Reader Interest in the Content of a Newspaper.' PhD dissertation, University of Iowa, 1928.
Jewett, Pauline. 'The Wartime Prices and Trade Board: A Case Study in Canadian Public Administration.' PhD dissertation, Harvard University, 1950.
Kreshel, Peggy Jean. 'Toward a Cultural History of Advertising Research: A Case Study of J. Walter Thompson, 1908–1925.' PhD dissertation, University of Illinois at Urbana-Champaign, 1989.
Rae, Saul Forbes. 'The Concept of Public Opinion and its Measurement.' PhD dissertation, London School of Economics, 1938.
Spence, Ernest J. 'Canada's Wartime Prices and Trade Board, 1941–1947.' PhD dissertation, Northwestern University, 1947.
Waddell, Christopher. 'The Wartime Prices and Trade Board: Price Control in Canada during World War II.' PhD dissertation, York University, 1981.
Ward, Douglas B. 'Tracking the Culture of Consumption: Curtis Publishing Company, Charles Coolidge Parlin, and the Origins of Market Research, 1911–1930.' PhD dissertation, University of Maryland, 1996.

Young, William R. 'Making the Truth Graphic: The Canadian Government's Home Front Information Structure and Programme during World War II.' PhD dissertation, University of British Columbia, 1978.

Selected Books and Articles

Abbott, Charles F. 'Market Analysis a First Requisite,' *Industrial Canada*, Oct. 1931.

Adams, Michael. *Sex in the Snow: Canadian Social Values at the End of the Millennium*. Toronto: Viking, 1997.

– 'Pro Polling.' *Policy Options*, July 1987.

Alpern, Sara, and Dale Baum. 'Female Ballots: The Impact of the Nineteenth Amendment.' *Journal of Interdisciplinary History*, 16, 1 (Summer 1985).

Anderson, Margo J. *The American Census: A Social History*. New Haven: Yale University Press, 1988.

Axford, Phillis. 'Marketing Canadian Magazines.' *Commerce Journal*, March 1939.

Barbour, Noel Robert. *Those Amazing People! The Story of the Canadian Magazine Industry, 1778–1967*. Toronto: Crucible Press, 1982.

Bartels, Robert. *The Development of Marketing Thought*. Homewood, Ill: R.D. Irwin, 1962.

Beauregard, Claude, Edwidge Munn, and Béatrice Richard. *Jack et Jacques*. Montreal: Comeau et Nadeau, 1996.

Beniger, James R. *The Control Revolution: Technological and Economic Origins of the Information Society*. Cambridge: Harvard University Press, 1986.

– 'The Popular Symbolic Repertoire and Mass Communication.' *Public Opinion Quarterly*, 47, 4 (Winter 1983).

Bercuson, David Jay. *True Patriot: The Life of Brooke Claxton, 1898–1960*. Toronto: University of Toronto Press, 1993.

Bernhardt, Karl S. 'Canadian Psychology – Past, Present and Future.' *Canadian Journal of Psychology*, 1, 2 (June 1947).

Blankenship, Albert. *Consumer and Opinion Research: The Questionnaire Technique*. New York: Harper and Brothers, 1943.

Blankenship, A.B., Chuck Chakrapani, and W. Harold Poole. *A History of Marketing Research in Canada*. Toronto: Professional Marketing Research Society, 1985.

Bliss, Michael. *Northern Enterprise: Five Centuries of Canadian Business*. Toronto: McClelland and Stewart, 1987.

Blumberg, Raoul, and Carroll Rheinstrom. 'How Advertising Techniques Are Rated by Gallup Survey.' *Printers' Ink*, 24 March 1932.

Blumer, Herbert. 'Public Opinion and Public Opinion Polling,' *American Sociological Review*, 13, 5 (October 1948).

Boorstin, Daniel J. *The Americans: The Democratic Experience*. New York: Vintage, 1973.

Bothwell, Robert, and John English. 'The View from Inside Out: Canadian Diplomats and Their Public.' *International Journal*, 39, 1 (Winter 1983–4).

Brady, Alexander. *Democracy in the Dominions*. 3rd edition. Toronto: University of Toronto Press, 1958.

Brown, G. Walter. 'Information, Please!' *Canadian Business*, 13 (Nov. 1940).

Brown, Lyndon O. *Market Research and Analysis*. New York: Ronald Press, 1937.

Bryce, James. *The American Commonwealth*. 2 vols. New York: Macmillan, 1888.

– *Modern Democracies*, vol. 2. New York: Macmillan, 1921.

Bunker, Harry S., George H. Gallup, W. Harry Harper, and Charles H. Stout. *The Business Department of School Publications*. Iowa City: Lombard Press, 1927.

Burt, F. Allen. *American Advertising Agencies: An Inquiry into Their Origin, Growth, Functions and Future*. New York: Harper and Brothers, 1940.

Burtt, Harold Ernest. *Psychology of Advertising*. Boston: Houghton Mifflin, 1938.

Canadian Daily Newspaper Association. *The Canadian Market: 1938 Supplement; A Graphic Summary of Canadian Statistics, and an Analysis of Retail Trade*. Toronto: CDNA, 1938.

Cantril, Hadley. *Gauging Public Opinion*. Princeton: Princeton University Press, 1944.

– *The Human Dimension: Experiences in Policy Research*. New Brunswick, NJ: Rutgers University Press, 1967.

Cantril, Hadley, ed. *Public Opinion, 1935–1946*. Princeton: Princeton University Press, 1951.

Caplan, Gerald D. *The Dilemma of Canadian Socialism: The CCF in Ontario*. Toronto: McClelland and Stewart, 1973.

Carey, James W. 'The Press, Public Opinion, and Public Discourse.' In Theodore L. Glasser and Charles T. Salmon, eds., *Public Opinion and the Communication of Consent*. New York: Guilford Press, 1995.

Childs, Harwood L. 'Rule by Public Opinion.' *Atlantic Monthly*, June 1936.

Clarke, Gilbert C. 'A Survey of Gasoline Consumer Buying Habits.' *Quarterly Review of Commerce*, 1, 2 (Winter 1934).

Clarke, Sally. 'Consumers, Information, and Marketing Efficiency at GM, 1921–1940.' *Business and Economic History*, 25 (1996).

Cleverdon, Catherine Lyle. *The Woman Suffrage Movement in Canada*. Toronto: University of Toronto Press, 1950.

Clokie, H. *Canadian Government and Politics*. Toronto: Longmans, Green and Co., 1944.

Coats, R.H. 'Beginnings in Canadian Statistics.' *Canadian Historical Review*, 27, 2 (June 1946).

– 'The Social Sciences and Public Administration,' *Canadian Journal of Economics and Political Science*, 11, 4 (Nov. 1945).
– 'Vital Statistics for National Advertisers.' *Canadian Advertising Data*, Dec. 1928.
Cockfield, H.R. 'Trend in Advertising Agency Practice (Part II).' *Canadian Advertising Data*, Jan. 1931.
Colwell, N.P. 'Avoiding Pitfalls in Marketing Research.' *Canadian Advertising*, fourth quarter, 1940.
Converse, Jean M. *Survey Research in the United States: Roots and Emergence, 1890–1960.* Berkeley: University of California Press, 1987.
Copp, Terry, and Bill McAndrew. *Battle Exhaustion: Soldiers and Psychiatrists in the Canadian Army, 1939–1945.* Montreal and Kingston: McGill-Queen's University Press, 1990.
Corry, J.A. *Democratic Government and Politics.* Toronto: University of Toronto Press, 1946.
Coutant, Frank R., and J. Russell Doubman. *Simplified Market Research.* Philadelphia: Walther Printing House, 1935.
Cowan, James A. 'Public Relations.' *Canadian Advertising*, April 1939.
Craick, W.A. *A History of Canadian Journalism*, vol. 2. Toronto: Ontario Publishing Company, 1959.
Craven, Paul. *'An Impartial Umpire': Industrial Relations and the Canadian State, 1900–1911.* Toronto: University of Toronto Press, 1980.
Crespi, Irving. *Public Opinion, Polls, and Democracy.* Boulder: Westview Press, 1989.
Crossley, Archibald M. 'Early Days of Public Opinion Research.' *Public Opinion Quarterly*, 21, 1 (Spring 1957).
– 'Straw Polls in 1936.' *Public Opinion Quarterly*, 1, 1 (Jan. 1937).
Cuff, Clarissa. 'Opinion Moulds Our Future.' *Saturday Night*, 25 Sept. 1943.
Curti, Merle. 'The Changing Concept of "Human Nature" in the Literature of American Advertising.' *Business History Review*, 41, 4 (Winter 1967).
Dryzek, John S. 'The Mismeasure of Political Man.' *Journal of Politics*, 50, 3 (Aug. 1988).
Duncan, Carson S. *Commercial Research.* New York: Macmillan, 1919.
Duverger, Maurice. *Political Parties.* New York: John Wiley and Sons, 1954.
Eaman, Ross A. *Channels of Influence: CBC Audience Research and the Canadian Public.* Toronto: University of Toronto Press, 1994.
Engelmann, Frederick C., and Mildred A. Schwartz. *Political Parties and the Canadian Social Structure.* Scarborough: Prentice-Hall, 1967.
Engle, N.H. 'Gaps in Marketing Research.' *Journal of Marketing*, 4, 1 (April 1940).
English, John. 'Politics and the War: Aspects of the Canadian National Experi-

ence.' In Sidney Aster, ed., *The Second World War as a National Experience*. Ottawa: Canadian Committee for the History of the Second World War, 1981.

Evans, Gary. *John Grierson and the National Film Board: The Politics of Wartime Propaganda*. Toronto: University of Toronto Press, 1984.

Ferguson, Barry. *Remaking Liberalism: The Intellectual Legacy of Adam Shortt, O.D. Skelton, W.C. Clark, and W.A. Mackintosh, 1890-1925*. Montreal and Kingston: McGill-Queen's University Press, 1993.

Ferguson, Barry, and Doug Owram. 'Social Scientists and Public Policy from the 1920s through World War II.' *Journal of Canadian Studies*, 15, 4 (Winter 1980–1).

Firth, L.E. *Testing Advertisements: A Study of Copy Testing Methods in Theory and Practice*. New York: McGraw-Hill, 1934.

Fisher, Donald. *The Social Sciences in Canada: Fifty Years of National Activity by the Social Science Federation of Canada*. Waterloo: Wilfrid Laurier University Press, 1991.

Fiske, Marjorie, and Leo Handel. 'Motion Picture Research: Content and Audience Analysis.' *Journal of Marketing*, 11, 2 (Oct. 1946).

Fulford, Robert. 'Election Frauds.' *Saturday Night*, Nov. 1992.

– 'This Brain for Hire.' *Saturday Night*, Dec. 1985.

Gallup, George. *A Guide to Public Opinion Polls*. Princeton: Princeton University Press, 1944.

– *Public Opinion in a Democracy*. Princeton: Princeton University Press, 1939.

– 'Can We Trust the Common People?' *Good Housekeeping*, Oct. 1940.

– 'Making Democracy Work Every Day: Public Opinion Polls.' *Scholastic*, 2 Oct. 1939.

– 'Measuring Public Opinion.' *Vital Speeches*, 9 March 1936.

– 'Polling Public Opinion.' In Asher Christensen and Evron Kirkpatrick, eds., *The People, Politics and the Politicians: Readings in American Government*. New York: Holt, 1941.

– 'Polls and Prophets.' *Current History and Forum*, 7 Nov. 1940.

– 'Public Opinion, 1941.' *Current History and Forum*, 23 Jan. 1941.

– 'Public Opinion in Our Cities.' *National Municipal Review*, 27, 2 (Feb. 1938).

– 'Putting Public Opinion to Work.' *Scribner's*, Nov. 1936.

– 'Reporting Public Opinion in Five Nations.' *Public Opinion Quarterly*, 6, 3 (Fall 1942).

– 'Testing Public Opinion.' *Public Opinion in a Democracy*. Special supplement to *Public Opinion Quarterly*, Jan. 1938.

– 'We, the People, Are Like This.' *New York Times Magazine*, 8 June 1941.

– 'What Do They Think?' *Maclean's*, 1 June 1944.

Gallup, George, ed. *The Gallup Poll: Public Opinion 1935–1971*, vol. 1, *1935–1948*. New York: Random House, 1972.

Gallup, George, and Claude Robinson. 'American Institute of Public Opinion – Surveys, 1935–38.' *Public Opinion Quarterly,* 2, 3 (July 1938).

Gallup, George, and Saul Forbes Rae. *The Pulse of Democracy: The Public-Opinion Poll and How It Works.* New York: Simon and Schuster, 1940.

Ginsberg, Benjamin. *The Captive Public: How Mass Opinion Promotes State Power.* New York: Basic Books, 1986.

Ginzburg, Benjamin. 'Dr. Gallup on the Mat.' *Nation,* 16 Dec. 1944.

Glasser, Theodore L., and Charles T. Salmon, eds. *Public Opinion and the Communication of Consent.* New York: Guilford Press, 1995.

Glenn, Norval D. 'Opportunities and Pitfalls.' In Philip K. Hastings, ed., *Survey Data for Trend Analysis.* Storrs, Conn.: Roper Center for Public Opinion Research, 1975.

Goldfarb, Martin, and Thomas Axworthy. *Marching to a Different Drummer: An Essay on the Liberals and Conservatives in Convention.* Toronto: Stoddart, 1988.

Granatstein, J.L. *Canada's War: The Politics of the Mackenzie King Government, 1939–1945.* Toronto: Oxford University Press, 1975.

– *The Politics of Survival: The Conservative Party of Canada, 1939–1945.* Toronto: University of Toronto Press, 1967.

– *The Ottawa Men: The Civil Service Mandarins, 1935–1957.* Toronto: Oxford University Press, 1982.

– 'Financing the Liberal Party, 1935–1945.' In Michael Cross and Robert Bothwell, eds., *Policy by Other Means: Essays in Honour of C.P. Stacey.* Toronto: Clarke, Irwin, 1972.

Granatstein, J.L., and J.M. Hitsman. *Broken Promises: A History of Conscription in Canada.* Toronto: Oxford University Press, 1977.

Granatstein, J.L., and Peter Stevens, eds. *Forum: Canadian Life and Letters, 1920–70: Selections from 'The Canadian Forum.'* Toronto: University of Toronto Press, 1972.

Gwyn, Richard. 'Ad-Men and Scientists Run This Election.' *Financial Post,* 28 April 1962.

Handel, Leo A. *Hollywood Looks at Its Audience: A Report of Film Audience Research.* Urbana: University of Illinois Press, 1950.

Hawbaker, Becky Wilson. 'Taking "the Pulse of Democracy": George Gallup, Iowa, and the Origin of the Gallup Poll.' *Palimpsest,* 74, 3 (Fall 1993).

Herbst, Susan. *Numbered Voices: How Opinion Polling Has Shaped American Politics.* Chicago: University of Chicago Press, 1993.

Herman, Ellen. *The Romance of American Psychology: Political Culture in the Age of Experts.* Berkeley: University of California, 1995.

Hitchens, Christopher. 'Voting in the Passive Voice.' *Harper's,* April 1992.

Hotchkiss, George Burton. *An Outline of Advertising: Its Philosophy, Science, Art and Strategy.* New York: Macmillan, 1940.

Hoy, Claire. *Margin of Error: Pollsters and the Manipulation of Canadian Politics.* Toronto: Key Porter Books, 1989.

Hubler, R.G. 'George Horace Gallup: Oracle in Tweed.' *Forum*, 103 (Fall 1940).

Hutchison, Paul. 'Who Makes Public Opinion?' *Survey Graphic*, June 1939.

Innis, Harold. *The Press: A Neglected Factor in the Economic History of the Twentieth Century.* London: Oxford University Press, 1949.

– 'The Necessity of Research in Marketing.' *Commerce Journal*, March 1940.

– 'Political Economy in the Modern State.' *Proceedings of the American Philosophical Society* 87, 4 (Jan. 1944).

Irving, John A. 'The Psychological Analysis of Wartime Rumor Patterns in Canada.' *Bulletin of the Canadian Psychological Association*, 3, 3 (Oct. 1943).

Jordan, John M. *Machine-Age Ideology: Social Engineering and American·Liberalism, 1911–1939.* Chapel Hill: University of North Carolina Press, 1994.

Katz, Daniel. 'Do Interviewers Bias Poll Results?' *Public Opinion Quarterly*, 6, 2 (Summer 1942).

Katz, Daniel, and Hadley Cantril. 'Public Opinion Polls.' *Sociometry*, 1, 1 (July-Oct. 1937).

Keshen, Jeff. 'One For All or All For One: Government Controls, Black Marketing and the Limits of Patriotism, 1939–1947.' *Journal of Canadian Studies* 29, 4 (Winter 1994–5).

Kesterton, H.R. *A History of Journalism in Canada.* Toronto: McClelland and Stewart, 1967.

Ketchum, J.D. 'Morale in Canada.' In Goodwin Watson, ed., *Civilian Morale: Second Yearbook of the Society for the Psychological Study of Social Issues*. Boston: Houghton, Mifflin, 1942.

– 'Psychology and Wartime Information.' *Bulletin of the Canadian Psychological Association* 3, 2 (April 1943).

King, Henry. 'The Beginning of Marketing Research in Canada.' in W.H. Mahatoo, ed., *Marketing Research in Canada.* Toronto: Thomas Nelson and Sons, 1968.

– 'New Problems in Advertising and Steps towards Their Solution.' In H.R. Kemp, ed., *Canadian Marketing Problems.* Toronto: University of Toronto Press, 1939.

– 'The Need for More Market Knowledge in Canada,' *Quarterly Review of Commerce*, 7, 3 (Spring 1940).

Kleppner, Paul. 'Were Women to Blame? Female Suffrage and Voter Turnout.' *Journal of Interdisciplinary History*, 12, 4 (Spring 1982).

Kornhauser, Arthur. 'Are Public Opinion Polls Fair to Organized Labor?' *Public Opinion Quarterly*, 10, 4 (Winter 1946).

Kruskal, William, and Frederick Mosteller. 'Representative Sampling, IV: The History of the Concept in Statistics, 1895–1939.' *International Statistical Review*, 48 (1980).

Kuna, David P. 'The Concept of Suggestion in the Early History of Advertising Psychology.' *Journal of the History of the Behavioral Sciences*, 12 (Oct. 1976).

Lachapelle, Guy. *Polls and the Media in Canadian Elections: Taking the Pulse.* Toronto: Dundurn Press, 1991.

– 'La Guerre de 1939–1945 dans l'Opinion Publique: Comparaison entre les Attitudes des Canadiens Français et des Canadiens Anglais,' *Bulletin d'Histoire Politique*, 3, 4 (Spring 1995).

Lasswell, Harold D. *Politics: Who Gets What, When, How.* New York: Peter Smith, 1936.

Lavin, Marilyn. 'Creating Consumers in the 1930s: Irna Phillips and the Radio Soap Opera.' *Journal of Consumer Research*, 22 (June 1995), 75–89.

Lazarsfeld, Paul, Bernard Berelson, and Hazel Guidet. *The People's Choice.* New York: Columbia University Press, 1944.

Lears, T.J. Jackson. 'Sherwood Anderson: Looking for the White Spot.' In Richard Wightman Fox and Lears, eds., *The Power of Culture: Critical Essays in American History.* Chicago: University of Chicago Press, 1993.

Leonard, Thomas C. *News for All: America's Coming-of-Age with the Press.* New York: Oxford University Press, 1995.

Lévesque, Albert. *Entrez donc. Analyse du comportement familial de la population de langue française au Canada.* Montreal: Les Informations Albert Lévesque, 1944.

Lewis, David. *The Good Fight: Political Memoirs, 1909–1958.* Toronto: Macmillan, 1981.

Link, Henry. *The New Psychology of Selling and Advertising.* New York: Macmillan, 1932.

– 'Some Milestones in Public Opinion Research.' *International Journal of Opinion and Attitude Research*, 1 (1947).

Lippmann, Walter. *The Phantom Public.* New York: Harcourt, Brace, 1925.

– *A Preface to Morals.* New York: Macmillan, 1929.

– *Public Opinion.* New York: Macmillan, 1922.

Lockley, Lawrence C. 'Notes on the History of Market Research.' *Journal of Marketing*, 14, 5 (April 1950).

London, P. 'Ringing Doorbells with a Gallup Reporter.' *New York Times Magazine*, 1 Sept. 1940.

Lower, A.R.M. 'The Origins of Democracy in Canada.' *Canadian Historical Association, Historical Papers* (1930).

MacKenzie, David. *Arthur Irwin: A Biography.* Toronto: University of Toronto Press, 1993.

– 'The Bren Gun Scandal and the Maclean Publishing Company's Investigation of Canadian Defence Contracts, 1938–1940.' *Journal of Canadian Studies*, 26, 3 (Fall 1991).

MacLeod, Robert B. *Psychology in Canadian Universities and Colleges.* Ottawa: Canadian Social Science Research Council, 1955.

Macpherson, C.B. *The Life and Times of Liberal Democracy.* London: Oxford University Press, 1977.

Marchand, Roland. *Advertising the American Dream: Making Way for Modernity.* Berkeley: University of California Press, 1985.

Marshall, Herbert. 'The Statistical Basis of Marketing Policy.' In H.R. Kemp, ed., *Canadian Marketing Problems.* Toronto: University of Toronto Press, 1939.

McNaught, Carlton. *Canada Gets the News.* Toronto: Ryerson Press, 1940.

Merriam, Charles Edward, and Harold Foote Gosnell. *Non-Voting: Causes and Methods of Control.* Chicago: University of Chicago Press, 1924.

Monod, David. *Store Wars: Shopkeepers and the Culture of Mass Marketing, 1890–1939.* Toronto: University of Toronto Press, 1996.

Morain, Thomas. *Prairie Grass Roots: An Iowa Small Town in the Early Twentieth Century.* Ames: Iowa State University Press, 1988.

Morton, W.L. 'The Extension of the Franchise in Canada: A Study in Democratic Nationalism.' *Canadian Historical Association, Historical Papers* (1943).

Murray, Kenneth. 'Radio Listening Habits.' *Quarterly Review of Commerce*, 5, 2 (Winter 1938).

Myers, C.R. 'Notes on the History of Psychology in Canada.' *Canadian Psychologist* 6a, 1 (Jan. 1965).

Myrdal, Gunnar. *An American Dilemma: The Negro Problem and Modern Democracy.* New York: Harper and Bros., 1944.

Nixon, H.K. *Principles of Advertising.* New York: McGraw-Hill, 1937.

Ohmann, Richard. *Selling Culture: Magazines, Markets, and Class at the Turn of the Century.* London: Verso, 1996.

O'Malley, J.J. 'Black Beans and White Beans.' *New Yorker*, 2 March 1940.

Owram, Doug. *The Government Generation: Canadian Intellectuals and the State, 1900–1945.* Toronto: University of Toronto Press, 1986.

Paltiel, Khayyam Zev. *Political Party Financing in Canada.* Toronto: McGraw-Hill, 1970.

– 'Political Marketing, Party Finance and the Decline of Canadian Parties.' In Alain G. Gagnon and A. Brian Tanguay, eds. *Canadian Parties in Transition.* Scarborough: Nelson Canada, 1989.

Peabody, Stuart. 'Research Big Development in Advertising.' *Canadian Advertising*, Dec. 1935.

Pickersgill, J.W., and D.F. Forster, eds. *The Mackenzie King Record*. Vol. 2: *1944–1945*. Toronto: University of Toronto Press, 1972.

Pierce, Walter M. 'Climbing on the Bandwagon.' *Public Opinion Quarterly*, 4, 2 (June 1940).

Poole, W.H. 'Marketing Research in Canada.' *Commerce Journal*, Feb. 1957.

Pope, Daniel. *The Making of Modern Advertising*. New York: Basic Books, 1983.

Porter, Arthur. 'After Victory, What ... ?' *Canadian Business*, Dec. 1942.

Raboy, Marc. *Missed Opportunities: The Story of Canada's Broadcasting Policy.* Montreal and Kingston: McGill-Queen's University Press, 1990.

Rae, Saul Forbes. 'The Oxford By-Election: A Study in the Straw-Vote.' *Political Quarterly*, 10, 2 (1939).

Richards, P.M. 'He Feels the Public Pulse.' *Saturday Night*, 5 Oct. 1940.

Robinson, Claude E. *Straw Votes: A Study of Political Prediction*. New York: Columbia University Press, 1932.

Rook, William G. *Their Purchasing Power*. Toronto: Canadian Woman's Magazine Publishing Co., 1912.

Roper, Elmo. 'Sampling Public Opinion.' *Journal of the American Statistical Association* (1940).

Ross, Dorothy. *The Origins of American Social Science*. New York: Cambridge University Press, 1991.

Rutherford, Paul. *The Making of the Canadian Media*. Toronto: McGraw-Hill Ryerson, 1978.

Sabato, Larry J. *The Rise of Political Consultants: New Ways of Winning Elections*. New York: Basic Books, 1981.

Sanders, Wilfrid. *Jack & Jacques: A Scientific Approach to the Study of French and Non-French Thought in Canada*. Toronto: Ryerson Press, 1943.

– 'American Opinion Swinging from Isolationism.' *Saturday Night*, 3 July 1943.

– 'Canada Looks toward Postwar.' *Public Opinion Quarterly* 8, 4 (Winter 1944–5).

– 'He's Ready to Take It.' *Maclean's*, 1 Jan. 1943.

– 'How Good Is the Canadian Gallup Poll?' *Public Affairs*, 6, 6 (1943).

– 'Pro-Votes and Con-Votes.' *Saturday Night*, 21 Aug. 1943.

– 'What Canadians Don't Know.' *Maclean's*, 15 Aug. 1945.

Sangster, Joan. *Dreams of Equality: Women on the Canadian Left, 1920–1950*. Toronto: McClelland and Stewart, 1989.

Schudson, Michael. *Advertising, The Uneasy Persuasion: Its Dubious Impact on American Society*. New York: Basic Books, 1984.

– *Discovering the News: A Social History of American Newspapers*. New York: Basic Books, 1978.

Schwartz, Mildred A. *Public Opinion and Canadian Identity.* Scarborough: Fitzhenry and Whiteside, 1967.

Simpson, Jeffrey. 'Pollstruck.' *Policy Options*, 8, 2 (March 1987).

Skott, Hans E. 'Attitude Research in the Department of Agriculture.' *Public Opinion Quarterly* 7, 2 (Summer 1943).

Sokal, Michael M. 'The Origins of the Psychological Corporation.' *Journal of the History of the Behavioral Sciences*, 17 (1981).

Spencer, Philip. 'Does It Sell the Stuff?' *Canadian Forum*, Oct. 1940.

– 'Pardon Me, Madam, How Often Do You Take a Bath?' *Canadian Forum*, Dec. 1940.

– 'We Went to the People.' *Canadian Forum*, Jan. 1941.

– 'We Went to the People – II.' *Canadian Forum*, Feb. 1941.

– 'We Went to the People – III.' *Canadian Forum*, March 1941.

– 'We Went to the People – IV.' *Canadian Forum*, April 1941.

Spingarn, Jerome H. 'These Public-Opinion Polls.' *Harper's*, Dec. 1938.

Stanner, H.T. 'Gallup Poll Comes to Canada.' *Canadian Business*, Dec. 1941.

Steele, Richard W. 'The Pulse of the People: Franklin D. Roosevelt and the Gauging of American Public Opinion.' *Journal of Contemporary History*, 9, 4 (Oct. 1974).

Stephan, Frederick F. 'History of the Uses of Modern Sampling Procedures.' *Journal of the American Statistical Association*, 43 (March 1948).

Stephenson, H.E., and Carlton McNaught. *The Story of Advertising in Canada: A Chronicle of Fifty Years.* Toronto: Ryerson Press, 1940.

Strasser, Susan. *Satisfaction Guaranteed: The Making of the American Mass Market.* New York: Pantheon, 1989.

Sudman, Seymour, and Norman M. Bradburn. 'The Organizational Growth of Public Opinion Research in the United States.' *Public Opinion Quarterly*, 51 (special issue, 1987).

Sutherland, Fraser. *The Monthly Epic: A History of Canadian Magazines, 1789–1989.* Markham: Fitzhenry and Whiteside, 1989.

Tedlow, Richard S. *New and Improved: The Story of Mass Marketing in America.* New York: Basic Books, 1990.

Thelen, David P. 'The Public against the Historians: The Gallup Poll, 1935–1971.' *Reviews in American History*, 4, 4 (Dec. 1976).

Thompson, Walter A. 'Brand Policy.' *Quarterly Review of Commerce* 1, 1 (Autumn 1933).

– 'Consumer Purchasing Outside the City of London.' *Quarterly Review of Commerce*, 2, 2 (Winter 1935).

– 'Retailing from the Consumer's Point of View.' In H.R. Kemp, ed., *Canadian Marketing Problems.* Toronto: University of Toronto Press, 1939.

- 'Tendencies toward a More Rational Approach to Marketing.' *Quarterly Review of Commerce*, 3, 1 (Autumn 1936).

Trestrail, B.A. *Stand Up and Be Counted*. Toronto: McClelland and Stewart, 1944.

Urquhart, M.C. 'Three Builders of Canada's Statistical System.' *Canadian Historical Review*, 68, 3 (Sept. 1987).

Urquhart, M.C., and K.A.H. Buckley, eds. *Historical Statistics of Canada*. Toronto: Macmillan, 1965.

Van Gogh, Lucy. 'The Gallup Poll System Has Its Limitations.' *Saturday Night*, 29 Nov. 1941.

Walker, David C. 'Pollsters, Consultants, and Party Politics in Canada.' In Alain G. Gagnon and A. Brian Tanguay, eds., *Canadian Parties in Transition*. Scarborough: Nelson Canada, 1989.

Weaver, Henry G. 'Educating the Consumer.' *Canadian Business*, Feb. 1937.

Whalen, Hugh. 'The Perils of Polling.' In Paul W. Fox, ed., *Politics: Canada*. 4th edition. Toronto: McGraw-Hill, 1977.

Wheeler, Ferdinand C., ed. *The Technique of Marketing Research*. New York: McGraw-Hill, 1937.

Wheeler, Michael. *Lies, Damn Lies, and Statistics: The Manipulation of Public Opinion in America*. New York: Liveright, 1977.

Whitaker, Reginald. *The Government Party: Organization and Financing the Liberal Party of Canada, 1930–1958*. Toronto: University of Toronto Press, 1977.

White, Percival. *Marketing Research Technique*. New York: Harper and Bros., 1931.

Whitehorn, Alan. *Canadian Socialism: Essays on the CCF-NDP*. Toronto: Oxford University Press, 1992.

Williams, John R. *The Conservative Party of Canada, 1920–1949*. Durham: Duke University Press, 1956.

Wright, Mary J., and C. Roger Myers. *History of Academic Psychology in Canada*. Toronto: C.J. Hogrefe, 1982.

Wright, Mary J. 'CPA: The First Ten Years.' *Canadian Psychologist*, 15, 2 (April 1974).

Young, Walter D. *The Anatomy of a Party: The National CCF, 1932–1961*. Toronto: University of Toronto Press, 1969.

Young, William R. 'Academics and Social Scientists versus the Press: The Policies of the Bureau of Public Information and the Wartime Information Board, 1939 to 1945.' *Historical Papers* (1978).

Index

Adams, Michael, 5

Adamson, Rodney, 141

advertising: comic-strip genre of, 26, 49; Conservative party and, 143–4; consumer surveys and, 10, 15; by Cooperative Commonwealth Federation (CCF), 135; early links to market research, 16; emotions and psyche as targets of, 49; growth in early twentieth century, 16, 47; newspaper dependence on, 32; soap and, 173n65

Anderson, Harry, 34, 43

Angus, H.F., 119

African Americans: disenfranchisement in South, 54; notable social scientists, 55; proportionate representation, 54; qualified interviewers, supposed lack of, 55; race-related survey questions, 188n84; undersampling of, 54, 160; white perceptions of, 55–6; women, parallel with, 55

American Association of Advertising Agencies, 34

American Institute of Public Opinion (AIPO), 3, 6; academic partnership with, 98; African Americans, undersampling of, 54; anti-union bias, 58; area probability sampling, 61; bandwagon electoral effect of, 59–60; business issues, lack of polling on, 59; Canadian questionnaire, 111; classes of respondents, 51; class biases in, 56–7; Congressional investigation of, 61; economic status, measure of, 57; election prediction and, 50; establishment of, 43; field workers of, 44; Gallup's work at, 44; international affiliates, 45, 65; job categories, 56; interview methodology, 44; issues polled, 45; labour issues and class, 58–9; low-education classes, undersampling of, 57; newspaper column, 43–4; postcard ballots methodology, 44; quota sampling, errors attributed to, 61; success of, 44; white collar vs blue collar interviewers, 58; women, undersampling of, 51, 53; value-neutral claim, 41; working-class interviewers, 57. *See also* opinion polling; Gallup, George